ONE WOMAN WALKS WALES

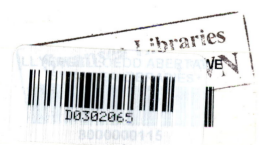

Owen; I'm glad you're alive

ONE WOMAN WALKS WALES

by
Ursula Martin

HONNO PRESS

First published by Honno Press in 2018

'Ailsa Craig', Heol y Cawl, Dinas Powys, Wales, CF64 4AH

1 2 3 4 5 6 7 8 9 10

A catalogue record for this book is available from the British Library.
Published with the financial support of the Welsh Books Council.

ISBN 978-1-909983-60-1 (paperback)
ISBN 978-1-909983-61-8 (ebook)

Honno Press is grateful to Faber and Faber Ltd. and the Estate of T.S. Eliot for
permission to reprint form 'Little Gidding', *Four Quartets*. And to Kobalt Music
Group Ltd. for permission to reprint from 'Break My Stride' by Matthew Wilder.

Cover design and illustration: Ruth Rowland
Maps: Leanne Cordingley-Wright www.StudioMayfly.co.uk
Text design: Elaine Sharples
Printed in Great Britain

FOREWORD

It is a great privilege to be asked to preface the story of such a personal journey of self-discovery. Ursula Martin's determination in the face of a diagnosis of ovarian cancer, and subsequent decision to walk many thousands of miles across Wales and tell as many people as she could about the symptoms of ovarian cancer, are incredible. I am in no doubt that Ursula's journey has helped a huge number of people to learn more about this disease and the work we must do to make sure women have the best chances of survival – every one of the 25,000 women living with ovarian cancer in the UK, and those diagnosed in the future.

Ovarian cancer can be devastating. One woman is diagnosed with ovarian cancer every day in Wales, and all too many die every year from the disease. Target Ovarian Cancer is the UK's leading ovarian cancer charity. We work to improve early diagnosis, we fund life-saving research and we provide much-needed support to women with ovarian cancer, across all four nations of the UK.

It is for women like Ursula that we exist. Her strength and determination know no bounds, and we are profoundly grateful to be a small part of her story.

Annwen Jones
Chief Executive, Target Ovarian Cancer

PROLOGUE

It started with a sharp pain, deep down in my side. A period pain, except I wasn't bleeding; I hadn't had periods for a few months. The recent extreme physical exertion I had put my body through meant it had stopped bleeding to conserve energy. It felt like a period pain except it was in the wrong place: too far to the right, almost at the top of my hip bone.

Late at night in a crumbling house in a small still village, remote in the brown plains of north-east Bulgaria, I lay on my sofa-bed rubbing my right hip and deep into my belly. There was a bulge there. A bubble of sensation slid into the centre of me as I pressed my fingers deeper. I didn't think this was a sign of something badly wrong, just strange; I had never noticed before that my body did this. I couldn't lie on my stomach, there was an uncomfortable pressure in there; but still I didn't realise there was anything really wrong

There was something pushing against my intestines, taking all the space. But I didn't know it was there. There was no conscious alarm, no clanging alert-signals or heart-fluttering realisation.

I hitchhiked back to the UK for Christmas. Borrowing a pair of Mum's jeans for a family gathering, I crowed about fitting into a size 12. I was the fittest I'd ever been. I'd just finished a three-month kayak journey, covering 1710 miles through seven European countries. I was bronzed golden-brown with blonde streaks in my curls of river-washed hair, and the technicolour memories had made my eyes blaze bright. As I swung in the motion of constant, economical paddle-movement, the kayaking had changed my body. Hours and hours, day after day I forced the bulbous plastic shell forward against oncoming winds and river conditions. I was full of muscle, my stomach lifted and flattened, my arms and shoulders strong and solid. Even my legs lost fat through daily pushing against the kayak body. I was healthy and beautiful. I was the most confident I had ever been. But there was a pain in my stomach and I didn't recognise it. I couldn't sit comfortably in a chair, there was something inside me that stopped me folding, made a bloated unpleasant pressure in my belly.

The family Christmas became New Year's Eve with friends in Bristol. I mentioned my strangeness to a few people. *I feel like I can't bend*, I said, blithely. *Go to the doctor*, they said, so I did, making an appointment as a temporary patient at the surgery around the corner. I was only passing through.

The doctor raised an eyebrow, said it was probably a large ovarian cyst, and sent me for a scan, to confirm it.

I was referred to a consultant who told me that I needed surgery, and scheduled it for twelve weeks' time. Then a blood test showed the cyst might actually be a tumour, that there might be a huge tumour inside me. I was bumped up the list, suddenly a priority. They'd used the word *tumour* and I had to ask, is that cancer? I'd attended the appointment alone, and a rise of tears grew up within me, my face scrunching in sudden emotion as the implications of that word sank in, becoming the clichéd trauma and all that suggested. There was a heaviness in that word, with all its implied suffering, finality and death. The consultant and nurse bent forward, patting a knee each as if choreographed; they'd been waiting for the ramifications to percolate through me.

I found myself waiting, my fluttering free life unexpectedly stilled by blooming uncertainty, waiting for the next appointment, waiting for another blood test, a scan, a pre-op assessment. I was waiting for a definition that never arrived, the name of the thing inside me, whether or not it was going to kill me. My stomach grew and grew. I couldn't shit, couldn't bend, couldn't tighten my clothes. My ovary was pressing against my diaphragm. There was fluid in my lungs. I couldn't breathe at night. My stomach distended. I felt the growth sloshing as I walked. It loomed silently, motives unreadable, like a jellyfish going about its unfathomable business, sculling slowly through the ocean. I reduced my gait to a gentle shuffle, careful to avoid shaking the bag of matter inside me.

I couldn't forget this was happening. Pain would cut through my belly, the cyst illuminating from within, a thundercloud flashing in sudden booms of white.

"If it bursts before the op, don't go to A&E," said the consultant. "Come straight to ward 78."

"How will I know if it bursts?" I said.

She looked at me sharply, assessing my naivety. "It will hurt."

I lay in bed and pressed my fingers against my swollen stomach. Something was growing inside me, the way a baby should. But it wasn't a child, it was a blank-eyed, brooding, poisonous thing: a growth of malicious and murderous intent, a malignancy. I decided it was an alien baby; I'd been abducted and probed, landing back to earth with a blank memory and a mystery growth that would burst open to reveal a pterodactyl, flapping and cawing before falling to ashes, killed in the bright light of the operating table.

Six weeks after the first doctor's visit, the operation date arrived. February 14th 2012. I joked about the date with the nurse in false, forced brightness, as I sat waiting for the needle that would put me to sleep. When I woke up, there was only pain and heaviness. I didn't know where my body was. I saw the ceiling, beige tiles full of holes, and felt a sense of busyness around me, machines beeping and people moving quickly, intently.

The muscles of my stomach began to ripple, then exploded into bursts of pain.

3

I was nothing but pain. My breathing stopped. My newly opened body was pulsing against its closure, raw edges stitched together moments previously were being pulled apart by involuntary muscle twitches. The wound screamed and I lay paralysed. I was caged by pain. I was the colour red. I was clay inside a fist.

The nurse found me lying there, immobile, my breathing caught at my throat. She looked into me and held me in her gaze. She was a tall, beautiful woman. I was a flat, heavy line of hurt.

The surgeon bent towards me and told me that as well as completely removing the right ovary, they had also scooped out a growth from my left ovary. In this knowledge came a flash of my future: chemotherapy, spreading cancer, no children. Infertility, hormone imbalance. I was a pair of listening eyes attached to a two-dimensional flat plane. I knew that she was telling me this to check my comprehension, to check that I was present.

My body was assessed for signs of internal bleeding, and the nurse rolled me to one side to administer a powerful painkiller. As she eased me down it came again, the paralysing red roar, but this time she was there, at my face, above me. The pain was dragging me inside myself but she told me to look into her eyes. I held onto her eyes; they were beams of light, a rope to cling to that pulled me out of my pain cage. She told me to breathe, I did and the pain receded. I smiled, and she smiled with me, we were together in that moment.

They took me to the organised murmur of a hospital ward. People muted by illness, curtailed to quietness. Intimacies conducted in full view, unspeakable acts removed behind curtains, privacy maintained through averted eyes.

Morphine dazed me, gave voices a cathedral-like echo, brought them from the other side of my room to speak at my bedside, awareness advancing and retreating at each blink of my eyelids. There were only pillows of sleep and the catching of shallow breaths that first night, my alarms beeping, bringing the nurse over to check I was alive. My body wasn't moving, it felt pressed down, muted, made heavy and quiet by a chemical cosh, lungs barely sipping at air. I was marooned in the night, eyes beaming out from my island bed.

They got me out of bed the day after the operation, body consumed by a fire at the centre, an awkward, hunched step to a chair where I sat for an hour, clicking at the morphine button, feeling my guts burn as they flopped against the raw sutures.

The first walks were to the toilet, struggling, stumbling stiff-legged, bowed at the waist with a hand supporting my stomach. I felt that if I let it hold its weight my belly would drop and burst open, spooling and spattering my insides down, out of the bottom of my gown and onto the mopped and trodden hospital floor. I was surrounded by shuffling patients, our reasons for being there bunched clumsily under the umbrella term "women's problems". At dinnertime an awkwardness of women would make their way down, carefully, gingerly, to the canteen, to be served an awful meal. We were looming, stumbling ghosts in long pale gowns.

A week after the surgery I was out of hospital and waiting for a diagnosis: shuffling around the house, sleeping, doing jigsaws. I had to keep my mind occupied without straining my body. I passed my birthday with my mum, watching films in a miserable hunch on the sofa, trying not to talk or think about how this was the worst birthday ever.

Time held me in a limbo of pre-diagnosis, cancer not confirmed. A week turned to two, my tumour embottled, the spooky floating potato sent to a specialist for another opinion. I was waiting for the hospital to tell me what they took out of me, waiting and suffering while they decided whether this hostile takeover was a cancer, checking what the growth on my other ovary was, whether cancer had spread, what stage of life limitation this infestation had been caught at.

I wrote postcards to friends; sending them was a way to leave the house. I aimed for the postbox, a scant 100m. Out of the house; turn left, pass three lampposts, cross the road and walk to the other side of the bus-shelter. I kissed the cards as I posted them, sending pieces of myself out into the world, small greetings soaring out beyond my agonised, reduced reach. On my way back I looked up and saw cherry blossom, pink and delicate against the pale blue winter sky. I breathed a fresh breath and remembered that the world was still there outside my personal agony. The season was turning and things were growing. It was only my life in flux, everything else remained the same. I realised how totally inward-looking I was, so focused on my own pain that I'd blocked out other sensory input. It didn't last long, but for a few seconds I came out of myself, admired the colours and breathed the clear air of coming spring before shuffling back to the house.

I was in shock, unexpectedly vulnerable. My world was based on freedom and vitality, facing the unknown and living with vigour, flitting between different exciting events, hitchhiking, travelling abroad. Now something unexpected had happened and it was awful, beyond the scope of my capabilities. Mentally I closed down. I'd learned to be spontaneous but I couldn't handle this. I'd deliberately removed from my life all the things I would need to cope with a serious, unexpected illness – regular income, community, home address, proximity to friends and family.

I was a nulled, dulled, traumatised person, miserable and weepy. I didn't know what was happening, just let it come. It was too huge and frightening to even work out how I felt, I just shut down and existed. It was never OK, I never coped, just lived through it until the trauma lessened.

Eventually the results came, after scans, blood tests, second opinions and weeks of waiting.

"Mucinous adenocarcinoma."

My right ovary had become a tumour.

"However, the growth we removed from your left ovary was a benign cyst, there's no evidence of cancer anywhere else in your body; we believe it hasn't spread."

No further treatment.

"Come back for a check-up in three months. You're free to go."

I was diagnosed with ovarian cancer, stage 1a. I had just turned 32.

TWO YEARS LATER

What do you dream about the night before starting a 3300 mile walk? You don't, because you barely sleep. There's a car to scrap, a flat to clean and a rucksack to pack. There are emails to send, a Facebook page to update, press coverage to arrange and donations to solicit. If you did dream, it would be of lists, of frantically scribbling down jobs in a small white notebook, each one an attempt to capture the fear-whipped frenzy of a thought whirlwind on paper, make it tamed and tangible.

Publish website
Add Glyndŵr's Way
Business card
Mail redirection
Preliminary route plan
Download route maps
Suma – apricots, Bombay mix, dried veg, peanuts, sultanas, muesli
Scan ID
Things to buy – boots, rucksack, sleeping bag, mat, keyboard,
socks, hand-warmer, bivvy bag, multi-vits, first aid kit
Phone BT
Phone council
Tax form
Buy one more mid-layer top
Type up press release...

You definitely don't think, dream or imagine what it's like to embark on a 3300-mile walk, because that's impossible. Unimaginable. You don't dream about tumbling down tired to watch clouds move large on the wind, of 500 sunsets seen from a sleeping bag, about the perfectly-balanced colouring of green fields, blue sky, white clouds, the delicacy of infinitesimal moss forests, the tingling swish of immersing dirty hair and face into the rarely realised treasure of a hot bath.

You don't dream about the pain of a 3300-mile walk; because you have no idea of how much it will hurt.

The reality of a 3300-mile walk is an idea too big to fully comprehend in its amorphous whole, so it must be broken down into component parts and dealt with that way. I knew that I could do this, I'd done it before. I could walk and camp, I could carry my things on my back, find sleeping spots, live with hardship. I could pack an assortment of clothes, kit and dried food into a thickly-strapped pack and leave. That knowledge was enough.

I was panicking, packing up my life, leaving my new-found home behind, heading out to travel. Was I strong enough, could I do this? I'd arrived in Machynlleth weak from cancer, in need of many things: of a home, of strength, of care and of support, of community. I found it all there, nurtured myself and grew strong again; I was strong enough to leave but it was frightening. I was out there when I fell ill, out there with nothing when I became weaker than I had ever been before. Was I really doing this again? Was I really leaving everything?

I'd gone travelling five years earlier, packing up my belongings in a huge Victorian room near the sea at Aberystwyth, leaving a job in a homeless shelter and becoming a hobo myself. I'd left to release my tightly wound self, let go of plans, expectations, definitions of self, let go of self-imposed restrictions. I wanted to learn to allow myself to just live, to simply exist, learning to cope at the uncertain edge, where safety met danger, where the spice of life lived.

Two years of journeying had begun with baby steps, volunteering on Welsh farms, and branched out into hitchhiking, beach-living and Spanish festivals, doing small jobs here and there to top up my carefully hoarded bank balance. I'd reached a life of freedom and spontaneity, kayaking the length of the Danube before living in Bulgaria for the winter, planning a walk back to Britain. However, with the surprise discovery of the tumour everything had changed. I'd been ripped away from a housesit in Bulgaria, all my belongings left neat and tidy for a two-week UK Christmas holiday that I didn't return from.

I was 32 years old and I'd come through a small but significant cancer. I had no job, no money, no husband and no children; just a slowly healing abdominal wound, a tearful and traumatised psyche, a group of friends in the Dyfi valley and no real idea of what to do next. Shipwrecked by a sudden storm of illness, a wave of cancer had washed over me and deposited me high up in the Uwchygarreg valley, shaken and discombobulated. The immediate danger had passed and there was only had a small chance of the cancer returning. But it had changed my life: my sense of strength and surety had gone, both in my body's reliability and of my place in the world. It took months to heal, to find myself again and remember that I was strong and free.

Walking 400 miles down the River Severn and back up the Wye six months after surgery had been part of that return to self. It had been a healing journey, a reminder that although this attack on my life had happened, although I'd been left weakened, I was still myself. I could still shoulder a bag and leave safety, go out and cope in the unknown.

I'd looked at a map and seen that the Severn started a few miles from my house. I could follow it all the way to Bristol, the city of my illness and treatment, the place I had to keep returning to for check-ups – regular scans and blood tests to see that the insidious sneak had not returned. That's what started the whole thing, going into follow-up treatment, facing a five-year schedule of appointments; I thought, I know, I'll walk to hospital, that will make an unpleasant and restrictive experience more bearable. From that idea this adventure grew and grew.

I planned a second walk, a public one this time: fundraising for charity. I'd loop down the Severn to Bristol in time for a hospital check-up, but this time I wouldn't head home. I would go up the Offa's Dyke Path and around the Wales Coastal Path back to Bristol in time for another appointment six months later.

But this didn't seem enough to fill the time. I added in the Glyndŵr's Way, an easy detour connecting at either end to Offa's Dyke. I'd been inspired by the proximity of the sources of the Severn and Wye and kept seeing pairs of rivers where I could trace my way up from the coast to the source, then walk a couple of miles to another source and down to the sea again somewhere completely different. I kept seeing paths that would slot nicely into my route: from Conwy to Cardiff via the mountainous Cambrian Way, then back to Conwy again via the Coast to Coast Path. Each piece of walking seemed essential: how could I walk Wales without covering the mountains or the coast? It was a surprise when I totted up the total and found that added together all these paths made up a 3300 mile walk.

8 months, two hospital appointments, 3300 miles. Or so I thought.

Now, on 2nd March 2014, two years after my illness, I was on the way to find the source of the Severn for the second time, fixated on a single idea: walking to hospital and telling people about the symptoms of ovarian cancer.

Survival rates for the disease were low. Wales was the only UK nation not to have paid for a national awareness-raising campaign; it also had the lowest UK survival rate (back in 2012): three per cent lower than England after the first year. At the time almost two-thirds of women diagnosed with ovarian cancer were dead within five years. Women were dying from ovarian cancer because they didn't know they had it until it was far too late to cure, and treatment was palliative rather than curative.

The ovarian cancer charity told me it was a sign of late diagnosis. I could change this by trying to encourage the Welsh government to mount a campaign, but I could also change it on a smaller scale by talking to as many people as possible.

In the aftermath of my serious illness I felt a need to Do Something. Ovarian cancer had claimed me, become my cause. The shock I felt that a tumour could grow inside me without my knowledge, almost guilt that I hadn't known, hadn't noticed what was happening to me, turned to a drive to make this experience different for other women. I felt that I could make a journey to tell women in Wales about the symptoms, which fitted in perfectly with my self-centred need to travel.

I had help from Target Ovarian Cancer during my illness, an information pack in the post and a poster in the hospital. I looked at the three ovarian cancer charities and it seemed that Target was a charity that campaigned for increased symptoms awareness at government level. I decided to fundraise for them and they were incredibly supportive throughout my journey.

I visited the Penny Brohn Cancer Care centre twice during my illness; they were an invaluable source of help, advice and support. I attended two of their residential courses for free and it's where I learned how to begin to cope with a cancer diagnosis. I felt I had to support them in return, to help provide free treatment for those who came after me.

I signed up for Facebook and Twitter during this time (Instagram felt like an app too far). I'd never used these things before, rejecting their inauthenticity, their disconnect from real human interaction. But these websites turned out to be invaluable for communicating my story to people – people who learned more about ovarian cancer from me, people who offered me beds, people who made donations and people who offered constant, uplifting, online support in response to my photos and updates.

If I talked about ovarian cancer on Twitter and Facebook, made a journey that got people's attention, got my posts shared, got my story into local newspapers and radio, if I scattered as many symptoms-information cards to the winds as I could, then that important info might nestle into the back of the right person's mind. Perhaps there would come a day when they were looking at themselves critically in the mirror, realising they'd felt bloated and heavy for a long time, or maybe they'd be talking to someone about a recurring pain in their pelvis, and my information, that dog-eared business card they'd found in a café, would form part of the critical mass that led to them making a doctor's appointment. That was the best I could hope for; this wasn't a journey which would save the lives of thousands of women, but it might increase the chances that ovarian cancer was caught earlier for the 350 women in Wales diagnosed with it every year.

Adrenaline had me bleary but alert at 6am after just a few scant hours of sleep. I'd named the day months ago and now it was here;

it was finally time to pack the last pieces into my rucksack, throw it on and make my way down to Machynlleth where there would – hopefully – be a group of people waiting to wave me off. I was a plump, unpractised woman in a raincoat and woollen hat; the only thing creating their belief in me was the fact that I was stating I would do this walk. I had no idea if I could, mainly because I had no idea what I was actually attempting.

I'd given myself a rough target of ten miles a day for the first few weeks, seeing it as a kind of on-the-job training. If I walked less than ten one day, I'd make it up the next. In my planning I'd imagined ten miles a day for the first month, fifteen miles a day for the next months and that left nineteen point six miles a day if I was going to complete my walk in the time I'd set for it, to fit into the six-month schedule of hospital appointments which had prompted the initial idea. Yes, you read that right. I actually planned this walk by making a list of all the paths I wanted to walk and then dividing that by the number of days between hospital appointments, and then nodding. *Yes, I can walk twenty miles a day.* What was I thinking?

I'd left no time to train for this monster challenge, focusing instead on working to earn money to live on as I travelled. A year of illness and living on benefits had reduced my savings to zero. I worked as hard as possible as a home carer, always making myself available for shifts and spending weeks at a time in the homes of dementia sufferers.

I gained fat, not muscle. My body was used to sitting in a car; the most effort I expended was getting down to the floor to towel dry elderly feet. But after buying kit and making preparations, I started with a fund of several thousand pounds. It was enough, as long as I was careful. I intended to live on £5 a day, finding dried food that I could carry and eat easily. I decided not to take a stove, trying to reduce weight and dirt in my bag. Couscous became a staple food, something I could rehydrate with cold water. Couscous and various vegetables and, eventually, tinned mackerel. My £5 budget was hard to stick to but I kept it there, the mental limit meaning I overspent up to £10 by sneaking occasional toast or chips in cafés, rather than going as far as spending £15 or £20 on whole meals.

My flat was bare but not bare enough. All the tiny pieces of my life needed to be attended to, tidied up, put somewhere. I'd almost made it. My flat cleaned and arranged, rucksack neat and jammed full, extra supplies stored at my friend Ruth's. Annie came to pick me up and drive us the four miles down to the clock tower, the monument that sits at the centre of Machynlleth, the gathering point where I'd decided to say goodbye.

"I've got this", I said to Annie when she arrived to collect me, waving a Welsh flag I'd picked out from the back of a drawer. "But I'm not sure where to put it."

"How about on the end of here," she said, plucking a length of bamboo from the stack in the still-untidy porch. And that's how my walking-pole was born, the first of a pair that I'd take the full distance, grinding them down so that they were significantly shorter by the end of the walk.

At the clock tower was a small group of my friends. We hugged and took pictures, not quite sure of what to do. Anna came with her three robust boys, playing chase around the legs of the Victorian monument. Heloise came ready to walk out of town with me, Ruth and Naps came to the edge of the golf course. We led a small procession down the centre of the road, the local news photographer catching people smiling and waving behind me.

It was exciting, not sad; my friends were used to saying goodbye to me.

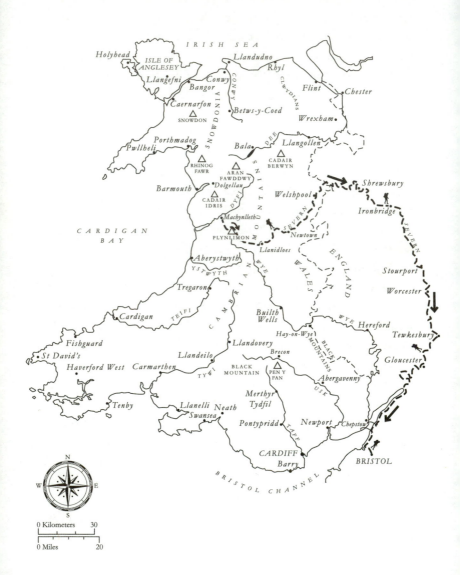

THE SEVERN WAY

Route description: The Severn Way traces Britain's longest river from source to sea. Starting in the wild uplands of Plynlimon it descends to the agricultural valleys of mid-Wales before widening and meandering through the floodplain of Shropshire and down to Worcester where it becomes tidal and huge. It ends under the two vast Severn bridges, where the estuary is almost four miles wide.

Length:	223.9 miles
Total ascent:	3,280m
Maximum height:	605m
Dates:	2 – 23 March 2014
Time taken:	22 days
Nights camping/nights hosted:	4/18
Days off:	1
Average miles per day:	10.67

The route away from Machynlleth towards the source of the Severn at Plynlimon led me up a single-track road, the houses falling away as I rose higher into the hills, ascending the Uwchygarreg valley. Eventually I would pass Talbontdrain, the house I'd been lucky enough to rent a part of: the wonderful place where I'd recovered from illness and then used as a dormitory as I worked all hours in walk preparation. Knowing I wouldn't see my neighbours again for months I detoured down the rocky track, through the trickling stream and up again to their secluded cottage, where I sat in their steamy kitchen to drink strong coffee.

They came out to walk along with me, my lovely friends – the baby strapped up against James' belly, Vicky taking photographs. We had a meander further along my path until the road ran out and turned into forestry track which started to climb, winding upwards through cleared plantation. As we said goodbye, hugs for luck, eating final pieces of cake, it started to rain – lightly at first, but as I trudged upwards, along the side of the valley, it became heavier. I had no idea this was coming; in the whirl and kerfuffle of preparation I hadn't even checked the weather-forecast. I'd taken my waterproof off and, after a while of trying to ignore the rain, decided it would be a better idea to stop and put it back on again.

The rain became heavier still as I stood in the faint shelter given by the thin line of trees at the edge of the beaten-stone track. They were wrongly aligned to keep the rain off me and it beat in, breezing and misting against my legs. I fumbled my rucksack-cover out of its zip pocket, but there was a concertina-like sleeping mat strapped to the back of my pack and the cover wouldn't stretch over it. I pulled and tugged at the inadequate cover until I'd centred it as best I could; the sides of my bag were still exposed but I decided that was good enough. I also decided not to put my waterproof trousers on. I couldn't be bothered with the faff of removing boots and balancing myself, the trousers felt clumsy and awkward.

I walked on, still following the forestry track, beaten yellow stone bleeding into rough muddy edges where ripped branches and churned earth marked the passage of huge, heavy machinery. It took another couple of hours to climb up to where the quiet ranks of pine forest met the grasses of Hyddgen. This was the open land that led towards the lump of Plynlimon, an amorphous overgrown hill that just squeezed, tip-toe, into the name of mountain.

I saw the mountain ahead, checked the time and noticed oncoming dark, way sooner than I'd expected. The friends, stop-offs and chats had been wonderful, but cost me time. I'd have to sleep on the mountain, or the moorlands this side of it, rather than in the woods on the other side, as I'd anticipated. This was an exposed and grassy kind of a place: no overhangs or clefts of rock, just wide open expanses of soggy grass and bog, waterlogged, wind rippled. No place to sleep.

Because I'd planned to wild camp, I didn't have a tent: just a tarpaulin to put underneath me to keep the wetness from soaking upwards and a bivvy bag to wriggle into as a damp-proof outer layer. It wasn't full preparation for all conditions, more a deliberate/calculated absence of planning. I'd always preferred to be under- rather than over-prepared, to allow for chance to aid as much as hinder. I hated the fussiness of 'what ifs', the overburdening of a bag full of objects for 'just in case'; it felt like using possessions to control fear of the unknown. In my frantic planning I'd tried to err towards the minimum of what I might need, sensing that I'd chop and change along the way, learning my true needs during the journey itself.

I'd learned this eighteen months previously, during my first long walk along the length of a river in Galicia, northern Spain. I'd hugely weighed myself down, leaving the UK with twenty-six kilos of suitcase and rucksack, carrying the gift of a lined army-issue winter overcoat, to use once I reached the colder winters of eastern Europe. How ridiculous to think that I couldn't buy a coat once I went further east. I'd travelled in this way, slow and over-weighted, for over six months, but once I started walking it became immediately apparent that I was physically incapable of walking long distances under so much strain. I remember finding a large, open-mouthed swing-top bin in the woods, and depositing eight vests, draping them over the edge for someone else to pick up. Why did I think I'd need eight vests?

Here in Wales I wasn't carrying any vests. I could feel the cold of my rain-soaked clothes as they clung against my skin, only the warmth of my efforts in climbing the stone track kept me from shivering.

Across the open grasses was a flatland where streams meandered, leading over towards where the mountain began to rise. This was where the Rheidol started, the river that ran its swiftest course towards the sea at Aberystwyth. Up there, on the slopes, began the trickling of the Severn and the Wye that I'd decided would be the beginning and end of the entire 3300-mile route. They ran away down the other side of this heap of rock and earth – one going north, the other south, heading out on their meandering routes to the sea, meeting again at the mouth of the Bristol Channel to mingle into the ocean. I'd walk away on one and home on the other, with all the other routes I'd planned in between. But first I needed to sleep somewhere; a storm was on the way and I decided not to chance it. There was one place of shelter – the sheep barns of Hyddgen, the only building in the entire landscape, away to my right.

I splashed into a puddle as I stumbled over the rock bridge leading to the barn, and my feet were instantly soaked. I didn't understand what I would months later, what months of wet walking would teach me, that without waterproof trousers the rain had run down into my boots and saturated them from the inside out.

Clambering over the puzzle of gates that enclosed the entrance to the barn, I saw an expanse of beaten-shit floor, separated into four pens. I walked down the row, searching for the pen that had the least damp patches, settling for the end one, closest to the mountain. I laid my tarpaulin on the ground and my sleeping-kit out on top of it, carefully trying not to let anything touch the sheep-shit. I searched further down into my bag for fresh clothing and pulled out wet clothes. The rain had leaked around the sides of the raincover into my rucksack. Oh damn, first day out and I was already fucking up. I didn't want to change my wet clothes for rucksack damp ones, again eschewing the awkward, uncomfortable fumbling. I felt dazed after four hours in the rain and just wanted to lie down. I got into my sleeping-bag and pulled it up around my head, and just lay there, staring. After a while I remembered my handwarmer: powered by lighter fluid, the perfect small heat source. I pulled myself out of my sleeping bag, shuddering in the cold air and fumbled it together, scraping the matches to start it.

I lay in my sleeping-bag, shivering in shock and stared at nothing, too worn out to move, too tense to sleep, listening to the rain rattling against the barn roof. The strong wind blowing water at me for the previous four hours had left me blasted, in stasis. I swapped the handwarmer from place to place, trying to warm my body. I was cold and seemed to be taking an age to warm up. My feet were solid cold, covered in slimy wet socks, damp with the water that had trickled down into my boots, I was too ignorant to take the socks off and let the dry sleeping-bag warm up. It was hard in the triple cocoon of sleeping-bag, liner and bivvy outer layer to get my hands down lower than my waist but I wriggled around, trying to place the handwarmer against every part of me in turn. It was a cold and wakeful night. The wind roared and whirled against the tin roof of the barn, I heard it bashing and blowing all night as I surfaced from my semi-sleep to change the position of my little heat bundle. I never really got any part of myself warm enough to slide into deep sleep, always having to keep moving the heat source round to the parts of me that were numb with cold.

I imagined myself out there, on the side of the wet, grassy mountain, nothing to string a tarp to for shelter against the rain and hail, and I was glad I'd come inside early. Not pressing ahead to camp in the dark later on was the right decision. If I'd carried on and tried to get as far as I could that day I would have been on the side of an exposed mountain in a rainstorm, close to freezing, with no tent. Disaster.

When shit got rough, when I was wet and tired, I made a decision that kept me safe. It was a good thing that I could do this, ill-equipped and unfit as I was. I was able to think clearly under pressure. That was something I'd do over and over again as I kept walking: coming to the end of a day, fuzzy-headed through low blood sugar, grimy, aching, exhausted. All I'd want to do was throw my bag down and stare into space. But I'd force myself to think, to decide what was necessary to keep myself fed, rested and safe – and do it. It's that skill, more than anything, more than the muscles in my legs, the cash in my bank account and the expensive kit on my back that made walking a total of 3700 miles possible.

It was fresh the following morning as I clambered out of the barn, sore and stiff, blinking at the glinting of the boggy plain ahead, tinged with dew and frosty edges. The sun shone a thin clear blue through a faint mist, and I looked over the shining grasses towards the mountain. It was draped in folds of mist that clung to the top like licks of whipped cream. I paused in wonder for a few breaths of crisp, cold air, and set off to climb it. Plynlimon is less a rocky peak of a mountain and more a lumpy heap of grass-covered water. Because the Rheidol, the Wye and the Severn rise from it, the ground where they gather is running, oozing, with water which collects until it is more than the earth and overflows, pulled by gravity towards the sea.

I crossed a small metal bridge lying next to the track that wound across the open plain and around the reservoir, eventually linking with the road on the other side of this open sheep-walk. Straight ahead of me lay the peak of the mountain, high behind a small lake.

But I was going to turn left and climb at a different point further north, towards the source of the Severn.

I trod my way carefully towards the first slope, following a stream that wound around the hill's base. Bog blanketed the valley, clumps of reeds or long grasses that had to be picked through carefully. Sometimes instead of earth there would be unexpected squelchy water and I would rebalance, using my single walking-pole to probe and find a better footstep.

My boots had been damp when I put them on, and they were soon soaked through, filling with icy water that took a while to heat to body temperature and become comfortable.

The stream took me past a rectangle of tumbled stone, remnants of a small cottage abandoned 120 years ago. Across on the other side of the valley there was another, with a wavering chimney-stack resolute against the destruction of the brutal wind and creeping, dripping rainwater. Hilary, my landlady and friend at Talbontdrain, had met the last woman to live in that house. She'd told me about the child walking eight miles to school on Monday and returning on a Friday, the visiting pedlars. I imagined the lumpy laden carts trundling, dipping and rising over that wild, lovely landscape and thought of the mother in that house, sending her children to school to spend days alone, her husband outside, fighting the weather, struggling to claim land from nature and turn it to other ends, with only grass, moss and changing skies to see from her windows.

I followed the stream onwards, splashing in and out of wet grass and plant clumps, until I came to an incoming stream running down from a fold in the land. It was too big for my clumsy, cumbersome body to jump over, so I hunted up and down like a frustrated dog nosing at the stream, trying to find a way to cross the obstacle. Every time I thought I could see a place to cross, where the stream narrowed invitingly with large rocks placed either side of a small rush of water, I'd walk to it and find a torrent lined with slippery moss. The huge rucksack unbalanced me, made me too scared to take a risk.

After moving fruitlessly up and down for ages, I finally found a crossing-point, heaved my pack over the stream and followed, splashing a gout of ice cold water over my already sodden feet.

From there it was just a long, slow, heave up the hill. I stopped often, utterly lacking in energy. Sometimes it was to stare back the way I'd come, marvelling at the hard-won footsteps, and sometimes it was to admire the lush mixed mosses that bulged out of the wiry green grass. There were starburst fronds, colours from deep green to icy pale lime, sometimes shocking like crusted lichen and sometimes green and fronded in miniature forests. There were craggy pillars of pale green, warped and knobbled, ending in bulbous bright red growths. These soft pillows of moss were beautiful, sometimes so big you could sink up to your knees if you stepped on them.

I wanted to lie down there, forget the cold mist and damp clothes, just to put my face to this tiny forest and sink into the luscious surface, to rest and look up through the moss trees. But I knew that it was only movement keeping me warm. Every time I stopped, my clothes would chill against my body, and it wasn't too long before I had to lumber up again and continue taking tiny steps against the slope, my calves burning in pain as I crept up the hill, bent against the weight of my pack.

Once the slope levelled out, I searched for landmarks in the mist. It's a pretty featureless place up there, just shaggy grass and occasional soggy-edged pools. There were crags of peat curl-topped like waves, shaped into smooth curves at the base: sheep-chosen resting places where they can lie contented, sheltered from the wind.

A fence ran the length of the mountain, and the source of the

Severn was on the other side of it. The official start of this huge river is marked by a wooden post, sticking up high in a sea of water and peat, brown water pooling in sticky mud, bottomless pools that are best avoided, lest you sink all the way down to the heart of the mountain. A trail of flagstones leads to it from the other side of my own approach, a safe path laid by humans. The mighty Severn, longest river in Britain, starts where crags and lumps of peat and mud crack and divide into islands, water trickling between them. It ends 220 miles away in the unstoppable four-mile-wide burst of the estuary. Not in a roar but a quiet hum, a near-silent force.

I took a few pics in celebration, grinning, rotund and sweating in black waterproofs, wreathed in a woollen headband, and set off downhill, trotting easily on the stone path down into the Hafren Forest. I came down through the pine trees to where the path joined a broader track running alongside the Severn. No longer a tumbling rushing stream, it had grown into a young river, too broad to jump across now. In the trees next to the path was a well-trodden area of flat ground, claimed from the forest before it made the earth impassable with soggy ruts and fallen branches. There was a small shelter there in the edge of the trees: just a branch leant up against a tree, others placed crosswise to form a skeleton shelter. When I'd walked the Severn two and a half years before, I'd slept in there on my first night, wriggling down into the length of the enclosed space, finding a way to shape my body around the lumps and rises of the root-riven ground. It had taken me almost a day longer to reach it this time and, discounting the rain and delayed start the previous day, I doubted my fitness.

Passing the waterfalls, I came down into an area of deep forest where the water lay thickly in the moss-choked grooves between pine trees. There was a wide boardwalk running by the river, slippery with creeping greenery, tinged with damp growth. It felt vaguely Germanic, a very wholesome way to come and enjoy the river, an organised viewing, wilderness tamed and made easy to access.

As I turned into the car park I saw people, dog-walkers. They were the first I'd seen in over twenty-four hours and I was shocked by the idea of interaction, almost recoiling from it. It had been an intense and solitary fight to get my lumpen and laden self over that mountain, and I'd forgotten there were other people on the planet. I smiled and spoke to them, the strangeness of human contact disappearing within seconds as I asked how to get to Llanidloes, the first town on the river.

My friend Heloise lived nearby and had offered to come and pick me up from the town, but I didn't want to stay with her that first time. I wasn't used to accepting help; I organised myself, looked after myself and shied away from any offer that suggested that what I could provide for myself was lacking. It wasn't a conscious rejection, I hadn't realised that was what I was doing. I instinctively brushed Heloise off, breezily telling her I'd probably be fine, would be past Llanidloes by the second day, no need for her help. As an afterthought, sensing that my rejection required softening, I added that I'd call her if I needed anything.

But, as I came down out of the Hafren Forest and onto the road I realised it would be stupid not to call Heloise. It was 4pm and there were seven more miles of hard painful tarmac before Llanidloes, another three hours of walking at my tired trudging speed. What was I doing? Why camp out so close to Llani when there was a friend's bed waiting nearby? I was wet, my spare clothes were wet and I'd spent a day and a half walking over a mountain. What was I trying to prove? Once I became so debilitated it seemed like a simple decision. I had no phone signal, so stopped at the first house I came to, knocking and asking to use the phone.

Heloise swooped, buzzing along the lane in her little red Punto and whisking me away from a damp night in the woods to her cluttered and comfortable rented house where I would be safe and looked after. She quickly organised cocktails, filling food, a bath and clean clothes. I just had to sit while she fluttered and cared for me, my clothes drying nicely on the airer and belongings scattered over every surface. I didn't know then that this would become a familiar routine. I hadn't imagined that this was how the journey was going to be.

The soaking wet boots had rubbed against my heel leaving a small, thumbnail sized blister, as well as others on my toes. I decided to tape my toes and put a blister-plaster on my heel, pulling it proudly from my first-aid kit. I'd never used one before, or even travelled with a first-aid kit. I felt very proud and well prepared.

I could walk another day of the route and come back to Heloise again; she'd ferry me back to yesterday's pick-up point and come back to collect me in the evening. I walked down the tarmac road into Llanidloes and out again the other side, stopping in a pub to have a strangely intimate conversation with the barmaid about female power and self-actualisation.

Coming out of a series of muddy, tiring fields that climbed up and out of a valley a few miles out of Llanidloes, I came to a crossroads where I could call Heloise and await a pick-up. No phone signal, though, so I walked to a nearby house and called from their landline, sat on a low grit-bin at the side of the road until I was cold, and watched the winding corner of the road for a while, waiting for her car to come into view, a tired and grateful walker.

Back at the house, the routine of cocktails and kit-washing well established, she gave me a bowl of water to soak my feet. We chatted as I drank a huge mojito, Heloise carefully squeezing the fresh lime, mixing it with rum and sugar. The plaster started to peel away from my heel and I unthinkingly bent down and pulled it further. Disaster. It seemed to have pulled the skin away entirely. I didn't just have a small blister anymore; the whole of my heel was raw. I had fundamentally misunderstood the way blister-plasters worked; where the plaster had bonded to my skin I'd just pulled it away, tripling the size of the skinless area. My thumbnail-sized blister had become an oval about two inches long.

Heloise phoned ahead to Newtown, running through her list of contacts to find someone I could stay with the following night. I accepted her help, not really knowing what else to do, not really able to process the idea that after only twenty miles of this huge journey I was hobbling and in need of aid. She would drop me back at the crossroads, then meet me later that night with my bag and introduce me to her friend Karen. All I had to do was walk fourteen miles in the meantime.

I looked ahead from the lonely crossroads. The path dipped down into a valley, going past a couple of small farmhouses and curving up to the right and around the hillside. I had to walk that. I had to get miles done that day, had to get to the next bed waiting for me, to the end of the section I'd set for myself, to Bristol in three weeks' time. It was too soon to stop. I'd set out to walk 3300 miles; how could I stop after twenty? It simply wasn't an option.

There was nothing to do but set off, agonising pain shooting through the raw skin at the back of my heel. The urge to limp was so strong, I had to force my steps into a stride, push my legs to walk in an ordinary, casual gait. After a couple of steps the agony would lessen and I could continue to walk normally, the pain reduced to a manageable background buzz.

"Come on, Ursula, it's just skin. It's not serious pain, of course I can walk like this, of course I can get to Newtown."

It was OK, just about. I walked through green fields, alongside pine copses, around small farmhouses, eventually coming high up alongside the Severn valley and dropping down to meet the river again as it looped wide and lazy through the flat flood-plain, the trace of the glacier carved wide and clear. I rested a while at the foot of a huge oak tree, curved and gnarly, roots flowing outwards to allow me a seat, eventually, hours later, stumping numbly into Newtown, feet like swollen stones in my boots.

That night at Karen's the pain was sharp and strong. I tried to make conversation with this friendly and interesting new person, but I couldn't focus away from the pain in my foot. Worry about the next few days kept stealing my attention, making me drift into silent thought. I rested on the sofa for a while, trying to chat or watch TV, but when I got up again I couldn't put any weight on it. My knee buckled and I had to catch myself on the chair and table edge. The skin was drying, trying to heal and I just broke the wound open again with every new movement.

The blister was huge and egg-shaped, taking up most of my heel. Excruciating pain shot through it the next morning as I tried to walk. It was an effort to straighten up, to avoid limping. I had to force myself to think of my posture, think of the weight on my back.

I marched forward, muttering orders to myself, forcing myself to stiffen my back and continue walking smoothly through the first few agonising steps as the raw skin pressed against the back of my boot, and pain screamed an urgent message to stop. If I could get into a regular pace then the pain lessened. If I curled my body against the pain, guarded the impact on that boot by limping, it would strain the rest of my body, which was already aching too much to take extra impact.

Not far out of Newtown the path turned to follow the Montgomery Canal, an arm of the UK canal network, reaching out into Wales as far as it could before the hills became too numerous.

It was a relief for me; eleven miles of a wide flat path gave me a wonderful chance to build up a steady pace, no changes of terrain or angle to force the raw skin against my boot in a shriek of pain and jerky hobbling. The canal was beautiful: underwater plants waving in glassy serenity, cows treading the opposite edge, dipping in to curl their tongues through the water. Small bridges, individually numbered, squatted low over the water, their bricks beautifully aged and flaking. I ducked under their curves, thinking of the horses, tethered to ever tug and plod their way to and from the big towns. The canal was impassable now, full of years of silt and plant-leavings.

Out of Newtown I could call on Laura. She'd picked me up the previous summer as I hitchhiked to Bristol.

"I'm on my way to hospital: ovarian cancer," I'd said proudly.

"I'm having treatment for breast cancer," she'd replied calmly.

I looked at the hat holding close to her bare head and breathed in. We piqued an interest in each other. She'd invited me home for tea and to share cancer stories: not in a flood of warmth or an outpouring of traumatic detail but in comfortable common knowledge, the bond already made, sharing only serving to cement it. It felt important to spend time with this woman who'd picked me up from the side of the road.

Her house turned out to be a sprawling ramshackle hall, pillars at the door and a high-ceilinged kitchen. She had six children, two adopted, plus years of fostering under her belt. Calm, surety and a sense of purpose were the cornerstones of this very strong woman, allowing her to provide a place where others could develop the same qualities. Laura approached her cancer with the same calmness and organisation, arranging childcare for the week of her chemo cycle when exhaustion took over.

"I just lie on the sofa and knit" she said, as if it wasn't too much trouble at all, light filtering dimly into the large room filled with sagging, comfortable sofas, an almost adult boy banging through in the background, saying hello.

I fitted quietly into the mix of teenagers filling her table, fostered, adopted and birthed, talking over each other, comparing selfies. An extra body to feed and house for one night was no bother here.

We walked a short way along the canal together to say goodbye, ending with talking about the false heroics of being a cancer survivor. I'm alive because of luck and doctors: the random way the tumour grew and because other people removed it and took care of me. I didn't fight cancer, I endured it and it knocked me sideways during the process. I wasn't brave, I was terrified and that made me a miserable, whining patient, prone to self-pity, petty anger and tears. Maybe that's not how it was for Laura; it's certainly not what I saw in her experience. We shared a rejection of the labelling, the tropes of being a brave warrior, battling cancer. My illness was a traumatic ordeal, but being labelled as a heroine and survivor was something it was hard to avoid, especially as my story became a public one through my own attempts to raise funds and symptoms awareness.

Shrewsbury came, and the welcome relief of my Auntie Susie with her warm hugs and loud laughs. She came out to get me when I came within a day's walk of the town, whisking me forward for a day to be fussed over. I could finally soak away the blister-plaster and show off my heel to appropriate shock and shrieks, revealing an egg-sized patch of fresh pink skin, frilled by thin scabs and tender to the slightest breath of air. I could sit on the sofa and read magazines, be brought cake and tea, cream for my heel, eventually sliding down into an afternoon nap, covered over by a soft, white, furry blanket.

I went to the boot shop and returned the pair I'd bought in haste. They were too small and leaking. I was fitted for a replacement pair, full leather to the ankles. Walking up and down a small, rubber-covered lump that was supposed to represent hill gradients, I tried to guess whether my toes were pressing against the front of the boots. These would do, I thought, grasping at straws again.

A day later, Susie and I went back out again and walked into Shrewsbury together, retracing the route I'd been spirited over by car, entering the town and walking underneath the huge bridges. I saw my first boats in Shrewsbury; the river would begin to be navigable below its huge weir.

I'd travelled from Wales to England and the differences began almost at the border. There were small thatched cottages and the villages became less stark, less dour, the difference of a richer country showing in small ways; a house could be kept for longer, a settlement allowed to grow naturally, rather than terraced houses clustered around some industrial edifice. The path between Wales and England had led away down a back road, and I'd come to a timbered house, worn and kinked with the weight of age, an arch leading through to a stable block and courtyard beyond. Crooked painted lettering above the door showed a date centuries ago. It was just a house on a back road – nothing special, no museum, no marker point, just one of many ancient dwelling places throughout this land. Suddenly I felt gossamer-thin ghosts, the weight of the history of England layered down upon me. Our present lives are built on so many that have gone before, mark upon mark of our history of living on the same land.

On the day I walked away from Shrewsbury I finished at Atcham. There I came across a pub that immediately made me feel uncomfortable. Too glossy and too many business clients giving me the side-eye: a place for meetings and important lunches, everyone driving there, not walking. I felt as if I would break things with the huge bag I carried on my back, lumber through the pub strange and wild, knocking over glasses and bumping against chairs. It was an unpleasant feeling and I walked quickly away from the posh pub and its judgemental customers, living within tightly bound strictures, too moneyed to allow space for my transience, nothing to define me except what I carried on my back.

Up the straight busy road and down a side turning, I saw a triangle of woodland on the map, just a small copse but it was more than enough to provide shelter for the night, dampen down the noise of traffic, and provide camouflage enough for any passing dog-walkers not to notice me. I found a gap in the barbed wire and slipped through, treading softly into the centre of the young wood. Small birch trees provided a soft carpet of copper leaves for my bed. I lay down, feeling happy and safe. This was my adventure, this was what I was setting out to do. At its core, my journey was to walk and to sleep, nothing more complex than that. The leafless fingers of the trees waved softly above me, and I felt at peace with the simplicity of my surroundings, snug and safe in my sleeping bag, well insulated against the March night.

All the fuss and effort of the first week released a little, the adrenaline buzz of walking and hum of online comments. When I camped alone I found calm, released from the effort of movement or the stimulation of having to talk to anyone at all. After a while of lying and listening to the wind sway the branches, all the chatter of thoughts disappeared. The scrolling lists of things I needed to do to make this walk a success, to inform as many people as I could about the symptoms of ovarian cancer – it all melted away.

As the day came and gentle light glowed around me, a light rain began to fall, just enough to make me hustle to pack away. A light mark on the ground where my body had been was the only trace of my sleeping-spot. A hidden night, invisible in public. I ducked out into the world again, cars passing, morning dog-walkers, continuing on the path.

At the point when I set out to walk 3300 miles I'd lived in Wales for almost sixteen years, moving between three different towns – more than long enough to have a diverse network of friends, many of whom were offering me places to stay when I reached their area, enough connections that I'd have someone to visit at least every couple of weeks, mainly when my routes took me back into mid-Wales.

I can't remember how long it was before the first message came, but it was surprisingly soon. Someone – a complete stranger, not even a friend of a friend, but someone who had received news of my journey through the myriad sharings of the internet – had reached out in return and invited me into their home. *Hi, when you get to x, you can come and stay with me.* The list grew and grew, I started to make a map, mark a star for each offer, so I could see when they came close. It meant more than just a bed; it meant a shower, washing my clothes, a safe place to close my eyes. I wouldn't say I was a mistrustful person but, during the planning and anticipation of this journey, it had just never occurred to me that so many people would offer me places to stay.

I did plenty of wild camping on this journey, sleeping in field corners, showering in leisure-centres and washing my socks in bathroom sinks, but I never went more than a week without a bed, usually having to camp for no more than two or three nights in a row. Many of my hosts were just strangers who'd decided to help me out, who found me through a variety of means: internet or radio or word of mouth or chance encounter. Whether inspired by the story of ovarian cancer or my travelling alone, they all reached out to aid me and it changed the nature of my journey completely.

At Ironbridge, where the folding of the land, a changing in the thickness of the stone, sent the Severn River turning south, I bought a pork pie in celebration. I'd walked 100 miles! When calculated in steps and effort this number was huge. A 100-mile walk, a massive effort, worth an "oooh" and a "well done". But it shrank down to nothing when I realised it was a thirty-third of what I'd set out to do. A thirty-third, a fraction barely worth mentioning. What was a thirty-third of an apple, one pip?

The weight of my walk settled down on me, and I felt sad and helpless as I walked over the bridge and down towards a pub where I would meet my next host. I struggled to make conversation with this woman I didn't know, only having admired her paintings on the internet: wanting only to sleep and rest, restore myself for the next day.

The way I'd been able to set out on a journey of this size was by not thinking about it; organising the whole thing at once was too enormous to comprehend so I faced little pieces of it, acted *as if* I was setting out on a long walk. *If* I was walking, what would I need? Well, I'd need a rucksack and a pair of boots. And so it began. Making the journey theoretical, reducing the terrifying task to small jobs meant I lined up a list of them that could be tackled in turn. The walk manifested invisibly in the background without my ever having to face up to the implications of the whole of it.

Now I had to do the same again with the route itself. I'm not sure it's possible to comprehend a journey of 3300 miles on foot. How can you imagine the size of your tracks, each step pressing against the ground, seeing a hill in the far distance and, hours later, standing on top of it, turning round and looking the way you've come, seeing your imaginary trace across the land, so many beads of sweat and heavy breaths? One day is hard to see, maybe ten or fifteen miles, but 3300? Huge, too huge. So I'd walk to Bristol, I thought to myself, focus on that and let the rest come later, when it needed to.

When I came close to Stourport I knew I was going to see Gaz and Steph again. I met them in September 2012, the first time I followed the River Severn to a hospital appointment in Bristol. They lived near a boatyard by Stourport, outside the entrance, on the river itself is a huge, rusting ferry. Something you can imagine as a steam powered craft on the Mississippi River, the kind that Huckleberry Finn found floating and abandoned.

Back then, at the end of one too-long day, I'd walked to Bewdley but had nowhere to sleep, walked a bit further, Stourport and the boatyard got in the way, still nowhere I could sleep. Past a lock and to a steep, dank wood: seventeen miles on the road by this point, rucksack cutting into my shoulders and feet like stones in my boots. I was ready to give up, but one last push and I came to a flat, grassy meadow with a weeping willow in the centre. Perfect. Just one problem: there was a caravan in the corner and it looked like there was someone inside it. Unusually, I decided to make myself known, risking the shouting and banishment to ask if I could sleep in the field. I was just too tired to go any further.

Wonderfully, as I approached the open door, a lovely friendly lion-head popped out of the doorway, golden-brown hair pushed back from a wide, calm face... Gaz.

"Hello, can I sleep in this field?"

"Of course you can, mate. Do you want a beer?"

We made a fire and drank cans of strong cheap lager, talking about silly things like feeding swans blackberries, making animal friendships. He was impressed with my story, in the way that cancer can sometimes be a magic word, and during the evening he went to fetch Steph from the first boat down on the river. I remember a light shining out of her face as she talked about being a nurse, and how enthusiastic she was about what I was doing. She gave me a little bag of food the next morning and a card that said I was a special person.

I spent the night in the caravan in the end, on the sofa while Gaz took the bed, telling each other bedtime stories and giggling ourselves to sleep. Gaz was saving up money to travel to South America, filling a van up with tatty goods for a car boot.

I'd loved that night and sent them a few postcards from further down the way, telling them where I'd got to downriver, keeping our connection open for a while longer.

The second time I met them was in August 2013. I'd decided to kayak to hospital this time, so I borrowed the kit and got a friend to lug me to the Severn, pushing me off where it became navigable at Pool Quay, near Welshpool. I didn't have their phone numbers but I wanted to stop by and say hello. I couldn't find a decent space to pull up by Gaz's grassy meadow so I floated on a bit towards Steph's canal boat and, shyly, looked to see if there was anyone in. There was, she was in the kitchen.

"Do you remember me?" I said, feeling proud to be coming to say hello in a kayak.

Yes, yes, of course she did, and she invited me in for a cup of tea and a bacon sandwich. Steph is like me, she'll get philosophical at the drop of a hat so we went off on great rambles for a few hours, talking about the world and getting to know each other a bit more. I met her husband and learned about how she'd cared for him during his serious illnesses. Gaz wasn't in the meadow any more, he'd moved his caravan back to the boatyard. We tried calling him but he was working that day. So off I went, with a hug from Steph, a phone number and another little parcel of food.

This time, another six months on, I walked into the boatyard for the first time, threading my way between hunks of metal. Cars, boats, lorry-trailers and caravans had been slotted into place, forming a rusty mosaic, built up over years. Empty canisters, bolts, torn pieces of metal scattered throughout the place, pushed into corners, up against bumpers. There was rust everywhere, like blown sand.

I found Gaz standing by an open fire, boiling some water in a dirty pan. Cleaning it, he said. He'd brought his caravan into the boatyard, painted it in the bright horizontal stripes of the Colombian flag and stuck pictures of tropical scenes on the outside, some kind of oval printed plastic. I looked closer.

"Gaz, are they toilet seat covers?"

"Yes, bab!" he said, thrilled that I'd noticed his ingenuity.

I asked about Steph and his face fell as he told me she had terminal lung cancer. This wonderful woman was dying. She was still living on her boat, pulled up beside the big ferry now, to make it easier for friends to come and see her. I went and showed my face but she had friends with her and it all felt a bit rushed; illness makes a person special and delicate and I didn't want to force her to talk to me.

Instead Gaz and I lounged around on a bench in front of the caravan and caught up on the last year. He'd been to Peru, fulfilling his latest travel passion. As various men appeared from corners, climbing down ladders from their boats or coming across the yard from caged-in lorry trailers, he'd introduce me proudly, tell the essence, the facts of my important self. I was the special guest, fresh with my story of a big adventure.

The man from across the way came out first, sitting in the sun underneath the hull of the huge yacht opposite, and talking about how hard his life was. Dave was past 65, had thick glasses and a bad leg. A couple of decrepit dogs followed him, languidly sniffing around, tennis-ball tumours swinging in the skin of their bellies. First he brought me tea, then two shortbread biscuits on a flowery plate. Finally, he shuffled away to his boat and came back with his change jar, two salt-pots full of coppers and leavings. Gaz opened a packet of crisps. Then Paul from the lifeboat around the corner brought out some olives.

Two more of them brought me their change collections, emptying jars and dishes of 5p and 10p pieces, taking back the spare screws and cigarette filters. I was awash with coppers and generosity, feted by these backwater urchins and honoured that they chose to give to me, paying their respects to my journey in unique style. Delapidated men, heavy drinkers, low-skilled, breadline lives, surviving at the edge of society; I didn't expect that they would dignify me in this way.

I had dinner with thin and twitchy Mike, squeezing into a mesh-roofed tunnel alongside his lorry-trailer, dogs skidding on the wooden floor he'd looted from an abandoned factory. The dogs were large and unruly, a hot pepper-smell coming from their short ginger hair, rare breed. Egyptian throne dogs, he called them. I was served dinner by Mike's partner: a huge pile of cauliflower cheese and gammon, thick oily slices overlapping on the plate. The dogs were everywhere, sniffing at plates, jumping ungainly onto chairs as they snapped at each other, wrestling and nipping on the foam cushions that lay out on the floor until they became too much and were banished to the large cage in the corner of the room.

After eating, I went back to Gaz, cheery and happy in his shambolic caravan, walls collaged with postcards and posters, ornaments crowding every surface. He had no bedding, just a thin sleeping bag on the foam-mattress bed. We sat close together as he told me about his experiences in Peru, this ponderous, gentle, heavy-drinking man. Our heads hovered close together in the magic distance where air prickles with possibility, just a slight turning together would mean our lips met. I wanted to kiss and love him, give him the tenderness he deserved, even just for one night, but he was too shy and used to being alone, a protective shell tucked and gathered tight around his vulnerability.

"You could live here if you wanted," said Gaz. "I can get you in. Tenner a week."

I thought about coming here, living an invisible existence. I could buy one of the rust-ridden boats and restore it, working to save money so I could leave again. I could use its dilapidation to spring myself to a better future, but only if I could hold out against the immobility of this boatyard, the depression. I knew, underneath, that I didn't want to pour my life into this fumbling, black place. I had a mission; time was too precious to waste.

The next morning I went to see Steph, alone, and this time it was easier to talk to her. She made tea, her skin stretched tight over her face, little bony body moving lightly in the small boat and first we talked about my journey. I showed her my shock blister photo and talked about how much I was enjoying myself. But soon enough we had to turn to what was happening to her. Cancer, once present in your life, is always there, hovering.

So we talked about her illness and at first it was the nuts-and-bolts stuff of where it is and how she's feeling, physically. What she's doing to treat it and when her next appointment is. Then after a while we got onto the real feelings, the things you can't say easily to most people. She talked of the chest-drain taking the liquid from her lungs, about hard days and easy days, about talking to people who don't have it, their struggles to understand, their crushingly awkward attempts to make conversation. Cancer is frightening and isolating and lonely. It's on your mind all the time, sitting in front of your face, taking up your consciousness. It turns your focus inwards, making you so self-centred that you can't bear to be polite to other people when they do something compassionate but misjudged, no matter how well meaning.

We understood exactly what the other was talking about, even from our different perspectives: hers that of a person who knows that the cancer has spread throughout her body with no hope of treatment, and mine that of someone who'd had an encapsulated tumour, easily removed and treated.

We didn't speak of death, so imminent yet so untouchable. I didn't bring it up, couldn't, really. *She* owned that conversation, no-one else. I walked away feeling saddened but uplifted by our connection. Somehow, when a person is dying in front of you, it charges every interaction with electric importance. There was nothing I could do for Steph, just spend time with her and take our conversation away, honour our small special connection.

The river took me directly south from Stourport and I could start looking ahead to Bristol. I was behind on my targeted mileage, thanks to the blister, but fortunately there was a woman ahead of me offering a bed for a few nights. If I could stay with her I'd make up the time, get a few days of easy, weight-free walking. I was noticing a small, strange pain in the base of my right foot, as if a piece of me wasn't stretching properly. Just walk to hospital I thought, get to Bristol, have a little rest and then worry about tackling the next bit.

Sally generously fed me and kept me for days, picking me up for the first time once I reached Worcester, driving 40 miles at a time to pick me up and drop me off. I was tracked by her as I made my way down the winding path, following the river-flow. She'll try and take over, warned my auntie in Shrewsbury, and she was right.

It felt excessive, the amount of trouble Sally was prepared to go to. It was really difficult to say no to this woman, her constant proffering of things I might need in an effort to be useful, and her hurt wheedling when I tried to turn them down. Accepting help was still a new feeling, and when I felt it pushed on me, it only made me more fiercely defend my independence. When I was resting in someone's house I had to remain pleasant, polite, making conversation. What I really wanted to do was to be alone, to squidge out and relax. I escaped as early as possible, each night, to my tiny bedroom.

Sally was nervous and loud, overbearing with her care and attention to detail, but her help was integral to my making it to Bristol on time. Though I'm grateful to her, at the time I found it heavy-going to be around someone so invasive. I couldn't leave early, it wasn't worth the angst. Plus, I needed this. I was only five days from Bristol, my appointment looming. My feet were tired and aching and I could walk further without my bag, no straps at shoulder and waist, restraining and weighting me down. My body was able to swing freely, loosening my tight muscles. The strange ache in the base of my feet continued, but I could walk seventeen miles a day bag-free, so fast compared to the agonised painful trudging at the beginning of the river.

South of Worcester, the ground I passed over was flat and agricultural. Small English villages with their squat black-and-white timbered cottages, ancient churches, antique towering oak trees in every field. The slow, fat river meandered alongside me. I passed my old favourite landmarks from previous journeys: the riverside pub with rare breed chickens pecking throughout the garden, the huge oak tree that leans to 90^0, a huge rising of earth holding the roots anchored where they tried to pull from the ground.

I stopped for a rest while walking the wide horseshoe loop of the Arlingham peninsula. I lay down and watched the sky, looked at the rain clouds massing on the other side of the wide river, and felt the wind ruffling the grasses at the top of the floodbank rising above my head. There were so many things rushing through my mind, as I wriggled my toes to ease the ache. I was distracted by thinking of emails to Assembly members, trying to get them to publicly support my awareness-raising. Then my thoughts moved swiftly to the chocolate in my rucksack. But for a small, precious piece of time I just lay there, feeling the grass gently prickling underneath me, and listening to the sound of it catching the wind.

As a carer, my days had been split into eight visits, each one a sequence of tasks that had to be accomplished within thirty minutes. The tasks had to be crammed in while not forgetting to take time for conversation with the service-user. Not too much though; don't forget yourself and get caught up in natural connection, it must remain surface conversation, easy to extricate yourself from. Get out in time, remember to write up your timesheet, list the jobs completed, and then rush away to the next house. If you're lucky you've got five minutes to pause before you repeat the process again. I was getting paid to be the person who didn't matter. The person who always bends her will, her personality and her time to the needs of others.

Each day was totally commanded by time constraints, I said yes to every piece of work I could and there was always somewhere I needed to be. In my scant spare time there was a to-do list to tackle, all the many small pieces of preparation for making a long-distance and very public journey with the aim of raising awareness of and funds for research into ovarian cancer.

Now I had time, entire days with only one thing to do. The clenched grip that my care-work schedule had upon my brain, the constant tick-tick of time passing, and the awareness of so many things I had to do was suddenly released, and I wobbled at the lack of structure. It was hard to have only one thing to do all day. What am I doing this afternoon? Walking. Tomorrow? Walking. I had nothing to do but walk, the rest of the spring and summer to fill with steps and fresh air. It felt strange, this release of pressure. I had to unwind, remember the travelling life once more, how to live with nothing to do.

The river had widened out into an unknowable blankness. Broad and smooth, moving in curling patterns, deep undertows of current coming to the surface in swirls and widening rings as sun-warmed surface-water mixed with cool immense depths. The path felt lonely and isolated, a thin strip of floodbank built up to protect the flat flood plain from rain-swollen river. The rare solitary houses crouched, blank-faced, behind the barrier. Constant wind shuttered their faces; they were closed, under attack. I passed a derelict pub, windows barred, grime climbing the grit-spattered walls. It was a strange area, walking down past Shepperdine, windy and abandoned, dominated by the blocky square bricks of two closed nuclear power stations.

An inlet in the mud banks led me inland to a bridge, and a boatyard where yachts lay marooned in the flatlands, and retreating tides had scored deep channels into the muddy banks, jagged like lightning strikes. There was a constant metallic music here, mixed tones of clanking cow-bells and tinkling cymbals or sleigh bells. The gentle cacophony of clinks and jingles came from the breeze, shaking ropes and linkages against masts and boat-sides. It was a beautiful background of calm, almost Buddhist, chiming and I took a break against the thick metal fence, leaning back to dream for a short while.

At last came my first sight of the Severn bridges, standing grand and calling to me, white and stately in the clear air. They were the marker of the end-point, just as the single lichen-coated pillar on Plynlimon stated the beginning of this wonderful river. I would walk all the way along the sheep-cropped river bank as the bridges grew awkwardly from small, faraway toys until they towered over me. They roared with traffic, braced against cars, holding the thread of transport over the river and connecting Wales and England. They were a soaring dream of wire-lines and concrete stilts, carrying a thread of road where car-ants ran. This was the end of the first part of my journey, and glee swelled within me.

I'd done it, I'd walked to Bristol.

THE OFFA'S DYKE PATH

Route description: A 177-mile National Trail, crossing the border country of England and Wales from Sedbury Cliffs in the south to Prestatyn, near the Dee Estuary. The route runs along or close to Offa's Dyke, a linear earthwork built in the late eighth century by the King of Mercia to mark out the western boundary of his kingdom.

Length:	176.8 miles
Total ascent:	9,085m
Maximum height:	700m
Dates:	24 March – 9 April and 26 April – 3 May 2014
Time taken:	26 days
Nights camping/nights hosted:	8 /18
Days off:	7
Average miles per day:	10.1

I went to hospital for my check-up, had a scan and was fine. No evil cellular squatters had nestled into my pelvis.

I felt pretty sober that day. This walk was mostly making me feel full of power and happiness. I could smile full-beam at everyone I met, wanting to chat, share things, hug people. Going to hospital was like tripping into a brick wall. The return to something scary, because it might happen, it might come back, and there in the hospital is where you go to begin to find out.

Sometimes it feels as if my cancer wasn't really cancer at all, just a near miss. But that's only true to a tired mind. I had a mucinous adenocarcinoma, stage 1a, grade 2. The important part is the stage 1a. It means I got lucky.

It took me about a year to feel good again. I came out of the illness part, through the recuperation and into the after stage where you put cancer behind you and stop being scared of it. It's just that it all comes back a bit when I go to hospital. Fear rises when the nurse leans forward to look closely at the ultrasound screen, or as I lie down, letting my body relax to horizontal vulnerability on the table, waiting for the doctor to loom over me and touch my stomach.

When I went into follow-up treatment, I was told that my cancer had a 6% chance of re-occurring within five years, and that 75% of recurrences happen in the first two years. That day, after achieving the first stage of my walk, I also crossed the line into the third year and it felt hugely significant. This wasn't quite over yet, I wasn't free of cancer, but it helped me to see that the fear barely needed to be with me anymore.

Looking back, with my repaired psyche, I can see that perhaps I was never in that much danger. That once I'd recovered from the surgery, it could have been so much worse. My body just lost a few minor organs; it was my tender and nervous brain that suffered in the long term. Maybe if I'd had a house and was financially stable, was supported by a partner and close community, this might have been a minor blip, a little operation to live though, and then later realise that everything was actually alright. I could look carefully at the statistics, my 94% chance of surviving for five years and onwards, snuggle down in a warm bed surrounded by people that I loved and be thankful that I was OK.

But there was no such OK for me. I had no home during my illness, I had no normal to return to from such a jagged interruption: no routine, no place of safety. The shock of such intense vulnerability was as difficult to get over as the cancer itself. A necessary part of my recovery was to teach myself to think positively: to focus on the 94%, rather than the 6%.

I came out of hospital, walked up Whiteladies Road and had a vanilla milkshake and a slice of Rocky Road brownie in a really nice café, and then found about six OS maps in a second-hand shop for 75p each. I felt better.

In Bristol, I stayed with friends who had done so much during my illness: friends of my parents, really. Pete had been my dad's best mate when he moved to Swansea for his first job after university, then best man at my parents' wedding in 1975. The last time I'd seen him and his wife Jenny had been at my father's funeral but, after a decade of silence, I phoned them while waiting for abdominal surgery, scared and homeless.

It was pure fluke that I had my treatment in Bristol. I'd arrived as an exciting, travelling wild person sleeping on a friend's sofa for a week but had turned unexpectedly into a weak and frightened woman who wanted to stay for a couple of months while awaiting a potential cancer diagnosis. My friends couldn't handle it and neither could I. I couldn't communicate in my time of stress, just shrank back and looked up studio-flats on the internet, wondering if I could find somewhere without stairs that would accept housing benefit, and imagining a food stockpile that would get me through the first few weeks of shuffling immobility. I was scared and didn't know what to do. The operation was too imminent to change hospitals; my brother phoned Pete and his immediate response, "How can we help?" was an incredible relief.

They welcomed an ill, traumatised woman into their home without reserve. I had my operation just a week after moving in, coming back to them a pale, quiet person, shuffling and in pain. They opened their home to me indefinitely and for that I was so grateful. Every time I returned to Bristol in the intervening two years, seven times, seven appointments, I'd returned to stay with Pete and Jenny, a long-standing friendship between families cemented by their aid.

A group came to walk out of Bristol with me that sunny March morning: Pete, Jenny, son George and his girlfriend Jenny, and my mum and her friend Leslie. They came with me as far as they could, stopping for breaks, aching feet; none of them worn-in like I was. We all made it to Severn Beach, though. I introduced them to the famous (in my eyes) Shirley's Café, an ancient wood-lined cabin with an equally venerable owner, too old for serious work now, her family bustling around her as she wiped the counter. I'd come in here every time I'd passed through and felt like it was an institution. After tea and cakes I hugged goodbye and left the others to catch the train home. I faced towards the windy Severn bridge, heading back to Wales and the start of the upcoming 3000 miles.

I stayed in Chepstow the first night, and then walked the day through the beautiful forests of the lower Wye, following the acorn markers of the Offa's Dyke path high above the winding river, and just catching a view of Tintern's ruins through a break in the trees far below. The path was easy to follow, popular, and well maintained as a result. Every stile brought another path-marker somewhere in the distance. I just had to scan the ground ahead and make a line for it, usually following the trodden marks of other feet.

After a night of camping, this time in the lushness of riverside woods surrounded by the strong smell of wild garlic, I made it all the way up to Monmouth, the next big town, walking into the streets as afternoon became evening. I bought food for a couple of days, knowing the path ahead held a Black Mountain crossing, no shops or villages, and two or three nights camping before I reached Hay-on-Wye. I stopped in at the leisure-centre, thinking I might be able to shower there, and was appalled when they wanted to charge me £3! I appealed for a charity-walker fee waiver and it worked, a tactic I would use all around the country, staying in the shower-room long enough to wash clothes as well as body.

I was heading out of town and ducked into a pub on a whim, thinking I'd charge my phone for a final half hour before heading out to walk. It was an upmarket wine bar, starting to fill with people at the end of their working day. A couple came in and obviously noticed me. They asked if they could sit with me, and we talked about cycle journeys. I told the usual story of cancer and hospitals and walking around Wales, and they looked at each other and then invited me to stay.

It felt strange. You're not supposed to do this, to trust strangers, just go home with people you meet in a bar. Part of me stayed alert all night, waiting for the creak of a door yawning open in the darkness of deep sleeping-hours. Travelling the way I do, having experienced wild camping for years, hitchhiking alone across Europe, a part of me must always remain cautious. But I also realised they were far more likely to be just genuinely lovely people.

The woman, Pat, was a particularly beautiful person. Both divorced, they'd met on a cruise ship and fallen in an immediate love that was strong enough to bring Pat here from her home country. I saw their first photo of them together, facing each other on deck, gesturing, locked into fascinated conversation. I realised that I really could trust them, that people could be nice for no reason other than they wanted to help me. We ate salmon frittata and talked about travelling – nothing more sinister than that.

I weighed my rucksack on their balance scales the next morning. 16 kilos! What was I doing, this was way too heavy. It was hurting my unfit body to drag this amount of weight along. Every item individually seemed essential but together they were far too much. I was carrying too much food – whey protein to put on my breakfast, a huge bag of trail mix, additional spare food, chocolate bars. It was as if I was scared to run out.

51

Arriving in Pandy late one afternoon I decided to camp there, rather than ascend the slopes of the Black Mountain and risk becoming exposed and vulnerable to weather changes as I slept. A long straight road separated scattered houses from a large hotel and between the houses and road lay a market garden. Just peeping over its high hedges was the pale half-moon of a polytunnel. The temptation to sleep in guaranteed rain-free comfort was hard to resist, and I sneaked over a gate in the corner, shrinking from the gaze of the houses as I walked across the field to the safety of the covered plastic. Warm and dry and giggling at my naughtiness I walked through the five large tunnels, until I found an unused area where I could lay out my sleeping-bag and prepare some food.

The light faded away to dimness as I sat waiting for the water to soak into my plain couscous. I had nothing to eat with it, just seasoning from an out-of-date salt-mill containing dried garlic and chilli flakes. I took a mouthful and put the bowl down. I felt defeated. This wasn't anywhere near good food, it was tasteless and unappetising. I needed to find something different. I needed to stop making do. All this meant was that when I became exhausted and couldn't face my unappetising, ill-planned rations, I spent money in cafés that I couldn't afford. I pushed the food aside, the light was almost gone and I was too tired to eat anything else. I lay down to sleep in the short space, buoyant on the rubbery earth beneath the black tarpaulin. I had muesli for the morning and would have to make sure I ate extra trail mix tomorrow too. I couldn't miss meals: calories meant strength.

Coming out of the polytunnel early, I blinked blearily. I'd packed up quickly, as a radio started droning Radio 4 in a shed nearby. I trod, light-footed, to the field's corner gate, skulking away before discovery. I was grateful for the early start as I planned a long seventeen miles up on the Black Mountain, a long finger of north- south hill, steep climbing to 700m and then a ten-mile plateau walk.

As I suspected, it had rained overnight, and as I came up through a sodden copse to the open land where the climb started, a mass of cloud and wetness draped around me, droplets hanging shining on gorse. The cloud stayed with me as I followed a trail through the peat and heather, flagstones laid where too many feet had ground away the soil. I saw no-one else that day, it was just me and the mist. There were grouse rattling in the background, and occasional wild and windblown ponies, steadfastly ignoring me, even as they sat directly beside the path, their manes hanging shaggy and glorious.

There was nowhere to shelter, no trees or scrub, nothing to tie my tarpaulin to. I had to walk the whole length of the hill before making camp, winding my way down off the flat-faced peak in search of a place to sleep. My aching and swollen toes pressed against the front of my boots, at their limits after a seventeen mile day. I lost the path somewhere down off Hay bluff which led me instead to a murky road nearby, almost in Hay itself. There, I saw a barn where I could gratefully bed down in the soft straw. There's peace inside a barn. An empty structure, made for shelter but half open, where the wind rustles the trees outside but inside all is soft and quiet and warm. Barn sleeping is my favourite kind of wild camping, the hay cushioning is an insulation to nestle down into. Human shelter normally excludes everything of the world – animals, weather – but a barn is open to these things. Mice rustle and burrow nearby, the rain blows into the open sides but doesn't touch me, and I snuggle comfortably, sharing my sleep with the natural world.

I slept long, wandered slowly into Hay and spent the morning lazily consuming a full English breakfast, perusing a few bookshop shelves, sneakily washing a full set of socks and knickers in a café toilet as a pot of tea cooled on a table outside. The clock struck 1pm as I left. 1pm and I'd walked half a mile. Terrible!

A few miles later I sat down for a bit then walked a few more over to Newchurch, sat down some more and decided to try for the final three to Gladestry. If I made it, there was only a hill to walk over to Kington the next morning, where I could have a day off with my mum.

The problem was that my feet were hurting and in a serious way. Sometimes I would experience a deep ache of tendon pain that went away after a while; alternatively, there was the sharp burning blister pain that was awful at first but which could be walked through. That day it was the kind of pressure pain that comes after you've pounded your feet onto the ground over and over again for far too long. A time-to-stop-walking-this-is-too-much-and-the-pain-will-not-stop kind of pain. I pulled a piece of plastic out of the hedge, one of those document-wallet type things. It was full of water and as I poured it out, out came the sad, saturated body of a mole. I was walking on painful feet, holding the plastic, irritated by there being no bin to put it in.

The sun was setting far away over the hillside and I could see that I would arrive in Gladestry after dark. Then the internet told me that it would rain before dawn. I thought maybe I would find a little piece of woodland where I could pitch a shelter or maybe go for the church-porch scenario.

These were the things that were running through my mind as I came to the sign announcing the start of the village.

There was a house by the road and a caravan in the garden opposite; it was a shabby trailer kind of caravan, not a shiny white pristine Caravan Club type. This probably influenced my decision, but as I stood there in the road, I suddenly thought *I am going to knock on the door of that house and ask if I can sleep in their caravan.*

A decision like that is a great departure from my usual self; I feel like an animal when I'm looking for a sleeping spot. I must be safe before I pass into unconsciousness, and with no walls or familiarity around me the animal part of my brain fusses and frets and won't lapse into sleep unless I'm absolutely certain that no other human knows where I am.

Before I could doublethink myself and slink away, with no more than a pause in my step to mark a decision made and reconsidered, I walked over to the house and knocked on the door. I wondered who'd be inside, what they'd say, what I'd say.

There were some faded postcards in the porch window, scattered feathers and a burnt-out tealight. I forecast potential friendly spirits within and felt hopeful.

It happened. A woman opened the door, about my age and with a very small baby sitting on her front in a carrier, a blanket wrapped around them both.

I took a deep breath to make sure I spoke calmly before I started an unstoppable chain of unknown actions and reactions.

"Hi there, I'm doing a long-distance walk around Wales and I'm camping as I go. It looks as if there's going to be rain tonight and I was wondering if I could sleep in your caravan across the road."

Pause.

That's how I wound up sleeping on a stranger's sofa, while she and her child slept in the next room. The people upstairs, the caravan owners, sent down an Indian takeaway and a £20 donation. They were all bright-eyed, relaxed and friendly; perfectly capable of coping with an outlandish stranger appearing in their lives.

As so many other times, we ate together and shared our stories, talked about the world and our learning of its intricacies. T was a single parent to this brand-new baby, alone and worried, admitting to her depressive history, asking me if I thought the baby was ugly. We were both confused people in our thirties, wondering how others have found it so easy to decide what they want to do with their lives.

I left her a postcard the next morning with the story of the crescent-moon bear on it: a woman is told to go looking for a cure for her woes in the form of a hair from the bear's throat but, in the end, discovers that the cure is the journey itself. It's the same for all seekers; there's nowhere to go and find yourself, all you can ever discover is that you were there all along.

The Offa's Dyke Path was more difficult than the Severn Way. When I was following a river down to the sea, it was either downhill or flat, whereas the Offa's Dyke Path was green and luscious and beautiful, but also very hilly and muddy. The ground was still saturated from winter, so it didn't take much rain before it became slippery everywhere. When I stopped walking and became silent, sometimes I could hear the glugs and gurgles as water slowly seeped into the ground or downhill to the waterways. The path switchbacked constantly, sometimes following a border, sometimes obeying the constraints of a long-distance footpath imposed on existing farmed land and around houses, but mostly following the dyke itself.

Offa's Dyke, the ancient monument, was always there: sometimes a winding heap alongside me, sometimes a rise too big to be climbed, sometimes imagined, sometimes disappearing altogether. It was a barrier to keep the Welsh out, or in, providing a platform to land a boot to the head of anyone in the wrong place. I thought of how many sentries would be needed to patrol this earthen defence, impossible to lead a horse up. This tangible mark of ancient history, too big to destroy, time has only blurred it. No more than a mound of earth: ploughed into flatness, cut through for tractor access, worn down by subsidence, rabbits eating away the insides, riddled by burrows. Sometimes it was tree-covered, sometimes it turned into a fence, a field boundary or sometimes it disappeared around me, with only a trace to be seen on the hillsides ahead, a groove carved across the land.

The walking started to become mundane here, in a way. Or maybe not the walking, not the stunning sights, but the rhythm of my days became repetitive enough to seem ordinary. It had been just over a month since I'd set out from Machynlleth, and my life of constant movement was becoming normal. I got up every day and walked, packing everything carefully into its place in my rucksack, safely strapped up and accessible during the day's journey. I'd started stretching since Bristol, making myself a list of all the different stretches to do. I stretched for twenty minutes before setting out every day and included a few after each rest stop. I was a ball of aches of different kinds and needed to release them, to make my body as fluid as it could be.

If I was staying with someone there would usually be some kind of delay, interesting conversation or a drive back to my drop-off point, meaning I'd start walking at ten o'clock or so. If I'd camped then I'd still delay, but instead this was self-imposed staring time; sleeping outside in the way that I do means I don't sleep as deeply as in a bed. So, even though I'd wake with the dawn, turning out of sleep to see the first pale washes of colour in the sky, it would take me a few hours of first dozing in and out, then sitting up and staring, then eating breakfast very slowly, then a little bit more staring, before I got up and walked, usually nine at the latest.

And then I walked, all day, for hours. That's what I did, every day. I just walked, sometimes at a moderate speed, sometimes slowly. I walked and looked at around me. Each day was stunning, surreal and memorable. I saw signposts stranded alone in fields, a faded medieval painting on the wall of a church, the sun rise over a castle, hundreds of spring flowers and three black-nosed lambs sitting by a stile. Every so often there was an abandoned, falling-down house that I wanted to buy and make my own, to live in and grow vegetables, be a hermit writer, learn to weave, set up an arts centre, a workspace, a B&B,

become self-sufficient, sell the place for a profit, leave it to rot and go travelling, never live in Britain, stay here forever. A thousand futures sprang before me. My mind raced more quickly than my body as I moved across the land at the slowest human pace.

A lot of walking is tiredness. It's stopping frequently, whenever the impetus slips a gear and the hovering pause pounces, compelling you to stop, turn around, watch the view and catch your breath.

A lot of walking is an utter empty-brained exhausted nothingness; especially at the end of a day, when it's important to find a flat place to lay your body that won't curve your back muscles into screaming discomfort. Ground that looks flat must be lain upon to be certain. Once there it becomes hard to get up; just lying down is a relief as you feel your body start to let go of the tension of ever-forward motion. You want to slide into sleep, but you haven't covered yourself to conserve body temperature, you haven't eaten to restore energy, you haven't rubbed your muscles to ease them and you haven't pissed to prevent the necessity of unwrapping your cocoon in the chill deep of night.

The bed, which looked flat, isn't. You know that if you lie here you'll feel your legs become bloodless as all your body fluids obey gravity and slide towards your head; it's a pressured and uncomfortable feeling, and you know you must change position. As daylight fades, the temperature is ebbing from the world and it won't come back. You must move, take action. But all of your being wants to be still on the floor, here, now, in this moment to lie and do nothing, to feel nothing, to lapse away from the effort and just stop. Your mind is dense and dark treacle, dipping into a coma of fatigue. To heave yourself back to vertical is a great and terrible effort.

A lot of walking is automatic; it's letting your body function while your mind wanders in its own realm, traversing tired old pain, inventing new and unusual scenarios with which to probe and torture long guarded scars. They're comfortable, these mental ruts: easy and smooth territory to glide in.

A lot of walking is time passing, small events amusing you for a second and then passing into insignificance. Climbing a hill that's marked by a line of larch, and realising that the branches carry rows of budding flowers that are shocking red, small red lapping coronets that nestle in the fresh green branch-tips, starkly contrasting against the previous year's deep green growth. The buds are at eye level because you're climbing up underneath them, and you stand for a second with your face close to these baby rubies, smelling the optimism of new growth, glowing in spring sunlight.

I walked and walked and walked. When it was easy, I strode along, feeling great, trying to lengthen my stride to work the muscles in my thighs instead of stomping on my calves. When it was hard, my feet hurt in multiple ways and it was time to stop for a rest. About every couple of hours I'd take twenty minutes or so to put my feet up, eat something from the never-shrinking bag of trail mix, drink some water.

Water was always on my mind. To limit the weight of my pack I only carried a litre bottle, but I needed to drink at least two litres a day. I had to find cafés or pubs to replenish my supply, or even knock on doors, feeling awkward whenever I did it, although I was never refused. If there was no water source then I had to conserve water, which I really shouldn't have. If I didn't keep topped up, I'd get tired and develop a blinding white-pain headache.

I started monitoring how much I pissed. If I didn't have a good long wee before bed, it meant I hadn't drunk enough that day. There was a time-delay with dehydration. If it came on, it was because I hadn't drunk enough the day before, not that day itself, meaning there was no quick fix of downing an immediate litre. Water took time to percolate through my body, and I learned to keep a constant supply of it going in, never leave it until later, never do without. During the first month, I'd tried to limit myself to a litre a day for the ease of getting to the next supply-point. But very bad headaches soon taught me that this was an awful idea. Food and water were fundamental; there was no going hungry for a day, or thinking, *wow, I didn't drink very much yesterday*. I didn't have the reserves to be able to deplete myself in that way.

There's a section in the middle of the Offa's Dyke Path that is the most arduous thirty miles of all. It's a sequence of numerous switchbacks, steep climbs and drops of 100m each time, an endless painful ache of rises and falls, making my calves burn, my ankles bent awkwardly against the gradient.

Someone came towards me and said hello in passing, then, an hour or so later into that day's gentle beauty of copses and streams, hedged fields, oak and hawthorn and curl-edged leaves, to my bemusement, the same man came towards me again. He explained that he was with a group that were following behind. He came a few miles in his car and walked back to meet them before walking to his car again and driving ahead, his hip too damaged to allow him to keep up with a full day's exercise.

The group caught up with me a few hours later and I tagged along with them for a couple of days, enjoying conversations with different members about children, retirement, cancer. They were a stalwart, experienced group of men, slowly becoming elderly. Years ago, in their thirties, they'd decided to get out and have adventures, feeling themselves decline and become soft, homely, as children made their lives more regulated and comfortable. Now, twenty-five years later, their level of adventure had declined to something I was capable of, walking the Offa's Dyke Path. Age notwithstanding, they were still faster and fitter than me and I struggled to keep up, especially on the steep hills. I happened to be walking next to the unofficial leader one time, the man who, so many years before had hustled this group of friends into getting out there, taking risks. Just take smaller steps and don't stop, he said. Solid advice from a solid man.

I was unexpectedly alone as I came up and into the ring of trees that marks the Iron Age fort at Beacon Ring above Welshpool, a couple of the men just ahead of me and the main group further behind. At this point there was a view of the wide valley below, where the Severn had carved a path curving away to the east. I stopped walking, struck with an image of my tiny self walking down there. My small steps had taken me in a wide curve all the way down to Bristol, and all the way up the humps and climbs of Offa's Dyke to return again, a dot in this land pushing and propelling my body to get here. A month of walking and sleeping: a month of effort, to bring myself round in this 300-mile loop. The completing of the circle flashed in my mind. I'd cross my own trail, the first of many invisible overlayings I'd make on this journey, and I felt proud of my new knowledge of the landscape.

I came down the hill, chatting to the friendliest of the men, trying to keep up with these two as they walked, long-legged and bagless, striding ahead of me. One began to run, he couldn't help himself, and I moved quickly, trying to keep up. It sent pain shooting into my left knee, feeling as if it would buckle backwards, wanting to bend in on itself. I had to stop, letting them go ahead while I raged at myself for trying to keep up with them and paying no attention to my personal pace or needs. I limped down the hill and into the pub at Buttington, sitting as dazed as they were, allowing ourselves a single pint before we all must keep moving: me to Welshpool where I'd begin Glyndŵr's Way and them to their pub lodgings further on. I'd follow them northwards but not for another fortnight. First came a 140 mile detour into Central Wales.

GLYNDŴR'S WAY

Route description: Named after the leader of the last Welsh rebellion, Glyndŵr's Way runs entirely through Powys in sparsely-populated countryside. One of three National Trails in Wales, it visits many sites associated with the Glyndŵr campaign against the English in the late 1300s.

Length:	135.5 miles
Total ascent:	7,180m
Maximum height:	504m
Dates:	10 – 23 April 2014
Time taken:	14 days
Nights camping/nights hosted:	4/10
Days off:	2
Average miles per day:	11.3

When I saw that Glyndŵr's Way made a C shape into mid-Wales, with the end of each arm perfectly lodged against the Offa's Dyke Path, I knew I had to include it. I could walk the Offa's Dyke Path up to Welshpool, turn off onto Glyndŵr's Way and, 136 miles later, wind up back on Offa's Dyke, thirty miles south at Knighton. It would be a journey to Machynlleth and back again, even passing through my old garden at Talbontdrain.

I used Couchsurfing for that first night in Welshpool, walking into a gift shop in the town centre and meeting the friendly face of Claire, who turned out to be a boisterous and big-hearted nurse, full of giggles and mild debauchery. She took me to a terraced house in a quiet cul-de-sac and we drank tea and smoked cigarettes, swapping tales of gin and foolishness. She was kind and friendly; I immediately felt like I'd found a friend, taking time to sit in her house the following morning before she set out to work, going back to boil the kettle again and again, just one more cup, topping up with tea and friendly chatter before I set out on the latest path.

The first afternoon I wound out through the parkland of Llanerchydol Hall, the ancient, tall trees carefully selected to fit the grounds of a grand home, the grounds-keepers carefully managing the estate. Peeping into a walled garden was the closest I came to the house itself: path edges crumbling, it had a stately aged beauty.

Here I began to see pheasants. They scooted awkwardly away from me, necks rigid with fear. Staying low and hidden until the last possible second of my approach when they were provoked into chirring alarm, signing their exit with a clatter. Rabbits glimmered at the edge of view, flicking away under the depths of gorse skirts. They all saw me well before I became aware of them, my contemplative ego separating me from a natural mindful state. It's a particularly human blindness, the laziness of the predator who buys pre-packaged prey.

A few miles later I came down a soggy and awkward field, claggy with loose earth: sheep snuffling at the brown, chewing away turnip lumps into white flat moons, all they could reach without eating the soil itself. It was a wide slope, tree-dotted but otherwise a blasted, over-trodden expanse. There was a rotting sheep corpse at the base of the field by the gate and more reedy soggy mud beyond.

It was an unfriendly place and I was glad to get beyond it, heading up a small rise and along a wooded field edge where tree roots had created shelters for sheep to lean against; their regular resting there had flattened out small rounded places. I looked at them longingly as I walked past, imagining myself sleeping there, curling my body into those spaces. Discomfort awaited, if I was desperate enough to try it, unable to roll over or stretch out beyond a very specific positioning. It wasn't so late, I wasn't that tired, so I carried on.

Another couple of fields ahead came a stream and a slope upwards above it, with a flat, almost-disappeared track running horizontally along the contour. It was a lovely space for me to sleep and I happily laid out my tarpaulin. There was still plenty of light in the sky and I surveyed my chosen bedroom: fallen tree nearby with intertwining bare branches, stream meandering along the bottom of the field and a rosy glow lighting the woods opposite. I was eating and relaxing, all until a group of horses trotted down the slope behind me, wheeling round into the space below my sleeping spot and spreading out to graze. They would wend their way closer and closer to me, pretending not to, so casual in their inquisitiveness, ready to wheel away at any sudden movement. Each horse took its turn to come nearer, each having their own particular comfortable distance. I watched them for a while, admiring the muscle and shining skin, in no particular hurry to get up and leave this calm and comfortable spot. But I knew I would; there was no way I could sleep in a field with loose horses, the fear of a hoof crashing against my prone body in the night meant I'd never be able to relax here. I had to pack away all my things again, stuff the puffed-up sleeping bag back into the base of my rucksack and fold away the tarpaulin.

Another space came within a quarter mile, after I'd paced up the hill to a road with, not long afterwards, a house at the end. The tarmac stopped with the last dwelling place, but caught between two high hedges, there was a hidden patch of land where a trackway continued. I could duck behind the grown-out holly bushes and make a nest on a bed of leaves, thickly fallen and held in the windless space between the thickets. It was a calm and quiet place, nothing human had come here, not for years, no path or vehicle, just an old place of passage, holding its space in charming wild decay, bushes hanging their sprouting arms down into the empty place. I lay down in perfect peace, and read until the last of the light had left the sky: *The Mayor of Casterbridge*, telling of a time when this road would have been used by carts and drovers. I imagined leaves layered over wheel-ruts.

I woke in the night to the rustles of rabbits and once when a spider ran over my face. I felt its first steps onto my neck and held still the urgent impulse to brush it away. I was rewarded by the feeling of a whisper of movement as its dainty legs touched faintly across my cheek and into my hairline. It was a moon explorer, a pod held high on spindly pins, delicately teetering through unknown territory, unaware of the sleeping giant that its landscape comprised. The taint of a spider's footsteps left no mark at all, just the feeling of being a complete part of this quiet hollow, one of the animals. For a few special seconds, I had quelled my blundering human presence to become just another piece of the natural landscape.

Hills crowded together in the distance as I lapped in and out of valleys, dipping and rising into different river routes. There was no single marker to follow, as I'd been doing with the broad snakes of the dyke and the Severn. The path wriggled, with no clear idea of a direction. It had obviously been invented, having no clear purpose other than tourism. A line had been drawn between places to incorporate possible daily stages and useful tourist-entertainment points, using existing footpaths and taking in small detours for views of a lake, or around a recalcitrant landowner not allowing access. This path feels very different to an old track, to a route that has been laid down by human feet for hundreds of years, that has a clear overall theme or purpose.

In Pontrobert, I sat on a bench for a while watching a blue tit bathe in the gutter of a bus shelter. It flung out intrusive moss pieces before fluttering and shaking wing shivers into water droplets, each catching a gleam of sunlight. Behind the grey metal roof came tips of pink blossom sprays peeping, delicate bravery in the fresh spring sun.

It was April, the time of spring flowers and new lambs. There was a brightness to the sunshine, bright and yellow and new, and my route was taking me through the heart of mid-Wales: sheep country. I came to lambs just born, feeling rude and insensitive blundering into the first moments of their life. I watched the lamb struggle to standing, legs askew in varying directions, nosing its way along the length of mother, not knowing its prize until it found the teat.

Sometimes lambs stayed behind when their mother bustled in alarm at my presence and trotted away. All the mother could do was call to her offspring and remain out of reach, pacing in the background, waiting for it to come further away from my stealthy, predatory stalking. But the lamb didn't know, wasn't looking up at the height of this interloper. The gigantic size of me was restricted to two thick dark tree trunks and an unusual smell: no sense of my marauding hands, ready to swoop and manhandle. It stayed at my knees while the mother paced and bleated and I couldn't resist kneeling to it, smelling its beginning scent of warm lanolin, watching the eyes blink against the light. Perhaps this lamb was blind, perhaps it was ill, perhaps it was too new to realise my threat. I wanted to stay with it longer, touch and cosset it, but took pity on the mother's worry and walked away.

I passed fragile lambs, tied by the farmer in protective plastic like a pensioner's rain bonnet, bone-thin and delicate, limbs shrunken below their shanks, below the knee puffed up by a legwarmer woollen coating.

Lambs rushed and vaulted up onto hawthorn roots, earth banks, food troughs, felled trunks, prizing the leap-gained height of a new perch before bucking down again in twisting ecstasy. Skittish and frisky they ran and paused together, enjoying the newness of mass movement. Heads tossing, the lambs formed groups that jumped and capered, a mini-horde at the mercy of impulse, with the potential to spread like liquid splashes in any direction.

Another new lamb still had the red cord hanging down from its belly, fresh and bright and blood-red, the last live line of contact from one body to the other. I squatted down and watched for a while as it wandered around its mother, nudging against her nuzzling licks, her pleasured grunts. It found its legs had taken it to the hawthorn shelter it was birthed against and I watched as this lamb closed its eyes, blinking dazedly as it absorbed the scent of this new thing. Crusted bark rough and dry, sap flow pushing, lichen-coated, beetle-tracked, swaying and creaking: tree.

I saw that lambs don't always easily find their mothers. I saw lambs start from their game, or knuckle up from a small snooze with no idea where their mother was. I watched as lambs called over and over, seemingly not hearing the answer from a patient parent. I saw them run towards a sound, only to divert to a nearer, grazing, white cloud. I saw them run towards any sheep and try to kneel and drink, only for the mother to smell their backsides and butt the interloper away from their dangling udder.

Coming through a field between Dolanog and Pont Llogel, towards a long, straight trackway that was probably once a railway line, I realised I was being followed by a herd of ewes. They were bundled together, unable to control their curiosity. I'd peep back over my shoulder as I walked, watching them take long languorous sniffs of the air where my scent was being wafted back towards them. Each flaring of their nostrils was their tasting of me, their learning about what exactly I might be. If I stopped and turned around, they stopped too, eyes flicking to one another, reading the group mood and watching for the next decision. They edged and twitched, wanting to come and investigate me but unable to step outside the group dynamic which has them to do as the others do: stay together, follow each other.

I was coming to know sheep. I saw the many ungainly ways in which they get stuck in their environment. I found sheep, alive and dead, twisted and trapped and wedged in wire fences. I was coming to know their calls, like a prehistoric herd of herbivores, opening their throats to blurt out a foghorn bleat. I came to know the way they communicate as a group, the ways in which they are curious, and the ways in which they are scared. I knew the smell of them and their marks and trackways, the ways they shape the ground.

Their faces were starting to tell me who they were. The brute, bulbous ugliness of a Texel ram, the inquisitive pointed rabbit-ears of a Blue-faced Leicester and startling clarity of the Badger-faced breed's black markings, a brown collar mark showing Welsh-mountain blood. Occasionally, I even saw the long, curled wool hanging over the smiling face of a Cotswold or the heavy-rolled layers of a robust and regal Merino ram. I knew I'd entered the higher places when I began to see the button eyes and small, cross-stitched mouth of a true Welsh mountain sheep.

I came to a hawthorn barrier between two fields, made obsolete by the wire fence, and allowed to grow from a thick, squat hedge into rippled trees, short and gnarled. Branches had become elegant grotesques, bark-scaled and moss-coated, like their bulging root fists. These are ancient trees, once placed to mark a holloway, to line a place of passage. Now they shelter grazers, their branches twisting and merging.

The wind is gentle and sweet, creaking in the rub of two branches together, humming the holes of each metal gate in the mellow pitch of panpipes. The low sound of a gate singing to itself, it's a beautiful thing to walk into.

Searching for an evening bed, I came at last upon a round flat mass of trodden hay, where seasons of sheep coming to devour a bale laid in the same place had trampled down a flat, yielding, and sweet-smelling base, their own threshing circle. I lay down, and watched the sky darken through the hazel branches, catkins shivering.

I watched two crows attack a red kite – a game of slow placement in the sky before a swooping, sudden attack. It looked like the crows had the best of the kite, hitting and bundling it downwards in an awkward falling movement that first drew my attention. I watched as they disengaged and circled each other before they swooped in again, their numbers putting the kite at a disadvantage. Incredibly, the kite was able to turn upside down in the air several times, presenting each diving crow with bared talons in a last second effort of aerobatics, forcing them to judder away and abandon the attack.

Water trickled behind me in a small cut at the side of the field, trees rooted deeply either side of it, drinking from it, their growth shaping the way the water ran downhill. I sat and looked over Lake Vyrnwy, the white rushes of water falling down the black stone dam, the turrets above it. Reeds ran away down the slope ahead of me, reeds and stunted hawthorn trees, their branches holding lichen as if they'd filtered it from the air. Ahead were the hills that surrounded the lake, green fields squared the sides or segments of dark pine; above the tree line there were bare tops that sustained only coarse grass and patches of bracken.

Vyrnwy is the first forced reservoir in Wales. England decided it needed water and that land in Wales could be drowned to provide it. The surveyors came, and then the Act of Parliament, and then the dam. Houses were built to replace the submerged village that now gave water to the thirsty city of Liverpool. Today the village is a memory, the outrage and broken homes forgotten in a lull of light on water, on small waves lapping at lake edge, quiet views, kayak holidays and picnic spots. Water forming infrastructure that was never any other way. A full third of the valley bottom was underwater bog over winter, they said, the land unusable, growing only reeds and willow groves. But still, the lives of 400 people were changed irrevocably, deemed unimportant, their feelings overridden in the search for water provision for tens of thousands.

I looked from the water to the pine darkening the hillside. Another forced land change; 100 years ago the UK government required wood for war, so bought up farms through compulsory acquisition and started a mass tree-planting operation to secure the country's timber supplies, employing up to a fifth of the country at times. Now, it's just another cash crop. Farmers plant their own fields, taking coarse land out of pasture, where the earth is stretched too thin over stone to support nutrition, and the sheep struggle to find good feeding. The pine has become normal; it's easy to forget that all here was once farms, without this cloaking plantation silence.

Patches of dark pine mix into the wilder grasses, and fields of undrained ground are left to be marshland, sporting longer grasses and reeds, and not artificially seeded by more palatable turf for pasture. I hadn't seen this landscape since I left home, and descended into the calmer farmlands of the English/Welsh border. As I turned away from the Severn Valley at Welshpool, onto Glyndŵr's Way and into the wilder territory of the mid-Wales uplands, it felt like a return to home territory; pine forestry wasn't beautiful to me but its presence was familiar and comforting.

Walking away from the lake and through Ddol Cownwy, the final small set of houses in the miles of pine forest on my route between Lake Vyrnwy and Llangadfan, I came to a broken-down chapel with an ancient K-reg car out front. The inside was a mess of moss, mould and tattered plastic, the tyres were flat and grass was growing up around it. A flattened front seat and greening

71

duvet proved that someone slept in here, once. The chapel door was open, a long-broken lock and useless length of chain hung from the tattered latch. I ducked under the clinging rosehip trails and into the building. Light filtered down through a gap in the roof, to where small plants had begun to grow in the mossy drip-hole beneath. The place was ragged, only remnants of chapel life clung to the broken building. There were pews at the front, a cross painted on the wall and a faded flower-border at the seated congregation's eye level. It was a small room, where the faithful of this small village in remote Powys had come to seek reassurance and a meaning to the direction of their lives. Now it sat as a holder for other dreams, for those who might come with little in the way of funds, to buy it, to scrape together tools and knowledge, repair and rebuild it, making it into a home where new dreams might come, new life from decay. The building waited in silence and held all these dreams, those of past and future, the repetition of years of hope and peaceful prayers layered into the walls, sunk through the peeling paint and into stone itself.

Arriving in Llangadfan I found the Cann Office Hotel and sat in the pub until it got dark outside, too tired and dazed to move. Two pints didn't help and I made a lazy bed-choice, squeezing an unsavoury sleeping spot out of a flat gravel bed alongside an electricity substation. It felt like a precarious place, I couldn't go too far away from the road or I'd be in view of the house next door, but equally, anyone walking along the pavement only had to turn their head at the right moment to see the whole of me lying there, exposed as a rough sleeper. It didn't feel pleasant, but once it was dark I'd rather sleep somewhere easy than begin the walk into the black unknown, stumbling over trip-hazards and nervous of what I couldn't see.

All the time I walked, I had intense and vivid dreams, swirls of surrealism about meetings and mafia members and Mexican violin maestros and felt-tip pens floating down a river. But waking up was even more surreal; I'd have to remember where I was each morning, allow the knowledge to trickle into my brain that yes, I'm sleeping on the ground, I'm in a field, it's because I'm doing a long distance walk, a few thousand miles. This is my life now, I've been walking for weeks and I'm going to be walking for months more. There'd be a split-second realisation, the blast where all this hit me. *Woah*, would go my half-asleep brain and I'd just lie there in wonderment, trying to absorb the insanity.

Once I left Llangadfan, the smaller twists of the path climbed and swivelled through muddy fields at first, then small stream-bottomed hollows levelled out to a wide, high plain, with higher hills lined along the horizon. It was the high lands, there were reeds throughout the fields, other undrained fields of long yellow marsh-grass, folded and lying on itself in a melted tangle. I looked at it, a trap to pull and hinder stumbling legs, and felt glad that the path followed the road here; that kind of terrain would take hours to walk through.

I came to the only houses on the long road in the Nant yr Eira valley: farm buildings and barns, with the road running between them, a small chapel next door. A woman was crossing and stopped to say hello, jumping in surprise when I said I was raising money for Penny Brohn.

"I had treatment there, fifteen years ago," she said. "For breast cancer."

Caroline invited me in for lunch. She and her husband were a warm and friendly couple, living a very basic smallholders' life, isolated subsistence living, people who'd escaped from expensive England and taken on a farmstead with geese and two cows. We ate a simple meal, soup and homemade bread. Caroline had warm round eyes and thick, centre-parted hair, Mick was grizzled and grey. They were good people.

They asked if there was anything they could do for me and I took a deep breath, unused to being so open about my needs.

"You could take my rucksack ahead for me? It would help me to walk more quickly and I've a big day today, over the high hills and down around the corner to my friend Annie's."

"Yes, we can do that" they said, and my heart sang.

I set off along the long thin road with lighter steps. It was so much easier without a bag; I could walk faster and more upright with no weight at my shoulders. The path turned away from the road and up into the winds, and with no more shelter from the valley I was blown and battered as I paced up the high hill towards the forest. Head down and shoulders set against the gusts, I crossed several fields, turning round to take one last look at the quiet valley, blue skies and scudding clouds, before heading towards a line of dark pine trees.

The wind stopped, as if at a switch, and I gasped and stopped to steady myself. The absence left a ringing in my ears, my head spinning in the aftermath. The silence in the forest was deep. Moss banks stretched away either side of a small stream that silvered between roots and thick peat overhangs. The branches of the trees brushed low, forcing me to bend and twist around them to follow the narrow path. The trees grasped at me and when I looked between their trunks I saw deep green moss-beds, scattered hillocks glowing phosphorescent lime in gleams of sunlight. There was silence, just faint flutters and flickers of birds dispersed throughout the foreign trees and in that silence there was a calling. The moss-beds were whispering to me, a siren song, inviting tired travellers to bed down in their thick, deep softness.

It felt as if there might be an entity pulsing at the heart of the forest, drawing living beings into its essence, down into its deep-held stillness. It was the forest itself that lived, each tree a tendril of the whole. If I turned from the path, ducking past branches, twisting between interlocking trees, into gaps of thinning needles until I couldn't turn back, maybe I'd never leave that place again.

I thought of a book of Swedish folk tales I'd read as a child, with its forever-remembered illustrations of bulbous trolls, gnarled hands and hanging curls of hair, tied-leather clothes and scattered rings and jewels. Then there was the tiny princess, frail and shining, who dropped her golden-heart necklace into a brown and shrouded forest pool and, in bending down to look for it, holding her long hair to either side of her face, forgot all else in existence and became a cottongrass plant, white fuzzy head bobbing in the wind.

Shaking away the illusion I walked on and came out of the trees high above Llanbrynmair, seeing many hills below me, lapping away to Machynlleth and the sea. The sun glinted on a tiny triangle of open water, away in the far distance. I'd walked to the edge of my home district. Down there, further along towards Cemmaes Road, began the places where my friends lived, where I'd go for visits, cups of tea and afternoons in the sun: the roads I knew, the farms and houses I'd visited to care for the elderly.

Home started in this view, where the River Rhiwsaeson curled down from the hills I stood in, met two others in Llanbrynmair and became the River Twymyn, running around to the west to join the River Dyfi at Cemmaes Road. The Dyfi Valley spread out all the way to Dinas Mawddwy, forming a scattered community of houses, farms and villages, centred on Machynlleth. Up in the forest wilds of Aberangell, or the sheltered peace of Aberhosan, people turned towards Machynlleth as the place they went to shop and gather together, and I'd follow Glyndŵr's Way from here to there the next day, walking back to the clock tower again after I'd left it six weeks before. It was the first time I'd return, but not the last; I was still several thousand miles away from that final finishing point.

From the top of the hills, wind blowing life at me and the sunshine dappling on the green expanse, I descended in and out of small pine plantations, following small green lanes, tree-blocked, no longer the places of passage they once were. Modern farmers' quad bikes could whizz up whichever incline they pleased. I came at last to the lane that held the road to the gateway to Annie's Land, Tir Heddwch, somewhere I'd been driving up to for the last two years and I could go to receive a warm hug and feel loved. Annie fed and petted me, showing me clippings about my journey she'd cut out of the local newspaper. My rucksack had arrived before me, like magic. I'd walked away from it up in Nant yr Eira and here it was again, safely carried round on the road by Caroline and Mick; they'd done the long tarmac trip while I took the high hills shortcut.

A day later, in Machynlleth I bought knee-supports and called in at the wholefood shop; they were really kind about my panicked over-ordering – 5kg of dried vegetables, 5kg of peanuts, 5 kg of sultanas, 5kg of Bombay mix, 5kg of dried apricots, 5kg of cacao nibs, 5kg of trail mix. They took back the peanuts and sultanas, split and packaged them to sell themselves; it was just the dried vegetables they couldn't sell. No-one would buy it and it wasn't surprising; I'd bought enough to start a pot-noodle company.

I'd already taken a lot of things back to Ruth's house; kept the apricots, the trail mix, the cacao nibs, added it to my supply dump: a huge storage-box full of scattered chocolate bars, books I'd saved from my previous flat, all the guidebooks I'd bought in advance, plus stores of odd things like extra socks or tins of lighter fluid for my handwarmer, packets of strange food that might be useful, Kendal mint cake, falafel powder, protein supplement to add to muesli, sold in strange, huge plastic jars as a weightlifter's muscle-building aid. I was constantly fighting against the weight of my rucksack, taking things out and sending them home, spending hundreds of pounds on postage over the duration of the journey: a foam roller for tense muscles, spare smartphone battery-pack, waterproof trousers... Too heavy, too bulky, not warm enough, not cooling enough, not used enough, not efficient. Scarf, hat and gloves had been necessary at the beginning of March but weren't in late April.

The boxes were silting up; they became a layered thing to root through, putting aside the discarded gloves, the extraneous insoles, the spare fleece waistcoat, maps and guidebooks that I no longer needed. There were things that I tried but didn't work for me; an orange, plastic emergency survival shelter that would coat the outside of my sleeping bag with all the moisture that escapes from my body overnight and a rucksack cover that didn't fit over the extra things I strapped to the outside of my bag. There were many different attempts at easing foot pain: discarded gel inserts, foot lotion, half-squeezed tubes of Deep Heat, ibuprofen gel and arnica cream. There were scattered boxes of matches, painkillers, bent sachets of Dioralyte, small lengths of rope, as well as things people gave me in the hope of easing my journey: gaiters to stop rain running into my boots, bicarbonate of soda to stop them smelling so awful, single-use handwarmers. There were stray postcards and scrawled children's drawings, carefully hoarded memories of a thousand special days. I'd sift through the detritus every time I passed, pick out a new book, pull out a couple of chocolate bars, a fresh stack of symptoms-cards, refill my puny bag of trail mix from the gigantic plastic sack that never seemed to lessen in volume.

The route from Machynlleth led to Llanidloes, where I could stay with Heloise again. But first I had to climb up and over a broad moorland gap, cross the heights of the uplands, where rippling grasses and scattered gorges and lakes led south to Plynlimon. After a day walking in the beautiful Dyfi valley and a sharp, sweaty climb up the 500m of Foel Fadian, I came out into a different world. This was the landscape I loved best, raw and difficult to control.

A complex mass of plants grew here, clumps growing and holding and supporting each other in twenty shades of green to delight my eyes. Only in the sheep-nibbled tracks could the ordinary green grass creep in. The textures palpated my vision – shaggy, bulbous, feathered mosses, samphire-like stalks of young bilberry bushes shooting upwards through rounded moss-clumps and purple heather. Occasional gorse grew in a sheltered space and, where the land truly dipped, in the curves that held still air, a gnarled and weathered tree, arthritic hawthorn or rowan, grown small and stunted.

I stayed for the night near Dylife, a wild place where the wind blows strong and bitter. Snow comes every winter, the houses are scattered, and scars have been cut into the ground by the diggings for lead. The Star Inn stands as a traveller's beacon, a respite on the journey over the pass for the drovers, the trudgers, the itinerant.

I'd walked as far as I could that day, but my host was still another village over so I thumbed a lift from a pleasant-faced farmer in a golf buggy, dogs rattling and barking in the caged back. He told me I'd accidentally picked a dead-end road to try and get to Pennant. I walked 100m back to the main road and he kindly came back ten minutes later in his pickup and took me the six miles to Pennant, telling me he was a fifth-generation moss-farmer, a fascinating detail.

I came gratefully to Felicity, my writers'-group friend from Machynlleth, finding a new appreciation for her hardworking days of mothering two children in a very isolated village, the intellectual escape of her editorial self-employment. Lambs rattled into the kitchen in the morning, searching for their bottle feeds, and I was joyous, spreading out my fingers for them each to take a suck, the ridges of their greedy mouths pulsing away at a finger, small teeth mouthing but not biting.

After the first couple of days of camping in the northern section of Glyndŵr's Way, I was hosted almost everywhere – so much so that I almost felt bad. Did I deserve this? This was supposed to be a tough adventure, inciting donations to charity, not a stroll from meal to meal. I'd sit down to eat food that friends had cooked for me and they wouldn't even let me wash up. I could just get up from the table and go straight to bath and bed, feeling selfish. I understood their compassion as they watched me though, just rising from my seat took a slow-motion effort of creaks and groans. Walking felt fine during the day, once I'd stretched and started, but as soon I sat down for the evening I'd solidify into an achy shuffling lump.

"I'm fine, I'm fine", I'd manage to blurt, as I hobbled up the stairs towards glorious immersion in hot water.

I was tired. Really, the groans were just a symptom of the effort I'd made to date: 395 miles covered in six weeks. The beginning stages of the walk brought the pain of blood swelling into my feet to cushion against the unexpected pounding, leading to a sharpened ache at the new internal pressure, feet feeling like clumsy stones at the end of every day, cells brutalised by the repeated thump and press.

After the final section of the ODP between Knighton and Montgomery, with steep hill after steep hill I'd toughened up. The ordinary hills felt easy, the flat sections felt like flying, my legs driving on by themselves. My body was developing muscle and I started to feel power inside me, a steely core that could walk and sleep and walk and sleep. I felt solid; my body didn't hurt in the same way as at the beginning of the walk. And yet I was heavy and tired, my thigh muscles starting to flicker into cramps on the day I reached Machynlleth. My body was growing to strength, yet under a duress that brought it close to breaking. The peace of sleep saved me, each morning bringing me fresh ability after the collapse of the previous night. The rhythmic rubbing and soothing of my muscles helped relax me into sleep, ritually removing the tension from the walk-formed cramps and knots.

Being hosted along this section, seeing friends, was lovely – but nevertheless I felt stressed. I was slow compared to the pace I'd planned, what I felt I should be doing. I fell prey to imposing the killer *should* upon my reality. I *should* be doing fifteen miles a day by now to reach to Bristol again by September. I'm not good enough, I'm pathetic, an idiot, a total failure.

But if I walked fifteen miles a day, I exhausted myself for the following day. I was carrying too much in my rucksack but didn't seem able to let go of it. I was carrying too much weight on my body, I hadn't prepared properly for this, I couldn't do it, I was useless and stupid. Twelve miles a day felt sluggish and slow, why was this all I could manage? I'd be laughed at by most long-distance walkers, the ones I read about on the internet, flying up USA trails with their 5kg pack-weights and their thirty-mile days. I felt like a fat amateur in comparison. I wanted to walk more but I was so, so tired, I could barely handle what I was doing now, struggling to get going in the mornings, squeezing in an extra rest-day with James and Vicky near Machynlleth.

I found it very easy to think negatively about myself, especially regarding comparison with others. It was something I'd been trying to conquer my whole life and now, as I pushed myself to achieve something extraordinary, the nasty thoughts of my inadequacy and weakness became a strong voice that was sometimes difficult to ignore.

Heloise took me in again, once the Glyndŵr's Way passed around Clywedog reservoir and into Llanidloes. I spent the day gradually descending from the high places and entering regular farmland, uniform enclosed fields green and seeded, winding around the spiked fingers of the reservoir, negotiating boardwalks over flooded valley corners, finally arriving at her place to be treated to more cocktails, flambéed banana pancakes and generally glorious food.

East of Llanidloes, almost at the end of Glyndŵr's Way, I spent two days walking from Llanbadarn Fynydd to Knighton with an old friend, Will, who visited from London on his way home from Pembrokeshire. He was a 6ft swimmer, cyclist and all-round athlete; he even carried my bag as well as his own so that we'd be equally paced. We stopped for lunch in a chapel, unlocked for once, enjoying the usually hidden space, feeling slightly criminal as we ate the sandwiches he'd brought from Pembrokeshire and looked at Sunday school outings photographs from the 50s, monuments to time long past. The importance of this chapel had faded, leaving behind an empty building, musty air and dusty windowsills, a lone loyal lady coming to hoover once a week. We spent the night in Will's tent, no sleep for me as an owl chose to make his perch in a tree directly above us, shrieking out a regular small-hours hoot.

The land turned to moorland on the way towards Llangunllo the next day, the last small piece of wilderness on our way back to Knighton and the smoothed-down borderlands. We climbed above the close-crowding, muddy-shanked cows and came to an open, misty land, tracking our way between two gentle hills. Resting there and eating Will's sweets, I bit into a lump of hard toffee and felt a tooth separate, splitting into two. A piece of filling had flaked away from there months earlier and I'd ignored it, even though I could occasionally feel the tooth creaking and aching. I was too caught up in the rush of journey preparation to acknowledge such impediments.

I hate dentists, avoid them, but I couldn't ignore this; the tooth had cracked open, half of it wobbling loose in my mouth.

I kept my fears to myself and walked on with Will to a small village near the train line where we said goodbye: him hitching back to London and an impending art exhibition, me to walk to Knighton and the end of Glyndŵr's Way. I knew I had to sort out the tooth problem immediately and as soon as I reached Knighton, I hitched to Machynlleth for an emergency appointment, taking a night's rest with Claire in Welshpool on the way.

I sat in Claire's kitchen. This time she'd gone to work and left me with a day to take time out before the dentist's visit later. I had a kitchen table, a sunny window, endless cups of tea and Radio 4 murmuring reassuringly – my favourite way to spend breakfast time. I had space to do some staring, think about plucking my eyebrows, look at the internet. All while the minutes slowly passed and the world burbled in the background, at a peaceful volume. Even though I hated the fact that I'd have to pay to experience pain (I had enough of it for free) it was nice to have an enforced rest. A day to look in shops, to hitchhike, to chat, relax my body and enjoy the day, no pressure to be anywhere else.

I'd been feeling nervous over the previous week. It felt as if I was going so slowly this would never be done. When I thought of the hundreds of miles I'd trudged over the last few weeks and how it was a very, very small fraction of the thousands still to come, the size, the enormity of what I was taking on, felt insurmountable. I felt rage at the total mileage, puny in the face of it. I'd found myself pushing for a few extra daily miles, always thinking ahead, panting to get to the next town, to the end of this path, to begin the next section. I wasn't walking any faster, just mentally throwing myself at the mileage, the equivalent of pushing your feet against the car floor as it bowls along the motorway. Do it, get it done, push onwards, so many miles to walk, so far to go. But my body simply wasn't capable. Too many miles one day meant more pain the next.

I had to recognise the time as well as the distance – this wasn't going to end quickly but would last, unequivocally, for months and months and months and no amount of push would get it over with. I was trying to sprint through a long-distance race and if I didn't go slowly, mentally as well as physically, it would break me.

The dentist put in a temporary filling. I imagined the line of amalgam snaking through my tooth in a Japanese Kintsugi style, mended but more beautiful for it. Then it was back to the walk. I felt grumpy at the thought of walking that tough section of the Offa's Dyke Path again, from Knighton to Welshpool and, at the last moment, as I hitched east out of Machynlleth, I decided to skip it. Sod it, I excused myself, I've already walked it once, it's an extra, an add-on, not part of any named routes. I felt bad about not walking a flowing route, the idea of what I'd designed was a route that never stopped and started, but I felt like I kept getting delayed – especially irritating when it was imposed on me by unwanted dentistry.

Back on the Offa's Dyke Path, heading north away from Welshpool, I spent a few nights camping in pub gardens. I was getting used to my new tooth, managing decent distances every day, things didn't feel too bad.

Val in Selattyn was the stepmother of a friend of my mum's: another typically tenuous and roundabout way for me to be invited to spend the night in the home of a complete stranger. She was careful and nervous, an almost-retired music teacher, leading a quiet widow's life, full of choir recitals and village meetings. She offered me a gin and tonic as I sat in her kitchen, taking in this new home, watching the cats waft in and out of their favourite sleeping-spots. I'm not sure welcoming strangers into her home was something she did very often, but Val had made a space for me in her life, and set out a small selection of snacks in my bedroom, next to the pile of towels. It was a wonderful welcome.

The night after walking away from kind, caring Val, I slept in a field again. I'd been able to walk without my rucksack for the morning and after I got it back at lunchtime it felt incredibly heavy. I trudged up and down the hills very, very slowly.

I walked into the grounds of Chirk Castle, through bluebell woods in full blossom, and on to the entrance where they had a second-hand bookshop. I couldn't resist picking up two books, one a hardback. Far too heavy! I'd finished Nelson Mandela's autobiography earlier that day and I was able to buy the biographies of Hannah Hauxwell and Malcolm X. Hannah's book must have weighed a kilo and a half, a ridiculous purchase but I vowed I'd read it that night and pass it on the next day.

I left the castle grounds and walked on, trudging by now, the rucksack feeling its full 16kg weight. It was early evening, the time of day where I should start looking for sleeping places.

I spent a long time looking at a dip down by a stone wall – very sheltered but stony at the bottom. Nope, right by the path, not quite the one for me. I walked on, past a house that had placed spikes along the top of all the gates (including the footpath gate); there were high walls, signs warning of dogs and telling me to close the gate and not trespass on private property. I wasn't going to knock on *that* door and ask to sleep in their garden, sure I'd get a very different reception to the one I'd had in Newbridge. On I went, along a road, passing a small copse where the brambles and nettles rose high beneath the close-crowding, human-planted larch. No comfy bed there.

Eventually I came off the road into a field of longish grass. The field went sloping gently downwards towards a fence, and at the bottom of the depression there was a hawthorn tree. It was secluded and beautiful, hidden from the road, no animals in the field. I decided I'd sleep underneath that tree the moment I saw it: protected by great thick roots rising from the ground, which pressed against the wire fence and made a solid wall for me to shelter behind. I could run the poncho off the fence to hide from the rain. The grass was long and soft, the field slightly sloping. Wonderful.

I sat there for a few hours, reading as the sun went down. The story of Hannah Hauxwell, the woman "discovered" in the '70s living a life of Dales isolation straight out of the 1930s. A black and white photo come to life. I wrapped my sleeping-bag round my legs and put my jacket on, but otherwise it wasn't so cold that I couldn't sit still. When I first started out in March, I'd have to get straight into the sleeping-bag and fire up my handwarmer as soon as I stopped for the night. The field was peaceful the whole time, no walkers, no animals, just the occasional call of a far-away pheasant. There were sheep in the adjacent field and sometimes a run of lambs would pelt towards the corner of the field where I sat, hidden by the tree. They would run until they saw me, an unknown animal sitting quietly; then they would stop, standing, unsure, until their mothers called them away.

I'd managed to find a patch of signal at the top of the rise so I'd checked the forecast which suggested rain between 8pm and 10pm, and dry the rest of the night. It was 9.30pm and still no rain; I kept checking the sky and the clouds weren't moving, they didn't look black or ominous, just a patchy covering of grey. I decided that I'd chance it without the shelter, but tied it to the fence at one corner so I could throw it over me if it started to rain in the night.

As it became too dark to read I tucked down into the three layers of sleeping cocoon. A bat flickered over me in the remaining grey blue light, and I could hear an owl somewhere a few fields away. I slept, not all night but tolerably well for a night outside. The ground was well shaped for my body; sometimes, when I sleep on hard, flat ground, the whole night can be spent shifting from side to side, trying to sleep in the gaps between the onset of hip pain. There was a small slope downwards from my head to feet, enough to be comfy but not so much that I started to slide downhill as soon as I relaxed. I woke at various points during the night to rearrange the sleeping bag: not so open that I got cold, not so closed that I couldn't breathe, the bag collapsing over my head as I relaxed down into sleep.

I first checked my phone at 5.45am and roused myself properly at about 7.30. The field was a new world of thick fog, dewdrops at the tip of every grass-blade. I don't just wild camp because of my budget, I do it because I love it. I love to open my eyes and directly see the sunrise, right in front of me. Beetles investigate my tarpaulin, rabbits come out to eat, owls hoot in the blackness of an unknowable world. Even a tent-wall feels as if I'm separating myself from that experience. I do greatly appreciate every chance I get to sleep in a bed and have a shower; wild camping is hard and tiring and difficult to keep clean in. But it also gives me a deep sense of peace.

Another wonderful camp came that night, at World's End. I'd walked past Llangollen, keeping alongside the canal at first, even as it crossed high above the River Dee on an aqueduct, boats floating through the thin channel, leaping into space forty metres above the tree-lined river gorge below. I climbed Castell Bran and took a celebratory photograph; I'd walked more than 500 miles to get here, the Proclaimers song echoing in my mind for a few days. The land changed on the way to World's End. I tiptoed on a thin strip of footpath, between high limestone cliffs, raw and rugged, and a flat valley below me, as if the land fell away to a sea bed.

Eventually the road bent into a U-turn and a path led straight up into the head of the valley: World's End, where the road turned back on itself and climbed to a moorland pass. There was nowhere further to go, it was a perfect place to sleep, the track running gently up between the pine trees and around a bend. There was a high rockface above the path and, sitting down on a bench to eat and wait for darkness, I heard shouts high above me and gradually discerned the small bodies of climbers, roped and belaying downwards.

I had to wait until they left, not wanting anyone to see my bed, so I ate a slightly forlorn meal of mackerel and couscous, squeezing stolen condiment sachets around the bowl edge and feeling the lack of private space.

Eventually the young, fit boys whooped and shouted their way down from the climb, fresh and bright-eyed, virile. Finally I was alone and could select a sleeping spot. A deep mattress of moss, nestled among the scattered, shattered fallings from the climbers' playground. A seeded pine, blown by the wind to root, became a totem, a sentinel to stand at my bed-head.

I lay in the open air as twilight darkened the sky, feeling vulnerable and scared of attack until I realised there was nothing in this environment that could hurt me; humans had killed all the dangerous animals. I had the luxury, in animal terms, of being able to lie down and lose consciousness wherever I liked. With no fear of predation, my survival instinct could lie dormant. It was a great and relaxing freedom.

Rain came early the next morning, driving me from my mossy nest. My eyes hurt, they weren't ready to be open yet, but rain was coming, the first gentle misty drops were tapping against my eyelids and I knew the longer I lay here the wetter I'd become. I packed away, unwillingly, and walked away from World's End.

The road led upwards, out of the gorge, around the corner and out of tree-cover altogether. I found myself on misty moorland, a thin tarmac line of road, surrounded on either side by gouts of heather and gorse and bilberries, thin sheep-nibbled tracks wavering away between bushes. I couldn't see into the far distance, grey mist held my viewpoint to the nearest thirty metres. It was a total change of terrain and I loved the sensory dissonance that came from such a quick transition.

I could hear something. The air vibrated with noise, shimmered. Liquid burbling came from everywhere at once, it was the air and it was inside me. Somewhere, there was a great population of birds in this stark landscape, happily pecking and breeding and living – ululating to each other, inhabiting the wet and grey. Searching them out, I could see one or two black round birds, pecking and busying themselves, not enough to account for the noise. I found out later they were black grouse. The rain brought me out of bed early enough to hear them, a special moment far away from normal life, walking along a grey and heathered moorland at 6am.

The moorland pathway, boardwalks and flagstones laid onto the soggy peat didn't last long before I descended into Llandegla Forest, and came out into the village on the other side. I breakfasted there, still early enough for only a few cars to be on the road, and walked the day away in the small hills leading to the Clwydian Range. I spent a miserable night in the forest up at Bwlch Penbarras, squirming down in my sleeping-bag to get away from the misty, penetrating rain, the tree roots and sloped ground underneath me not allowing my body to relax into deep sleep. I left my meal, couldn't face more cold couscous, and was visited by a mouse in the night which whisked in from the pine-needle desert to nibble at my congealed dinner, leaving small grains of black poo at the mouth of my food bag. I was visible to early morning dog-walkers but they steadfastly ignored me, looking away from this seemingly homeless and desperate shadow in the woods.

The next day was up and down in the high hills that dropped away either side of me to the Denbigh valley and the north eastern coast, Dee estuary and views of England. I tucked down to read a book in the shelter of a stone wall, rain speckling and darkening the pages. I didn't care about getting wet, just wanted to stop for a while. I had a window of time to sit and read and dream until the cold drained the comfort out of my body and I was forced to continue.

Fortunately, coming over the next hill I was greeted unexpectedly by my hosts for that night, Morg and Nige, who'd come with a view to encountering me as they made their daily dog-walk. I could have asked them to come back later and walked for another hour over the final hill and down to Bodfari, but I caved in and went home with them for an early finish, snuggling on the sofa with their friendly dogs. I could stay with these guys for two nights, so the following day was rucksack-free and I made the most of it, coming over the up-and-down rises of the Clwydian hill range, getting larger glimpses of the sea each time. I'd almost made it to the top of Wales.

The second day of walking away from Morg and Nige I felt awful and I didn't know why. Every step was an effort, I just had no energy. I came down Moel Maenefa, turning left and right through leafy lanes and seeing the invasive A55 dual carriageway cutting through obstacles, splitting the land open for blind cars to pass without the time to pay attention.

There was a caravan park ahead and I turned into it, knowing it would have a pub somewhere. It was a strange, unfriendly place, done up like a posh bar, thereby removing any semblance of character. The drinks were overpriced and the clientele steadfastly avoided eye-contact. I took my crisps and pint of John Smiths over to a table and sat back to dream for a while. The relief was short-lived. I crunched into a crisp and my damned tooth cracked right open. I felt the gum stretch in pain and a warm wash of blood spread a tang through my mouth. The tooth had broken completely and I spat out a small nugget into my palm, much smaller than what felt, to my nervous, probing tongue, like a gaping hole left behind.

I sat in the expensive pub, with its high-backed, uncomfortable bench seats, upholstered and tanned caravan-owners crowding around me, and wanted to cry. I'd only walked nine miles that day before giving up. My kneecaps felt as if they were floating away from my knees and my tooth had fallen apart. So much for the filling – ten lousy days. I needed to go back to the dentist immediately and the walk would be interrupted, again. I felt as if I was crawling sluggishly across the land, never actually achieving any goals or getting anywhere at all. I had an urge to get wildly, blindly, destructively drunk. Instead I called Morg and went back to her and Nige's house, lay on the sofa enfeebled and sorry for myself, wrapped in a blanket watching *Britain's Got Talent*.

It was the Saturday of the Easter bank holiday weekend; I couldn't even phone the dentist for another three days. Yet again, a night's rest strengthened me and I could think more clearly. The tooth didn't hurt anymore so I kept walking.

I made it down to Prestatyn and the end of my third path. I'd walked 551 miles along the Severn Way, Offa's Dyke Path and Glyndŵr's Way. At the end of my day I arrived in Rhyl. Broken glass, vomit-stained seafront, bad burgers, casinos and candyfloss, this was a desperate and heavy-drinking town, dazed by alcohol, edges blurring into miles of blank-faced caravans. There was no secluded place for a wild camper. I needed a safe sleeping-spot so I got on the train. Conwy, a few stops down the line, provided a quiet field opposite the castle wall, and I came back to Rhyl the next morning to complete the concrete seafront miles to Colwyn Bay, the smell of sick and bins floating through the shuttered town as I hurriedly made my way to the seafront.

It was a pretty uneventful day, just a strip of tarmac path between road and sea, the blank line of the flat water and the rush and roar of cars alongside me. I couldn't escape Rhyl, it was there hovering in the dusty skyline whenever I looked behind me. I waved my flags, I chatted to people, I took donations: all normal, until I reached Vicky the Couchsurfer's house and sat down to rest. Once I got up I couldn't walk properly. I couldn't bear any weight on my right heel – sharp pain shot through my foot whenever I put it to the ground.

I'd intended to stop the next morning and go back to Machynlleth, anyway. The tooth needed attention and now it seemed I'd injured my foot too. I felt scared. Allowing the idea of stopping the walk to deal with the tooth and the foot meant admitting the possibility of stopping permanently was out there too. The only way I could continue this effort in the face of such hardship was to completely deny it.

The dentist pulled out the remnants of the break and filled it again.

"You'll have to come back next week for the permanent filling," she said. "The gum needs to heal first."

I decided to rest for the week. Limping and tired as I was, I couldn't face returning to walk with the final dentist ordeal still to come.

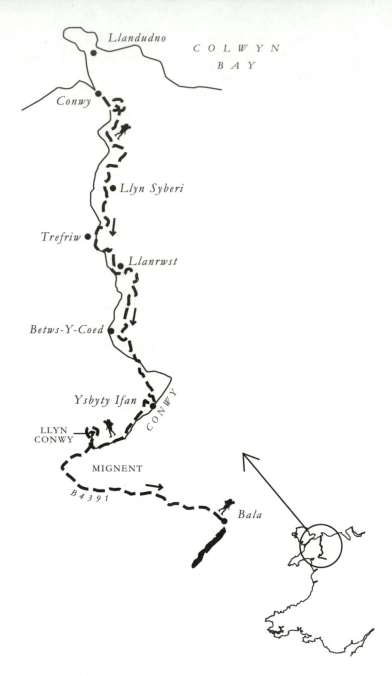

CONWY VALLEY

Route description: A path that follows the length of the Conwy River from the estuary at the castle walls of Conwy through open farmland of the flat Conwy valley, past the tree-lined gorges of Betws y Coed and through the upland pasture of Ysbyty Ifan and on to the wild moorland of the Migneint where it rises from Llyn Conwy.

Length:	41 miles
Total ascent:	unknown
Maximum height:	473m
Dates:	15 – 22 May 2014
Time taken:	8 days
Nights camping/nights hosted:	1/7
Days off:	1
Average miles per day:	5.85

Annie's yurt embraced me. I bought food from the town – cheese, pâté, bread, tomatoes – collected my post from a friend, and hitched the ten miles back out of Machynlleth, up to the land. Annie had a yurt on the acres that climbed behind her barn, and she graciously offered it to me. After a polite cup of tea and a chat I could escape up there, falling, dazed, into a luxurious double bed. I drifted into unconsciousness, waking only to eat cheese on toast or read for a while. I dozed and dreamed, watching the sunlight dapple against the circular roof opening, coming to shine on me and then passing again, the darkness of the green canvas enclosing me. Four full days passed this way, before I tottered down to the barn to say hello to Annie and drink tea with her again. It was the first time in eight weeks, 500 miles of walking, that I'd been truly alone in my own private space and could let go, release into total exhaustion. I hadn't realised that something was missing, that single rest-days weren't enough and I was slowly depleting myself.

This walk was overwhelming, I was always busy. Days were spent walking in public, nowhere to retreat from people, the world. Nights of wild camping were beautiful but not relaxing; nights in houses were comfortable but I still had to interact with people. I hadn't realised I felt this way, caught up in the intensity and adrenalin of daily walking and social media interaction, the necessary elements of a public journey. It wasn't a conscious state of alert, more the realisation – once I got to an empty house and could shut the door on the world – that a small part of me had remained tense, buried too deep to notice.

Annie gave me energetic healing, running her hands through the air above my feet and coming up with a worried look on her face.

"They're fucked," she said. "Your earth chakra was frozen, I restarted it moving, I brought the lines of energy which were trapped in your legs back down into your feet. The lines were broken and the energy transfer was jumbled."

She was right, in her way. My feet weren't communicating properly, they weren't flowing. Whether they were lacking the full relaxation of muscles and tendons to allow efficient flexing and function or a more spiritual energy transfer, they were broken. She looked at me tenderly, my wise friend.

"Ursula, you'll permanently damage your feet if you carry on. Continuing to walk won't heal them, it will only do further harm to your body."

I knew she was right, at least the risk of what she was saying was right, but I had to put it away as a possibility; there was only a *chance* that I'd permanently harm myself. I respected Annie's statement for the care and gravitas she put into it but I couldn't accept it as the truth, not if that meant cancelling the walk.

On the final morning of my dream retreat, dentistry done and no major excuse to keep resting, I could feel pain in my feet as I walked down the short grass path to the main barn, a dull ache underneath the arches, threatening to ripple out into sharper pain if I moved too suddenly. My rest time hadn't worked – they weren't healed. I'd have to continue this way. I hitched up to Conwy town, limping slightly as I gathered supplies together. I wasn't really ready to start again, but every day resting was a day of procrastination. The target remained and I had to face it.

Sun setting slowly over a calm Conwy estuary, I walked across the bridge from the town and into the narrow strip of nature reserve which ran between river and road. I had a vague idea that I'd sleep there, find a bird hide perhaps, endure a hard wooden bed in exchange for the calm, enclosed air of a shelter. Sun shone colours across the endless grey-brown mud-widths that bordered the receding water, draining channels and cracks silver outlined pale orange and white illuminating the rustle of tall thick banks of reeds. It was a calm and inviting place, perfect for wild camping. Except that there was a man walking about the place. I'm not sure what unsettled me about him but I kept seeing him as we walked the twisting, crossing paths and there was a dark, lurking air about him. I didn't like the feeling and knew I couldn't stay there without trying to hide from this person, feeling nervous about him finding me sleeping. The reserve was edged by fences; I took a muddy skip-and-hop over the fence, then stepped carefully along the edge of the deep mud washes and ducked down to squeeze through a flood channel under the railway and into the village of Glan Conwy. I sat with a half pint, slightly forlorn, in a pub, the sky darkening through the windows, coming to the dangerous time where it was dark and difficult to find a camping-spot.

As I sat wondering what next, my phone started to buzz; it was my old next door neighbour Deri who had an Auntie Shân in Capel Curig and she was firing off messages of support, calling in her contacts to help me out. I had beds waiting for me all along the Conwy valley. All I had to do was wait another twenty minutes in the pub, staring dazedly at the quiz machine, and Irene pulled up.

"Feminism in action," she exclaimed, and I was taken home by this chain-smoking ovarian-cancer survivor, ex-college head, a woman of power, both in personality and influence, now passing her retirement in a pleasant haze of gin and cigarette smoke, trailing sentences and crinkle-eyed smiles.

Next day was tough: dropped back at the pub, for my first real day of walking in ten days, and it hurt. My feet, my feet, my feet... it's all the problems there ever were. They felt hobbled, clawed and pained. It wasn't the sort of injury that could stop me walking, and the pain was mild most of the time, it's just that it was always there. A bruised ache underneath the arch of my foot, spreading in a line across my heel, pain turning from tender through to sharp, depending on how much I walked that day. The sharpness was that of tearing, of separation of tissue from bone. I knew what it was, I'd Googled it: plantar fasciitis. The only way to keep on was to stop every hour for a long rest, raising my feet, reading a book. The enforced stillness was frustrating. I wanted to walk, to get on and do this. But sometimes, as I lay back against a gate, by the side of a back road, chestnut tree shading me as I read about George Eliot, I looked around and thought about how lucky I was.

There was part of this enforced stillness that was OK. Being able to walk amongst such beautiful scenery, my breaks were the time to truly absorb these surroundings, no matter how much pain I was in.

I walked all day, small steps, birdlike, feeling the pain in my feet throb, trying not to aggravate or worsen it. The busy road down below traced the river bends, but high up on a small winding road above the River Conwy there were no cars, just me and my rucksack all morning, taking our time about it, not pushing too hard, just staying aware of each movement. The pain had come when I walked from Rhyl, as I lengthened my stride on the tarmac, striking to the ground heel first. So to avoid it I walked in small steps, placing each foot gently to the ground, hobbling myself with a mentally-imposed restraint.

Bluebells thronged the banks around me, pushing over unfurling bracken. The sun shone on a haze of blue. There were thousands of bluebells pouring over the ground in a breath of blue mist. I turned in a slow circle, trying to count the bells, to distinguish the number contained in the blue blanket, but the number became meaningless, hundreds of thousands, a million. Uncountable. There were infinite bluebells, all coming up in response to the same temperature, the turning of the planet changing the amount of light in the sky and stirring them to growth. It was stunningly beautiful.

I'd told myself while I was resting in Annie's yurt that I'd just set off and take it easy: five miles a day would be fine. I'd walk slowly up the Conwy Valley, letting go of timings and targets. The thing is, it's different while I'm doing it. My body may be walking slowly, but my poor over-active brain moves at a quicker pace than my feet and there are minutes, hours filled with thinking. Entire scenarios flash before me, quick as blinking. Five miles a day is awful, I tell myself. I'm not quick enough, I'm stupid and ponderous and slow, my stomach flops over the belt of my rucksack, I'm chubby and ridiculous, I'm the worst walker ever. No, I'm not. I am a strong, powerful woman. I am wonderful and amazing and at the end of this walk, when I finish triumphant, I'll be able to write a book and never work again, I'll be able to sit in fields and read books forever. I've damaged my foot, I'll have to stop, next month, at the end of the week, tomorrow, right now. What will I do? I'll have to go back to work, it's the end of the walk, no more adventure. No, it's OK; I just need to take it easy, don't worry, pace yourself, five miles is fine... All this within the space of a few steps. My mind lit up with extra energy, occupied by the walk, flashing neurons, over-activity, nothing to distract me from myself. You can do this, you can't do this, you can, you can't.

I would come out of my brain sometimes and realise that the birds were singing; they'd been singing the whole time and I wasn't listening. My head was down and I was staring at the road, blindly replaying old arguments or forging fresh imaginary relationships. What was I doing? There were flowers to look at, a river to follow. The air was thick with heat and the plants around me were bursting, fecund, spewing seed heads into space to float hopeful in the air. There was a whole world here for me to savour, and I was shutting the blinds and disappearing into my imagination.

Each day was hard, is what I'm saying. The walk was about so much more than a physical challenge, it was about pushing my mind to constant acceptance and assimilation of change. I had to push forward, strive to achieve what was extraordinary (for me and my body), accept pain as normal, accept throbbing feet, clicking knees, a heavy rucksack, the discomfort of sleeping outside, of turning an ankle in an uneven field, of finding my way across the countryside, of walking every day for eight hours, of keeping going, being stubborn, not stopping, focused onward, always pushing onward.

Conversely however, I also had to, *had to*, if this walk was to succeed, practice self-care, give myself time, give myself rest, listen to myself, know when to pause. I was forever teetering on the tightrope between pushing myself beyond my normal capabilities and simultaneously knowing when to stop. It felt like an impossible balance.

In late afternoon, after taking six hours to cover just four miles, I came to a small lake, high up on the hillside: Llyn Syberi, lying still and calm, surrounded by trees, with floating ducks and small wooden jetties for fishers. I'd heard that ice and cold were good for plantar fasciitis – restrict the blood flowing to the area and restrict the pain – so I stripped off my boots and dunked my feet into the water, resolving to sit there for twenty minutes, to allow the inflammation to lessen. Light lay on the surface of the water like smoothed-out foil, wavering and rippled, holding the Easter egg-printing of tree branches and white clouds, blue sky and golden light. I felt desperate, spun into nervous over-thinking, in fear about the constant pain. The whole walk was falling to pieces in front of me; what could I do if I couldn't complete this? I had a plan to walk back to hospital, an appointment in five months' time, and I'd set daily mileages so I could make that. I should have been walking nineteen miles a day by now. Every day I didn't do that I fell further behind schedule. There didn't seem to be any piece of the walk I could cut short, it didn't even occur to me to do that; the route I'd decided had formed as a whole. It existed, entire and integral: mountains, rivers, coast. I couldn't miss any of that out. I was going to walk around Wales, I was going to walk 3300 miles. Every inch of me was focused on this idea. In order to force myself to achieve it I had to allow it to obsess me, take me over, to become all that I was. When it started to seem as if I couldn't do it, I couldn't change the image; it just shattered around me like a broken mirror, exposing a vortex. My mind distorted at the idea of my incapability.

Illness had ambushed me, smashed my life sideways, turning strong and fearless into weak and vulnerable within a matter of weeks. When everything had been made uncertain, the thought of the walk had been something to fix onto in the aftermath, a thread that I could follow into the future. I couldn't imagine going back to Machynlleth and getting a job – in no way was that how I wanted to live. I wanted to go back out into the world and adventure again, but I was temporarily tied to this country, tied to hospital. Plus I couldn't really return to my previous life in Bulgaria, I was too fragile, too weakened by shock of illness. Cancer stopped my life as it was but didn't give me another one to continue with. I had to make one up and I chose to walk. If I couldn't walk I had no idea what to do next.

I called my brother Owen, talking to him as I dabbled my feet in the lake, sending ripples out across the reflected blue and green, and he calmed me.

"Bro, my feet are hurting too much to walk more than five or six miles a day, what can I do? I'm scared; the whole thing's collapsing around me and I've put so much effort into telling people about it and trying to raise money and I can't just stop. What a let-down that would be, what a failure, what a disappointment; the whole walk just disappears because I can't do it anymore. I've set myself the target of 3300 miles in eight months and now I can't complete that, what can I do?"

Owen listened, like he always does, and then told me about his running, about when he started to take it seriously, to run harder, and decided to run a marathon, entered training, set his focus on personal bests and trying to beat himself every run. He found he was always pushing himself onwards to get better every time, all his focus became about the clock and he had stopped enjoying himself any more. So he decided to tell himself he was just going for a run, that's all, nothing more, no training, no PBs, no competition, no failure, just a nice piece of exercise somewhere beautiful.

"That's what you could do, sis," he said. "Just go for a walk."

There it was, this challenge reduced to its essence – just go for a walk. I could do it, I'd get to hospital, even if I walked a mile a day. It might take years but I'd still get there. I was still capable of movement, even though it was sometimes a painful hobble, at night reduced to an aching shuffle. I could still do this, I just had to get rid of time as a target, stop caring about my speed, about my miles per hour, my daily total. I had to stop comparing myself to other public journeys – Ffyona Campbell walking around the world, Carrot Quinn speeding up and down the trails of the USA, all the ramblers, all the pilgrims to Santiago, all the people who could walk faster than three mph, all the people who could walk twenty miles a day. Stop.

There was no-one else creating or judging this walk, it was only me who truly cared about what it contained. Everyone else just saw a huge charity walk, the details varied according to how accurate each local journalist was. No-one knew when my next hospital appointment was, no-one really knew where I was or where I was going, the route was too complex for that, my Facebook updates too infrequent. I'd veer off one path and onto another, make sudden detours inland to follow rivers: no-one cared that much, they just knew I was walking Wales. The definition of the walk only existed inside my head *and I could change it*. I'd return to Bristol and home again: it didn't matter how fast I went. I *would* do this, I *could* do this, just at my own speed, that's all. My mind calmed, panicked ripples fading to stillness. This was OK. This was possible.

There was nothing else to do but walk, so I did. I walked incredibly slowly along the Conwy Valley, not allowing it to matter how far I travelled in any given day. Shân helped me out from afar, arranging a free hotel room in Llanrwst, then finally a farmhouse host at the top of the Conwy Valley, near Ysbyty Ifan.

I was so lost in the difficulty of this walk sometimes, struggling along by myself in the hot sun or dribbling rain, just me and my mind and the pain of my body. Then a car would stop or someone would recognise me, tell me I was doing really well, that they were inspired or amazed or other superlative compliments that I was embarrassed to hear. It helped to break me out of the hard slog, give me a little boost, know that what I was doing was acknowledged. People saw me, they appreciated how difficult this was. That day it was a car full of children on their way home from school who stopped for me on a long thin road that ran high above the Conwy River as it curled around from east to north running. They'd been talking about me in school that day, the Wales bush telegraph had zipped ahead of me, and all the mums knew I was coming, thanks to Shân and Facebook. The children piled out, it felt as if there were at least six of them in the car, and I showed them my flags and rucksack, chatted to the woman driving, smiled for a photograph before they all scrambled back in, on their way home to various farms.

Down off the hilltop in the Vale of Conwy, coming close to the valley's head where the river wriggled down from its source, Elin and Alun's was the first working farmhouse I was welcomed into. It was also the first place where the household's very young children chattered in Welsh around me, only able to speak the school-learned English phrases that were the beginning of their bilingual fluency.

I'd come to this place because Shân had put the call out on Facebook, in Welsh: *Helpwch y ddynes yma!* Help this woman! And Welsh people had responded; I'd made it to the inner circle. It takes a lot, in some ways, to break through to the other side of the Welsh/English divide. I don't mean a divide that exists in that nervous, get-off-my-land type of way, and I don't believe the tales of people changing language as soon as an English person walks in. No, the English/Welsh divide is two subtly separate circles that make up a community and overlap at school gates and in workplaces. It's not a question of overt discrimination, more a slight turning of the shoulder. I see it as the historical way to deal with the total governance of your country by a foreign nationality. Every time you let in an outsider, your culture is diluted and there's a danger your differences will fade away to the point of subtlety. So you turn the shoulder, keep your known circle to itself.

Through my work as a carer, going into the farmhouses of the Dyfi Valley, being for the first time in environments where Welsh was the first language, I realised the breadth and depth of the Welsh cultural world. I'd never appreciated before how it was possible to conduct your whole life in the Welsh language, listening to radio, TV, speaking it to your friends and family. Only strangers and acquaintances needing to be spoken to in English, so closely-knit are parts of the Welsh community.

Now I was there, in a farmhouse with a couple and four children, the children excited to speak to me but nervous about practising their English, breaking into giggles when they couldn't think of words. The youngest, Gwydion, a boy just into school age, wanted to play with me but he spoke no English at all. We muddled by though. I could just about understand nursery Welsh; my few scattered words like 'hot', 'cold' 'shirt' and 'outside' helped a tiny bit.

I read him a bedtime story one night. The words were scattered, just a single sentence per thick cardboard page. Reading slowly and carefully, I sounded out the thick Welsh pronunciations, so lush and gloopy, using the whole roundness of my mouth. He seemed to enjoy it.

I stayed there for two nights, my slowness keeping me in the valley for longer than I thought. Alun had sheep up on the land near Llyn Conwy and he took me back one morning to where my walk had finished the night before. It was a hard and slow day, that one. The lake was an almost circle. No particular stream running into it seemed to be identified as the Conwy, so I decided to call the lake the source and walk around it in a ceremonial fashion. If the day hadn't been so stark and wild and beautiful it would have been totally awful. There was no path, I just picked my way through the bilberry and heathered edge of the lake, cottongrass waving its white tendrils in the wind.

That part was fine, but the boggy parts were awful. I was wet to the knees, picking my way at the edges where water met soil and they blended into soggy, wet awfulness, no handy rocks to jump between, just a swamp with no discernible safe spots, extending too far inland for me to walk around it. It took a full day to cover maybe five miles. But I didn't mind, I'd really enjoyed the raw and wild beauty, just me and the wind and the water all day, taking a break to sit in the shell of a boathouse on the opposite side of the lake, admiring the framing of the view through an empty hole where a window had been.

Alun drove me up to Llyn Conwy again the following day, after we waved his children off on the school bus. I was due to walk directly south towards Bala, heading from the source of one river to the start of another, the River Dee. Looking ahead to the Migneint I saw an expanse of bog and cloud, mist drifting across the reedy, grassy, slurping ground. There weren't any footpaths crossing here, I'd have to walk to the end of a track and then take my chances, weaving from rise to rise, always trying to find the driest ground, following sheep-tracks between the twin rises of Migneint and Bryn Glas. Thin weaving lines, faintly trodden, that could easily disappear or take me in the wrong direction.

I thought of yesterday, my struggle against the terrain of Llyn Conwy, my sopping feet, the age that bogs take to cross, the careful picking and shuffling. Today I was lurching and overloaded and would take hours to cross a few miles of ground. I balked at this, using the excuse of mist and rain to take the tarmac way round, enduring a long day of road walking instead, getting wet through in the mist and soft, wetting rain, stopping for a few hours of sanctuary in a steamy café oasis. I knew I wouldn't make it all the way to Bala and would have to camp somewhere out in this blank expanse of damp pine and grass.

I had dumped my tarpaulin in favour of a poncho which would double as a shelter when strung up with ropes, excited to lose another few hundred grams from my pack. I'd mostly used it as a rain-cover during the day but now was the time to test it out as a camping shelter. I came off the road into the forest and decided to duck underneath the wide-spreading skirt of a larch, hoping the thick spiked branches would provide some shelter from the misty, drop-laden air. I put the poncho up as best I could, tying each corner far out to branches, stringing up the centre-hood above me. But it wasn't working. Keeping the central hood hole cinched tight meant that the material wouldn't stretch flat. I watched as water droplets ran together into the folds of the material, and started to ooze through. A drop fell on my face. I was tired, my body hurt, I was wet through from the day's walking and there was nowhere I could go that was drier or easier to shelter. I couldn't get the poncho any straighter; it had a hole in it anyway. I'd come out here with the wrong kit.

It was only 8pm, still an hour until sunset, but I'd stopped because I couldn't walk any further. There was nothing I could do, not without an effort I was too exhausted to make. I decided to leave it, allowing the water to drip through the stupid, badly-put-up shelter onto my bivvy bag. I lay there and felt miserable, in a fuck-this and fuck-everything kind of way. Time stood still as I watched the rain drip down, eating all the chocolate that Elin had packed for me that morning. I was warm in my multi-layered cocoon, and knew I wasn't in danger, just uncomfortable. I stayed warm all night, just got increasingly wet as dampness slowly soaked in from the outside.

The next day was hard as I came slowly down the road from the mountains into Bala, a defiantly Welsh town tucked down by a huge lake. Llyn Tegid is the largest natural lake in Wales, its flat shallow edges lapping into warm shallows, trees and jetties. It also contains the River Dee, which runs into and out of the long, thin lake. From here the Dee would curl around through north-east Wales, heading into England and ending in Chester and the wide estuary between the Wirral and North Wales. I'd arrived at my next river, but before I could follow it east out of Bala, first I had to go west, around the lake and up into the forestry to find the source.

I gave in to tiredness and paid for a B&B on the night I limped into Bala. It was something I could barely afford if I was going to keep walking for months, but my sleeping bag was damp and clammy. I lay in bed, showered, clothes rinsed in the bath, sleeping-kit strewn around the room to dry out, feeling miserable and eating ice cream, then realised I'd started my period. I instantly felt better about everything; it's hard to cope with such strain when you're experiencing hormonal peaks and troughs as well.

RIVER DEE

Route description: The River Dee starts in the wilderness of the mountains south west of Llanuwchllyn and ends at the estuary between North Wales and the Wirral, passing through the wooded valleys of Llangollen and the flat flood-plain farmlands of Cheshire on the way, leading to the urban environs of Chester, before turning tidal and becoming estuary.

Length:	127 miles
Total ascent:	unknown
Maximum height:	134m
Dates:	25 May – 12 June 2014
Time taken:	18 days
Nights camping/nights hosted:	5/13
Days off:	4
Average miles per day:	9.07

I set off around the south side of Bala Lake, crossing the steam-railway line and keeping on for a mundane day of road walking. Someone contacted me on Facebook to tell me their auntie worked at a campsite further on, and I should go and ask for a cup of tea. I paused at the roadside sign that marked the turnoff; was I really going to do this? Just barge in on strangers and say *someone on the internet told me you'd give me a cup of tea*. Why not, I decided. Worth a try. I wound my way through the fields down towards the lakeside campsite and there I found the really relaxed and friendly Paul, Jane, Molly and James. They were bemused but welcoming, and fitted me in nicely to the chaos of a family campsite in the summertime, letting me bed down on the leather office sofa, James coming to pick me up after I'd walked another few miles onwards. I walked in the rain but didn't mind, it made such a difference knowing I had a dry place to sleep in later. Another really random but very nice experience, thanks to a woman I didn't know making contact online.

The next day, pausing at the garage in Llanuwchllyn before heading into the Penaran Forest, I found myself in conversation. First, Heledd recognised me from Facebook and offered to host me that night, further up the valley. Then Non popped out of nowhere, wife of Gareth, who farms the land around my old house in Machynlleth, and we were all recognition and excited chatter.

"Do you have somewhere to stay?" Non said. "You could stay at my mum's."

"She's coming to mine", Heledd said.

It turned out they were sisters, had grown up in this village where the road turned a corner to wriggle around the lake to Bala. I told them I was going to search for the source of the Dee and they looked at each other and giggled. Non gently teased Heledd about a mention of the big cat, out there in the Penaran Forest, close to the river source. An old story barely believed, the kind that involves an earnest teller and a scoffing family.

It seemed to me that I'd come a very long way from home. I'd walked away from Machynlleth months ago and left it 600 miles away, but really it was just over a few hills. Wales feels like it's a very separate country but each area is incredibly close to the other; north and south Wales have barely a hundred miles between them. The start of the Dyfi River was high up on the side of Aran Fawddwy, the mountain that Heledd lived under, but I wouldn't be coming to find it for another few months. I was going to walk another 1500 miles before it became time to trace my home river to its beginnings.

Once I walked deep into the Penaran forest, a few miles west of Llanuwchllyn, I had to leave the stone forestry road. There was no man-made path leading to the source of the river, I'd have to split away and follow the water through the forest and into the boggy wilderness beyond. There were bulbous clumps of grass, sprouting long sharp reeds from gooey, squelching ground which drained copper, clear water into the bubbling, vibrant Dee, ice cold and faintly peaty.

There were scattered young trees tenderly beginning to live, yearlings, unsure yet of their footing. I saw curls of scat on the ground and thought about Non and Heledd's warning of the big cat: the Llanuwchllyn leopard. It was really hard ground to cover, trying to stay close to the infant river as it wound and wiggled through the marshy, pine-seeded field. The ground was a mix of water and plants, and I never knew where was safe to put my feet, resorting to stepping from one bulky bubble of grass to another. There I knew the matted roots would hold my weight, would keep me out of the lurking, greedy water. It was incredibly slow, twisting and balancing, often on one leg as I probed and tested the ground ahead to find another footstep.

I realised, there, just how much humans have tamed the world, how much of it we've made safe for ourselves to walk on. Even our countryside footpaths are a laid-down ribbon of safe ground. I couldn't see the inhospitability of the truly wild world until I left the manicured human paths, and found plants wildly overlapping, no safe passage, nothing cleared or laid down ahead. I felt as if I was a settler in a new world, forging ahead where others had never trodden, experiencing the difficulty of being the first human. It was time-consuming and tiresome. I felt intimidated by the wildness only metres away from the human-laid trackway, equal to the irritation at how difficult it was to cross.

My feet felt better, though. The twisting and balancing, precarious as it was, was forcing my feet to stretch in unaccustomed movements. Rather than thudding them repeatedly onto flat, unyielding ground I was tiptoe and precarious, using my poles to steady myself as I twisted from side to side, bringing the trailing leg slowly forward to hop towards the next dry pedestal.

I took hours to follow the river, coming at last to the edge of the pine plantation where the ground became too wet for trees. Across the plain, where sheep roamed their own winding, unfenced ways, the mountain loomed ahead. From this view Dduallt was a huge crag of rock, sheer-sided, dribbling with pebble falls and water droplets. I squelched and plodded my way towards it, my feet long since soaked through. There was no source, just the place where the water ran together and became more than the land, started an overflowing and outpouring until it became a channel. There a stream began, which would find its way to sea sixty-eight miles away.

At the base of the mountain there was a small building. The remnant of a building really, just low walls and scattered rubble but, for me, potential shelter. One side was a huge round stone, the rest balanced and built onto that. *A Celtic place of ritual*, said the guidebook. A place of reassurance, of obeisance, a place to say hello, check in with the gods of the water. I sat in the edge of the shelter and ate, taking silly selfies in the starkness, just me and the grasses and the mountain, scattered sheep far away. I made myself small against the cold wind until I felt no need to be there anymore. There was nowhere I could sleep, I had to plod my way away from the water, to find safe, dry ground to lie on.

I took the direct route back, no longer feeling tied to the water's winding. To reach the nearest track, I had to pick through cleared pine, a mass of ankle-twisting booby-traps, never knowing how the wood would act beneath my feet, whether it would hold strong or sink away, crumbling and rotting in peace. I knew I wouldn't make it back to pasture that night, I'd have to sleep in the forestry somewhere. I also knew it was going to rain and worried, end-of-day footsore, about where I'd rest. I was thrilled to spot, then, by the side of the forestry track, where beaten stone dropped off to a ditch and a morass of inhospitable cleared plantation, a series of thick black plastic pipes, big enough to kneel up in. They were long and dusty and empty, apart from a lost, confused slug, dehydrating in the dusty interior. It was heaven, apart from the midges. I pulled the sleeping bag around me, my hair over my face as a midge deterrent and read happily until bedtime. The rain in the night didn't touch me. Bliss.

When I reached Bala again, the annual Urdd Eisteddfod was in town. Children, schools and parents gathered from all over Wales to compete in Welsh-speaking singing, dance and performance. It was a huge deal; two of Elin and Alun's children were competing. I'd been listening to them practise. Elin had said she'd see me there, I could go to the enclosure and find the Ysbyty Ifan area, where their caravans and tents were grouped. Heledd was proud, her son had won first place in a singing category. It was the only time during the whole trip that I truly felt like a foreigner, a visitor, someone who didn't understand the culture she was in. I suppose it's the effect of entering into a tight-knit community, and this really was the time for the Ysbyty Ifan families to celebrate together, to come and camp and watch their children perform, popping in and out of each other's caravans, chattering and excited, a festival atmosphere, the village holidaying together.

I sensed that they didn't want to speak Welsh in front of me because they felt it rude, but their English conversation was awkward and stilted. It didn't feel natural them prioritising my inclusion, especially as I was the quiet stranger in the corner, zoned out and half asleep with exhaustion. Why speak a second language to your own mother just because a foreigner is in the room? I thought it best to excuse myself and go to bed early. Elin had put me a bed in the awning of their caravan. '*Gwely Ursula hon,*' said Gwydion, showing me to it. 'This is Ursula's bed'.

I met nice people as I walked along the back roads and hillsides from Bala to Glyndyfrdwy to Rhewl to Horseshoe Falls, joining the canal which ran flat and straight towards Llangollen and past it, for an easy nine miles further, towards Chirk. There were aged brick bridges, trailing trees, and sometimes the canal was chipped out of a tall rock-face, just a narrow horse track alongside a steep descent to the Dee valley. Some of the people mentioned a hostel in Llangollen and it piqued my interest; the forecast was for rain and I was tired of getting wet.

Descending into pretty and touristy-twee Llangollen from the canal I passed horse-drawn tourist boats, fudge shops and hanging baskets, painted metal railings and riverside pubs. I walked into the suburbs to find the hostel and, as I came closer to the door, a small child came running across the road to me, clutching a pound to put into my collection tin. She asked what I was doing, and as I started to tell her the story she turned and yelled across the road.

"Muuuuuum. This lady's doing something awesome," bringing the waiting family over to hear my tale.

Suddenly there were phone calls to the hostel owner, money was pressed into my hand and I was beckoned to the hostel door, finding myself with a bed for almost nothing and an invitation to breakfast the following morning. I stood stunned and amused, inside the grand, empty kitchen, to cook my sparse rice and fish, nabbing extra spices from the communal leftovers cupboard. The world of possibilities had opened up out of nowhere and great things had happened, yet again.

Sarah, the girl's mother, came to meet me the following morning. She wore her hair cropped close to her head as she'd donated it all for wig-making. The more I looked into her steady, direct gaze, the more I saw how stunningly beautiful she was; a woman who felt strongly that she must do all she could to make the world better, to raise money for charities. She had something deeply strong and wonderful inside her, but seemed to have no idea of it herself.

She'd read through my blog overnight and saw that I was having foot trouble. She'd been suffering the same plantar fasciitis while standing at work, preventing her training for fifty-mile endurance walks, and had brought something that she used to ease it. Rocktape is a strip of adhesive, elasticated fabric that stretches in only one direction, and it would save my walk in all its smallness and simplicity. Sarah stuck a short length to the sole of my foot, covering the arch lengthways, from the heel to the ball. I took away a short strip of what she gave me and ordered my own online, discovering that it came in a variety of colours and patterns: tiger print, cow print, British flag, pink camouflage, skulls and crossbones. Although I didn't know it at the time, I would walk for another fourteen months, and wore my feet strapped for every single day of that, cycling through as many prints as I could.

The day Sarah strapped my feet over breakfast, I walked nine miles. It was a revelation. I felt so happy as I walked gently along the canal towards Chirk; this was much further than I'd been able to walk recently, and with no pain!

Val was very accommodating and picked me up a day early at short notice. I felt unworthy of all this care, a gauche invader in her tidy life. Not only had she gone to all this trouble, I'd phoned up and asked to come off-schedule, just using her according to whatever I wanted, paying no attention to the careful way in which she planned her life. I made excuses and went to bed early.

As I lay down, showered and clean, an unexpected sentence spoke itself in my mind. *She's doing this because she feels sorry for you*, and all I could be certain of fell away. My body tensed as something dipped within me, as if the bed dropped away beneath me to reveal a howling chasm of my deepest fears. I was fooling myself if I thought that I was doing something worthwhile. I wasn't impressive, thinking I was on an epic adventure, I was homeless and in need of help, a deluded hobo, ranting of cancer.

I struggled and clung to the edges of the bed, telling myself it wasn't true, doing my best not to fall into that space where all was self-hatred and unworthiness. I clung to scraps of reality, people online told me I was inspiring, I'd received generous donations, this wasn't real, my old patterns of thinking were trying to hook me back into the safety of not doing anything, not challenging myself, not risking any failure by never trying at all. It was a sabotage attempt from my low self-esteem, my historic traitor within. The fact that the chasm had opened so clearly and unexpectedly helped me to withstand it. The surprise attack was its very downfall, I could see that it was just another state of mind, not the absolute, just something to be considered and let go. It was unsettling, that this deep self-loathing could surface in the face of exhilaration. The walk was wonderful and positive, a constant flow of beauty and good things happening. I was totally buoyed up by the online reaction and support I'd received, yet I contained the poison that would render all my positivity void. Thankfully I'd been able to see it for what it was this time.

I set off the next day, thinking I'd head into a stretch of small villages. With no contacts organised this was a chance to really get back into wild camping, re-enter the journey I'd set out to make, just me and the countryside. I walked from Chirk to Overton through the morning, where I stopped in at the library, intending to spend a couple of hours sitting, resting, writing. I'd come through fields of soggy clay which excitable calves had trodden completely to muck, a slow and frustrating morning trying to pick through an inhospitable mess.

The librarian asked what I was doing; the flags and large rucksack tended to inspire a raised eyebrow or two. I got people approaching me to say *Umm...err...* and I'd fill in the question they were too embarrassed to ask.

"What am I doing?"

"Yes," they'd say, and laugh. "What's it all about?"

So I'd give the usual spiel about cancer, long-distance walking, hospital appointments, Wales.

"Where are you sleeping?"

"Well, I'm set up to camp but people keep offering me places to sleep, which is really unexpected but a massive help."

The librarian, Rebecca, offered me a cup of hot chocolate which was very nice. I was clearly tired after my tough and muddy morning.

"I know someone who'll take you in. They're kind of drop-outs, and they regularly have people to stay. He might come in later."

And he did. Rebecca placed him at the computer next to me, just saying, "This is a special lady that you need to talk to."

It was a very awkward way to begin a conversation, but eventually we started chatting about what I was doing and Steve asked if I had anywhere to stay that night, and if I wanted to stay with them. I agreed, following this unexpected turn of events with no real wariness.

We agreed that he'd pick me up a couple of miles down the road and I walked on down the river without my rucksack, feeling a wonderful lightness in my body. The air was warm and thick with thistledown; it floated like fat snowflakes against the trees. A cow

117

stood close to me, I stopped still, said hello, and she trotted over, enthusiastically licking my outstretched hand, even letting me scratch her tufty forehead.

I waited at a pub, was picked up by Steve and taken to his home. There I found a Christian family, driven by a message from God to give up their IT business, stop working or paying their mortgage and attempt to live self-sufficiently, keeping pigs, growing vegetables. They were living in a big and beautiful home, bought when they were still working, but now the house was without electricity, mostly without hot water, completely without gadgets. God had told them to show people that we are deadened by over-consumption, headed down an oil-addicted dead end that will lead to the collapse of civilisation within our lifetimes. "A person who believes we can keep a finite system in constant growth is either a madman or an economist," said Steve.

God had told them to keep an open house and accept anyone referred to them in spiritual trauma, after suicide attempts or mental illness, devil-worshipping or other moral repugnancy. Steve told me stories of challenging paedophiles and Satanists, a constant ramble of words tumbling from him, I felt he was close to mania.

They showed me the pigs, sniffing around a bare sty. The family would root in skips to find all the food the animals needed, regularly bringing remnants from the local cheese factory. The family were eating basic food, but they were always eating. "This is a bag of wonky carrots, they're supposed to be for horses but they're perfectly fine for humans too!"

"Whenever we really seem to feel like we've got nothing left, the nuns come and bring us food," his wife, whose name I have forgotten, told me proudly. "They always seem to pick exactly the right time." Jars of dried food lined a bookshelf: pasta, chickpeas and lentils. They showed me the milk kept at the top of the cellar steps; the fridge had been turned off along with all the other electrical gadgets. In the winter, they tried making lamps from pig fat but were forced to buy fuel for oil lamps instead.

Steve was practised at breaking people down, keeping me answering questions over the dinner table, stopping the conversation when I avoided them – such as a question about whether I was traumatised by my cancer – and so forcing me to answer. I felt uncomfortable in the face of his forceful personality, their angelic, home-schooled children looking on interestedly, as they would have done with all the reprobates who'd come through the doors, chiming in with their own particular memories of certain characters. I felt as if I was being treated like the morally questionable people who came to have their minds rearranged, their beliefs turned upside down. Steve appeared to have forgotten I was a guest who was invited home because she needed a bed, not because she needed reprogramming.

I went to shower that evening, the bedroom door closing behind me on a darkly-polished wooden bed with lacework bedding, thick carpet softening my footsteps, and the shower water beating down on me as I stood in a huge Jacuzzi bath that wouldn't work because the electricity had been disconnected. I lay in bed, listening to the sound of Steve praying with a woman on the phone in the chapel they'd created on the top floor. They'd taken her from being homeless and she was now in a psychiatric ward; he repeated the Lord's Prayer with her over and over. It wasn't relaxing.

It was an unsettling, strange and out-of-the-ordinary evening that I'm completely glad I experienced. Sometimes you have to leave yourself open to chance and deal with what you find out there. It's the same with hitchhiking; I stand by the side of the road, stick my thumb out and wait for people to stop, then I deal with their idiosyncrasies, trusting I have the skills to deal with any danger. I open my arms wide and allow the possibilities of the world to flow through me. Threads of lives pass through my outstretched fingers until I catch one and am tugged along with it, experiencing their story until I let go and float free once more. It gives me a taste of the full variety of the human race. It's never been too dangerous thus far: sometimes exceedingly strange but never too dangerous.

I set out to walk along the riverside from Bangor-on-Dee to Holt, following footpaths set out in the guidebook. It soon became apparent that the paths weren't there anymore. Farmers had planted their fields full of crops, stiles were overgrown and blocked, field corners thick with nettles. If people were walking their dogs in this area, it wasn't along the river, which was wide and fast here, high banks with trodden-down pits where cows stooped to drink. It wound in sinuous curves through the fields, almost doubling back on itself with an embankment alongside it covered, mostly, in nettles. The rest of the landscape was flat and wide, just trees dotted around, the mark of ancient boundaries now rendered gaping and meaningless.

The grass was high, waist-height, lush and thick growth, dotted with thistles, nettles as well as other, less aggressive plants. This was rich farmland. I had to step high with each stride forward, lifting my arms to drag my poles behind me. It was a very inefficient way to move but there was nothing else I could do, nowhere else to go. I'd committed to this path and finding another would waste even more time and energy. I just had to keep on trudging slowly through this strange and inhospitable landscape, looking at the shape of the section of winding river that was in view, and trying to relate it to the black line drawn across my map that sometimes touched the river and sometimes set off at an angle to cut across a horseshoe loop.

The sun shone hot on me and my dwindling water supply. Sometimes I came to patches of grass that would shoot out fluffs of white powder and seeds as I moved against them and I began to sneeze, the inside of my mouth itching.

I came to a fence where the book said there should be a double stile. *Fuck it*, I thought and laboriously climbed over. A field of Friesians came into view, languorously lying, relaxing, chewing cud – where I had to cross. They stood up as I approached and ran away, apart from one. Near to her feet was a newborn calf, lying apparently dead on the ground.

It was still warm, so I slapped it in a pathetic, ignorant attempt to make its sides move, trying to make it breathe, take air into its lungs, to live. The mother hovered, making warning, grumbling noises. There was nothing I could do: a dead baby calf in front of me on the floor, in a puddle of blood and mucus, blue tongue lolling from its mouth, body wet and sticky. I felt helpless in the face of my complete inability to fix death, my lack of knowledge revealed. I walked away, looking back to see the mother nosing her child, trying to bring it to consciousness. I held it together until I reached the next stile and found a fallen tree blocking it. It was the final frustration I needed to burst into loud tears. I sobbed and told the cow I was sorry her child was dead, then set about picking and clambering through the dead branches. I looked back moments later to see the cow eating the placenta, chewing vacantly on a string of bloody gore.

There was another fence, another stile, another field with no path, just long frustrating grasses and me with no option but to pick my way through the tangled mess. I was looking for a gate leading to a stone bridge crossing a stream. But what's this? The river in front of me. I looked to see which way it was flowing, confused. OK, the water's flowing left so I'll follow it left. I didn't understand where the bridge was but kind of gave up. If the river's flowing towards the sea from the source, it made sense to follow it towards the sea. So I continued, picking my way towards the sea. Then came a cut through a hedge boundary, a driftwood log lying on the floor. *I recognise that log*, I thought. *Am I going in a circle?* The river looped round in a way I didn't recognise. If I was going in a circle there'd be a fallen tree up there, so I couldn't be going in a circle, there had just been so much grass and fields that it had sent me slightly loopy. I carried on, cutting across a field to miss out a curve of a river and came to a fence boundary. The same one I'd climbed over an hour ago. I'd gone in a fucking circle.

I shouted and screamed in frustration; would I ever be able to leave this stupid overgrown silage patch? I climbed over the fence again, this time managing to rip my top open on the barbed wire.

Another six miles of riverside struggle? No thanks. I was done. I gave up on the river, cutting away and walking through the next field until I found a gate and then the beginning of a track. I cut across west to a field with sheep in it and then, finally a house, a road. Civilisation! It was a four-mile straight tarmac stride to Holt, the last Deeside town in Wales: Farndon, its English twin, across the bridge. I walked into the Peal O'Bells and started swearing about what a crap day I'd had until the landlord bought me a drink!

I'd crossed the border into England, as proved by a mid-afternoon stop in a pub that charged £2.50 for a cup of tea! I drank it and felt aggrieved, making sure that I discreetly charged my phone up at the same time. Chester came next and it was ugly. A town that started gently with flat, riverside fields full of dog-walkers and shimmering, trailing willow trees, turned to grey concrete and blank faces, a typical bustling English town, all uniform shopfronts and bland unoriginality.

I spent a couple of days travelling in and out of Chester, going to see a few different friends and family, a leaving do that I couldn't miss, a day out with my auntie and an afternoon with my granny in nearby Manchester. Every time I walked from the train station to the hostel or around the city at all I seemed to see the same group of scruffy street homeless. I recognised the types of person from my time working in a homeless hostel: grubby, disreputable, hard-drinking, probably junkies. The regular committers of petty crimes that would occasionally break out into violent ones.

I chatted to one of them on the first afternoon, as I made my way out of the train station, and so word got around and they knew I was doing a long-distance walk, my rucksack marking me out whenever they saw me, and my walking speed meaning they could easily catch me up.

The final time, on my way out of Chester, as I came to the waste patch where I would cut away from grey streets through undergrowth, and out to the strange untended parts by the river where people didn't go, they were coming single file, up out of the bushes. The leader came close to me.

"Still going," he said. "What's this?" He grasped my donation tin, pulling gently, face grimaced. "Only joking," he said, as I shied away from him, but I'd caught a snarl of clenched teeth and it left my heart thumping.

I walked along the seemingly everlasting straight riverside path, along the New Cut to Connah's Quay, checking behind me for unwanted followers. On the edge of town, where trees overhung and the path was secluded, three lads came towards me. Rolling shoulders, big dog, shaved heads, wild-looking, pushing each other, tripping along. I crossed to the other side of the path so my donation tin was away from them, kept on walking, keeping up a good stride.

"Nice flag, love, what's the other one?"

"It's my own."

"Nice one, keep going, good flag."

And I was left to examine my prejudices, yet again.

There was a lot of flag love that day, the tattered dragon proclaiming my status once I crossed the border back into Wales, people making a point of saying *Nice Flag*.

I rested for a while in a pub in Connah's Quay, a scruffy place, where all the hefty, tattooed blokes at the bar put money in my tin; a woman up the road, friend of the barmaid, had just been diagnosed. This was my purpose, to walk and talk about ovarian cancer.

It felt good to be back in Wales.

I came to the end of my time with the River Dee, walking up the coast to Holywell over a couple of hot days, tentatively changing from long sleeves to vests. Brilliant for keeping cool, not so good for sunburn. My shoulders burned and peeled and burned again, causing me to be patchy, like a giraffe.

The river had widened to a great grey estuary when I said goodbye to it here, the Wirral still faintly visible on the other side of the long inlet that marked the beginning separation of Wales from England.

I'd been walking for over three months now, covering over 650 miles. I felt good, mostly; I'd grown a lot of muscle and felt strong and capable, it was just this painful foot that was slowing me down. I was already behind schedule, knowing for certain that I wouldn't complete the mileage in the time I'd planned. What I didn't know was what I'd do about it. Did I walk the distance or walk the time? I knew what I wanted to do, I wanted to walk all the way, the full thousands of miles that I'd planned, but it depended on my body coping with the task. If I wasn't physically capable there was no way to push myself beyond breaking. I decided to walk through the summer and then decide properly. It didn't matter now – I could carry on regardless, get as far as I could before the real decision had to be made.

I'd felt a bit emotional over the previous week, as I travelled the length of the River Dee. I missed the feeling of staying in one place, the familiarity, the restfulness. It was hard to be on the move all the time, hard to keep washed and dry and in clean clothes, hard to meet new people every day and hard to carry your life on your back.

There was constant stimulation, beautiful sights like a field of white horses, wheeling and snorting, or turning to a tickling sensation and finding it's a delicate green lacewing resting on your shoulder. All this was beautiful and wonderful, so it felt strange to find a yearning for home creeping in amongst the uplifting interest, support and generosity I was receiving.

I never used to feel like that; before I knew I had cancer I had been travelling free and unfettered for almost three years. Maybe age was changing me, or maybe it was the residue of having been through a life-threatening illness. Or maybe I shouldn't underestimate the effect of being in mild pain all the time. I'd been jarred by this foot injury, the future of the journey thrown into doubt.

I had no plans to stop, obviously. I would complete this walk if I had to build a home and drag it behind me on wheels. It was just another new part of me to listen to and take into account.

CISTERCIAN WAY

Route description: Back in 1998, a Newport university professor decided to create a route that linked all the Welsh Cistercian abbeys, medieval and modern, to mark the 900th anniversary of the founding of the Cistercian order. It resulted in a walk around the heart of Wales, a loop connecting Holywell, Tintern, Tenby and Conwy.

Length:	602 miles
Total ascent:	26,861m
Maximum height:	550m
Dates:	12 June – 29 August 2014
Time taken:	75 days
Nights camping/nights hosted:	28/47
Days off:	20
Average miles per day:	10.94

The Cistercian Way is a little-known route that I'd picked based on its huge 602-mile length – the third-longest Welsh path on the list. There weren't any formal guidebooks, just a written route description on a website, last updated in 2006 (at the time of walking). It was wordy and indistinct, containing such instructions as:

Take the minor road which bears right from the crossroads. In little over half a mile turn left then immediately right. Just after a block of trees to the right a track goes to the right along the edge of the woods. When the track divides, take the left fork and follow the bridleway up into Wentwood.

I found it really hard to follow but had to print out the description and try my best to take the landmarks it mentioned and link them to the footpaths I could find on the OS maps. There was plenty of road-walking, the most out of all the routes I'd included, and the paths it used were frequently underwalked and overgrown. As is the case with the majority of footpaths in this country, councils can only afford to spend money on maintaining the most popular routes. On the Cistercian Way, I regularly found myself fighting through brambles or nettles, climbing over fences and occasionally losing the path altogether and resorting to yet more road-walking. It was slow and sometimes frustrating, although there was a deep satisfaction in tracing an infrequently-walked 602-mile path through inland Wales. Although this historically-themed route didn't include scenic high points like my other choices of mountains and coast, it complemented them somehow and felt worth the struggle.

At Holywell there's a small concrete inlet, a boat launch for the tiny dinghies that were dotted about the harbour, and that was where I turned inland, stopping to chat for a while to a friendly man in a baseball cap, coming down to the sea with his stiff-legged white dog. I was saying goodbye to the coast for a while; now I'd walk from landmark to landmark, heading down the eastern side of Wales to Tintern, then across inland to Tenby, then up to Conwy and across to Holywell again, a four-pointed star, curving inwards between each outstretched arm to wriggle between the major Cistercian sites of Wales – the ruined abbeys of Strata Florida, Tintern, Valle Crucis, Abbeycwmhir, Cymer Abbey, the living community of Caldey Island – plus following as many pilgrim routes and ancient trackways as could be made part of the route.

I came over the Clwydian range from Holywell to Denbigh where I slept my most urban night out so far: in the doorway of the Denbigh ex-servicemen's club, tucking myself down behind a pillar in the covered archway entrance, all tiles and concrete and cigarette-ash blown into the corners. I'd bought a takeaway and didn't want to walk too far before eating it, then the skies promised rain and at 9pm it was too late to go searching for a more salubrious resting place outside the town. I felt pretty safe, slowly eating my disgusting Chinese takeaway: tasteless, water-injected chicken, sloppy sauce and hard chips – a meal that had been much better in the anticipation. There were plenty of passers-by cutting across the open grass inside the grounds to get into the town centre, but only one noticed me. It's amazing how invisible you can make yourself in a public space, just by hunkering down and staying still.

I felt bored for the few days it took me to walk down the Vale of Clwyd. It all seemed very samey somehow: just a long flat valley, faraway hills on both sides, hot sun, no shade and footpaths through field upon field upon field. Occasional animal interactions brightened the monotony: a couple of young birds, the size of hen chicks, with a mix of fluff and feathers, too young to fly away so they just hopped along the path in front of me, cheeping, before burrowing into the long grass. Then there was the first stuck sheep. I thought it was dead at first but then it twitched, lying on its back with all four legs in the air; it had rolled down a bank beside the wire fence and couldn't right itself. I took a good grip on its wool and pulled it over to a more reasonable position, relieved to see it immediately get up and trot away.

With the long climb up to pass over the Llantysilio mountains, I was back in more dramatic scenery, and I revelled in my surroundings again. I turned round to see the way I'd come and to my right was the invisible line of the Offa's Dyke, rising and falling with the Clwydian hills. Ahead lay the sea and my path from Prestatyn along the coast; somewhere in the mass of rising mountains of Snowdonia to my left lay the beautiful Conwy valley and behind me, over the Llantysilio range lay the Dee valley. My paths had covered these lands, tracing an invisible line of footsteps around me, the journey made visible in my mind's eye.

I took a weekend out to attend a writing course, and I met a man for a short-term fling. We kissed a lot, walking to a quiet place, finding a grove of young trees high up in a field. He was ponderous and slow: a deep thinker and steady, silent mover. He was writing a book and talked about finishing it in a year or two. I asked him how long he'd been working on it: more than five years. Fresh from the exhilaration of constant movement, I was incredulous that he could spend so long on the same project and teased him in our rush of flirtation.

"Don't you want to progress? Write, do it, you might die at any moment." And suddenly I realised this was the answer to the irritating journalist's cliché, *How has cancer changed you?*

I hadn't received any national coverage by this point, and didn't receive much press attention at all, other than a few articles about my journey in *Wales Online*, but could guarantee a column in each local paper. I'd usually phone them up for an interview which ticked off a checklist of standard questions – name, age, where from, charities raising money for, amount raised. If I was lucky (or unlucky), I'd get a question about cancer and how it had affected me. All I ever wanted to answer was, "NO, it hasn't changed me at all! I'm still the same and I'm not going to be affected by this stupid illness. I just had a hole ripped in my belly, that's all, I just lost a couple of minor organs. I'm still the same person, I am all the things I was before."

But there was a difference, here was the change. It made me aware of time, of the blunt ending of death, its indifference to circumstances. I'm aware that my precious life could end at any

All routes

Curious sheep on Glyndwr's Way

Wonderfully surreal signpost near Llangollen

1000 mile celebration

Source of the Dee

My favourite of all the
sheep I rescued

Motorboat trails near Tenby

One of my better tarp shelters on Sarn Helen

Soaking my feet to reduce pain and inflammation

Looking back at Rhinog Fach from Y Llethr

Top of Plynlimon in the cloud

Airing out my kit

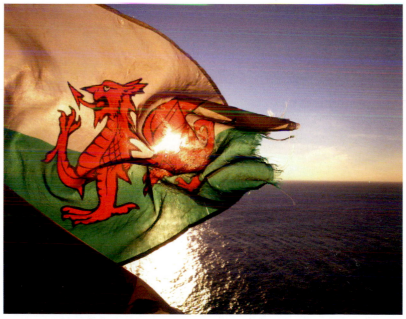

Flag flickering against the sunset at the tip of Gower

Autumn in the Elan Valley

Pont Scethin north of Barmouth

moment and I need to make use of it because I'll never get it back. I felt the need to get on, the need to achieve now, because no-one knows when death might come. Every month must be movement towards achievement, there was no time to let focus slide. I hadn't thought like this before cancer.

South of Llangollen, I joined the Offa's Dyke Path at Rhydycroesau where it skirted around Oswestry. I woke up in the house of a couple I'd met when I'd walked into the Barley Mow, Trefonen, the previous night. Michelle, Steve, baby Charlotte and three big dogs welcomed me into their home, after chatting to me for a while in the pub as I helped myself to the buffet plates of party food scattered around, the remnants of a birthday. We chatted, ate a slow breakfast together, and somehow I didn't start walking until ten.

I followed the Offa's Dyke Path again, in reverse this time, down from Trefonen towards Welshpool. I wanted to get to Welshpool but knew it was too far, so I texted Jen in Guilsfield to see if I could stay with her. She was a Facebook follower who I didn't know at all but had messaged to offer me a bed when my path brought me close to her. *No probs*, she said. Great.

Offa's Dyke is signed at every junction and also very heavily walked so you never have to think about where you're going, just follow the clear pathway worn down into the grass, the tread of feet noticeably thinning the undergrowth. It was very different to my recent struggles with Ordnance Survey maps, invisible stiles and banks of nettles. I felt like I was on a walker's motorway, an ambulatory fast track, allowing me to walk much faster than I'd been able to in recent weeks. I came to Llanymynech Hill and could see over the Welshpool valley. It was so satisfying to think that I'd traversed this landscape three times already, on the Severn Way, the Offa's Dyke path and Glyndŵr's Way, all in one sequential journey.

I reached Arddlin at six, to meet Jen. She walked along the path a little way to meet me, waving as we walked towards each other. We chatted a bit and I said how I really wanted to get to Welshpool tonight, it would make tomorrow so much easier – allowing me to walk to Llanfair Caereinion in a day, to stay with my mother's friends.

"Well, why don't you?" she said. "It's only another four miles and I'll come and pick you up when you're done."

I thought about it. It was much further than I'd recently been attempting, but I could give Jen the rucksack and it would be great to get all the way to Welshpool. So I set off.

A girl called Lou wanted to meet me, too, a friend of Jen's. She'd meet me in Welshpool and take me to Jen's. Half seven, I said, maybe eight.

Definitely eight, I amended, a bit later on, Facebook messages flicking between us all.

It was 9pm by the time I got into Lou's car. She came along the towpath to find me, fed me banana and chocolate and was a great companion for the last hour. Meeting me was important to her; her mother had died from ovarian cancer and, in response, she had done a lot of symptoms-awareness and fundraising work in Wales.

At Jen's we drank beer and ate together. The girls told me I'd walked somewhere between seventeen and twenty miles that day. I couldn't believe them, asking a few times for confirmation; I didn't think my bad foot was capable of that. It's astounding. I would never have pushed for that last section on my own. It was hard, and I definitely felt the pain once I'd stopped, but nowhere near as badly as I'd thought.

I was so grateful to Jen and Lou for that day. They were a brilliant support team, coming out to walk alongside me.

From Welshpool to Llanfair Caereinion to Caersws to Abbeycwmhir to Glastonbury; I met strong women everywhere I went. Sarah in

Llangollen facing down a potential cancer diagnosis, Lou and Jen in Welshpool helping me through a twenty-mile day, their own bereavements very present, Claire the Couchsurfer in Welshpool leading a nursing team, and Rebecca the 1000-mile walker who would support me through the Knighton area. Maybe it was walking as a single woman that invited care from the women who wanted to help me, or the ovarian cancer I'd suffered that inspired female solidarity. Each of them, in their own particular way, inspired me in return.

The day before I left for the Glastonbury Festival, taking a week out for a yearly commitment to serve pizza and earn some much needed wages, I walked over the high hills from Caersws towards Abbeycwmhir through gently roaring wind-farms. I was very late starting but it didn't matter at all as in Caersws I was given an ice-cream by the nice lady from the café, and saw Dee Doody driving past, whose house I stayed in as a guest of Heloise in Llanidloes. Plus, Shân Ashton, who'd done so much for me in the Conwy valley, called excitedly to me as she pulled a minibus over to the side of the road on her way to Merthyr Tydfil. Wales felt like a big village that day, and I was coming to know all of it, my adventure making so many new connections for me.

Abbeycwmhir was a hidden village, hanging trees obscuring the views of most of the houses. I first saw the ornate tower top of a church, then descended a steep hillside to find an interesting pub at the winding roadside.

I sat alone in the Happy Union Inn for a couple of hours until, after 10pm, the customers drifted in. Working farmers, still in the comfortable grime of their working clothes, drinking and refreshing themselves after a long day of haymaking, vibrating tractors and dusty grasses. It was a comfortable and ancient place, with people doing as they had done for many decades. I sat in their atmosphere for as long as I could stay awake, absorbing their relaxation and joviality, until I went to find a field to sleep in and hitched out the next morning to head for Glastonbury.

My friend sponsored me with a pizza, a Festival special: the Wonderwoman! 50p from every one sold would go to my charities. It was a strange thing, taking a break. While I was there, in the packed-out glorious Glastonbury, I couldn't imagine being able to journey again, to return to that world of constant outside, where my legs strode across the land in automatic steps. Loud music was all around me, people rushing past to collect supplies to feed the waiting queues. I reversed my body clock completely, smoked a bit, drank a lot, chatted, joked, made up stories, flirted, grinned, received tips and slung pizza at a variety of drunken, happy, glitter-covered festie-goers. Right there, in that chair behind the food stall, in the centre of the festival buzz, the solitary dreamer of my walking days seemed very far away.

I always have a lovely time working at Glastonbury – intense but lovely. I chatted a lot of late-night rubbish with happy drunken people and came away with £213 for my two charities, another few hundred pounds income to keep me walking, and a warm glow.

I hitched back to Abbeycwmhir, happily wearing the remnants of my festival facepaint. Other after-effects lasted a bit longer, though. I'd spent the week drinking lager rather than water, sleeping during the day and staying awake all night.

I woke the next morning in the long grass on the edge of a field containing the remnants of Cwmhir Abbey. Over time most of the stones and monastic works had been taken away to adorn other churches or build houses. I was up with the light but it wasn't a good day. Sickness, diarrhoea, fuzzy head. Rebecca and Phil came to meet me. Rebecca had finished her 1000 miles around Wales two months previously; we'd been in contact during that time, sending each other messages and postcards without ever meeting. She and I walked a slow eight miles over the hills down to Llanfihangel Rhydithon before they whisked me home for rest and recuperation. They were wonderful hosts. Phil was a jolly bear of a man, loud and comforting to be around, complementing the quiet Rebecca. In their provision of good food and joviality they made me feel completely welcome.

I had a morning off in their house, frantically trying to do as many computer things as I could. Emailing newspapers to work up some publicity, updating my blog, buying supplies, making online payments, uploading photos. It was days like this that I missed having a support team, people working away in the background to make everything run smoothly so that I didn't have to worry about things like a broken shampoo bottle or a dress that needed mending or where to buy sun-cream.

My shoes were damaged again, the soles separating away from the uppers. They'd not done badly, I'd walked about 800 miles in this pair of fell-running trainers. In Hay-on-Wye I could buy glue in an outdoor shop and make a temporary repair while I arranged to receive a new pair in the post. Accessing an address for parcel delivery was the complicated part, I had to try to find a friendly person online who wouldn't mind receiving post for me and keeping it until I arrived on foot.

I got up early, unpacked my rucksack and packed it again, trying, as always, to find something I could take out to lighten the load. Maybe it was warm enough now to lose a pair of gloves or even my fleece waistcoat? I took it downstairs to where Rebecca and Phil were babysitting a neighbour's boy, entertaining him with wooden trains. They weighed my rucksack and it came out at a stonking 17kg, far more than I wanted on my shoulders. We took some food out and got it down to a more manageable fifteen. I aimed to carry between 12kg and 14kg, including food and water. There were so many small things that seemed to slip in as essentials that took me over that, though; symptoms awareness cards and postcards to send to supporters were a significant weight. Plus, it was difficult to buy small packets of certain foods; if I wanted more muesli I had to buy a kilo at a time, when I ate roughly 350g a week. With the packing, rearranging and discussing it was gone 10am before we got in the car to go to the drop-off, pretty typical for most days I spend being hosted. I usually have great intentions to get going but pottering happens, interesting conversations over breakfast, and I never make it out early.

I set off across the hills from Llanfihangel Nant Melan towards Hay-on-Wye. First came a high steep climb behind some farm buildings over to a mix of moorland and forestry. I got lost within half a mile and it started to rain, not a great beginning to the day. I decided to stop for lunch early (cunningly lightening my load still further): oily bacon and potatoes eaten straight out of a vacuum packed silver bag as I sat on soft moss, pine fronds tickling my neck. I wiped my fork on the moss, then on my leggings and cracked on in the drizzle. It would have been a glorious landscape to walk through in the dry: high pasture and moorland, with lakes and sheep and tiny isolated houses, small wind-turbines whirling. As it was I only saw glimpses of this through rain-studded spectacles as I walked as fast as I could, the bridleway stretching out ahead of me and curling around a hillside. I needed to get out of the rain for a bit, so I decided to stop in the next barn for half an hour. Just my luck it had people in it! I asked if I could shelter for a bit and they didn't mind, even made me a cup of tea before continuing with their shearing. I hung my sodden waterproofs from various protruding pieces of metal machinery, took my boots off, squeezing them, squelching from each foot and sat, steaming slightly, as I drank the good hot tea.

I came down into Newchurch at about 5pm, a place I remembered from the Offa's Dyke Path. It has about fifteen houses and a small church where they lay out drinks and biscuits for walkers, according to a tradition started in the time of Charles II. I sat in the church for several hours, drying out and rehydrating, as the rain fell outside. 7pm came and went, nobody came to lock up the church. 8pm passed and I hadn't seen anyone. I might sleep in here, I thought, not looking forward to the thought of a soggy bed outside. 9pm passed – still no-one. So I made my bed in the aisle. I felt slightly nervous about ghosts and spirits, the atmospheric humming of the ancient building affecting me until I lay down and sleepy feelings took over. I looked at the ceiling and thought about the hundreds of years of weekly wishes spiralling up into the rafters.

The next day I absolutely stormed the seven miles into Hay-on-Wye. A nice lady came in to clean the church at 7.30am, making me very glad I was already up and packed! I don't think she would have minded anyway, but it was good to get out walking by eight. The Offa's Dyke Path is great for fast walking; I saw plenty of other walkers coming my way too, a nice change to say hello and have the odd conversation. I saw the Black Mountains again. It felt slightly less awe-inspiring to look across the landscape and think that I'd walked that three months ago. Was this experience in danger of becoming mundane? Was everything finally blurring into one long year of walking, like routine days in an office job that all became the same?

In a Hay café I did a bit of internet surfing and stuff, washed my socks in the sink, blagged a free bit of cheesecake and put my shoes on the windowsill to dry out. I used the break to put up a social media post celebrating 1000 miles walked. Whoop!

It felt good, it felt official. Even though I was overweight, even though I didn't train, even though I was carrying too much in my pack, even though I hurt my foot, I'd walked 1000 miles because I'm stubborn and determined. It felt great. If it all went wrong next week I'd still have walked 1000 miles and that was enough to be proud of. I'd celebrated with Rebecca the night before, opening a bottle of Prosecco in our honour, two female 1000-mile walkers. Reaching this milestone also gave me hope for the future. If I could walk 1000 miles, I could walk any distance. I might be walking for an entire year but I was going to walk 3000 miles. Fuck. Yeah.

That night I knew, for a too-brief overnight stay, what it felt like to do a supported walk. I came up onto the high land out of Hay-on-Wye, following the Offa's Dyke Path again. It was coming to sundown and I wanted to get a few miles done before the light faded. I came to the long, flat plateau overlooking the Wye Valley, the Black Mountains towering to my left and a long clear view of the land beyond me, the lights of Hay glimmering down to the right, and the squares and fields of farmland, cut outs, lines and markings, the division of land into owned pieces and the lights that marked the human dwellings.

A van overtook me, windows in the back marked it as a camper. *There's a cup of tea in that van*, I thought, and watched as it pulled in about 200m ahead of me. As I trod closer, in steady paces, a silver-haired woman called out to me.

"Do you want a cup of tea?" Magic.

I ended up in there for the evening, sitting with my feet outstretched as a slender and graceful woman cooked me a meal, kneading chapatti dough in a bowl, giving me banana and fried vegetables to scoop with my fingers. Her story started with a fact; she'd been abandoned by her partner. He'd unexpectedly ended the relationship, the man she thought was hers forever had dumped her for a younger woman. She'd settled into this partnership, thought it was a certainty and then she had to learn that they'd been taking each other for granted. They'd lost the spark, stopped trying and he'd sneakily, weakly, fallen in love with someone else.

I listened to her stages of denial and grief. Grief at the fact of the younger woman, at her own unattractiveness, her uncertainty. Pain at the way they had to untangle their shared lives, communal properties, bringing new people into old beds. Her sadness at becoming the hag, the crone, the woman whose love life is over, wrinkled and shrivelled, replaced by plump and dewy youth. Discarded, no good. She bemoaned his immaturity, his shallowness, but acknowledged that they'd both stopped trying. They were ignoring their deeper sexual selves and taking each other for granted. I was listening to a woman who'd had her life broken apart and was choosing to get wise and deal with it, picking up the pieces, finding herself in the shards, putting together a new person in light of this huge imposed, unwanted change.

I wanted to stay talking to her all night, listening to her life story, an amazing tale of psychosis and hidden gardens, of shattering and healing, but tore myself away to go to bed. If I was camping alone, I would generally choose to be in bed by 9pm. That night was late, late, late, almost 11pm before I snuggled on one of my benefactor's sofa cushions outside the van, a beautiful late night skyline beside me. The light was almost gone from the sky, just a line of colours at the black horizon bleeding between red, yellow, pink and then blue, deepening down to the velvet violet darkness where stars were beginning to show. I had to tuck down inside the sleeping bag to get my head out of the brisk wind that came off the wide landscape before me.

The next morning I was up by 7am; the lovely lady made me chapattis with marmite, tahini and banana, delicious energy-giving food, as well as zingy coffee. We talked some more about the nature of love. All love involves need, we decided. What if love could be given freely, without leaving you wanting something in return. Was that possible? Altruistic love?

It was a wonderful evening, just being able to walk up to a van, sit and talk and receive food and hot drinks. This happens every day to someone being supported. It made me realise that what I'm doing, the way I'm doing it, is REALLY BLOODY HARD!!

My route that day lay over the Black Mountains, a steep climb up to the west of Lord Hereford's Knob then down the valley along into Capel-y-ffin, and on towards Llanthony Priory. I revelled in the wilderness of the high hills, the long views out behind me and the easy-to-follow path, spending the night sleeping out near the remains of the priory. I woke at 6am, sitting for a while, slowly coming back to life, then ate breakfast and set off, following the contour line around the hillside down to Cwmyoy. There was a fantastic church there, the ground settling underneath it over the centuries, leaving it leaning south at one end and north at the other. I sat inside for a rest, admiring the visibly twisted archways and door jambs, but soon the view started to spin and I realised I had an awful headache. The longer I sat there the less I felt like walking. I slumped over in one of the pews and went to sleep for an hour. It's very hard being vulnerable in public, with nowhere safe to go when you feel peculiar. The painkillers kicked in while I slept, and once I woke up I could think more clearly. I realised I hadn't eaten very much the previous day and had only drunk a single litre of water. I slowly chewed my way through a big meal of couscous, chopping beetroot and tomatoes into the bowl, and felt much better. I went to see the woman in the house next door to ask for water and, wonderfully, she invited me in for a cup of tea and made me some sandwiches.

I carried on south out of the valley in sunshine, coming out of the enclosure of the Black Mountains and out onto the Offa's Dyke Path again, to follow this familiar route all the way down to Monmouth. It was 4pm; I'd walked maybe six miles so far and spent about three hours feeling ill in the church.

I decided to walk the final two miles to the next village, maybe sleep in the church porch there, but when I arrived I found a sweet little pub full of people interested in my walk. I sat and chatted, got given plenty of donations and even a couple of beers and a free meal. The owners were interesting;:a pair of brothers who'd clearly done a lot of travelling and wild living over the years. I got invited to the house of one of them, quirking an eyebrow as he took two bottles of wine from the fridge on our way out of the pub. We drank late into the night, swapping stories across the kitchen table, refilling glasses and hunting out more bottles. He'd spent years abroad but had run away from his adopted country, a midnight flit to avoid a failing business and the looming bankruptcy of an unpayable tax bill. He'd brought his wife back here and now she hated him, he said. She resented their fall from grace, frustrated with their small life here and being unable to return to her home country.

We were unafraid to get down to the bare bones of our experiences, telling details of sexual partners, his time with a much older woman, my time on the banks of the Danube, with the freedom of expression that comes when the person you're talking to will never be part of your daily life again.

There came the moment where all the wine was finished and the hours had long since dropped into small numbers and begun to grow again, where the conversation dwindled into silence and we looked into each other's eyes for a long pause, where the spark of another energy began to grow between us and time hung still in the split second before action, the moment before we leapt together and ripped at each other, biting, pressing and tugging, mingling spit and sweat.

"Shall we go to bed?" he asked, and all the potential for an alternate reality where we fucked gathered and formed until I shook my head, retreating from instinct into sensibility. He was married and not all that attractive; it was just an animalistic thing.

I collapsed into his teenage daughter's bed, all pastels and pillows and slept like an animal instead, drooling and snoring. I felt far too rough for walking, spending the next day on a zebra-print sofa, extremely hungover, watching bad TV and enjoying this unexpected time. The man went to work and came home late and drunk, I didn't see him until I went into his bedroom the following morning to say goodbye.

I looked at him, the way his hair curled greasily into a little flick at the base of his neck, the smell of booze seeping out of him as he sat blearily in a black T-shirt, sheets carelessly rumpled around his near-nakedness, and was glad I hadn't submitted to that tremble of lust. It wasn't that I didn't want to have sex, didn't feel horny or crave physical contact. It's just that it wasn't important enough to share with just anyone I had a momentary lust for. I was becoming animal-like on this walk, turning wild and growing in physical power, but this was still a behavioural boundary that my human ethics kept me from crossing over.

I slept outside Monmouth in a straw field shaved down to bristles. I'd headed for the patch of grass left long in the centre, hoping for camouflage from the dog-walkers who patrolled the field edges. It was a mistake; twenty slugs were all over my kit within an hour of lying down. I deeply love camping without a tent, the immediacy of the experience, waking up to see the moon beholding me, my night-time companion. But I do wake up with dew all over everything, slugs as bedfellows, and avoiding rain is a permanent problem. As this journey lengthened – and it seemed that I'd be walking for at least ten months, through into November at least – I

142

knew I'd have to sort a tent out for the autumn/winter. I could avoid the issue by creeping into church porches or hay barns, but they wouldn't always be available.

After spending a morning in Monmouth, sorting out my non-charging phone, new maps, a food top-up, I headed for Tintern, where I'd turn a corner and walk through south Wales to Tenby following, as far as possible, a medieval pilgrimage route described by John Leland in 1540. The modern guide contained such descriptions as, *The main track, once the way between Pontypridd and Ynys-y-Bwl before the modern road was built, has been badly eroded by rain and is blocked in places by burnt-out cars but it's still passable with care.* My first time in South Wales, the most heavily-populated part of the country. What would I find there?

It was so hot in the few days I spent around Tintern, I felt as if I could never drink enough water to maintain myself. I felt achy and stinky almost all the time; it was coming to the end of July and the full summer heat that came with it. I was always sweating, my skin crusted with salt, my rucksack odorous, the heat of the thick bag pressing the full length of my spine. I was covered in insect bites; horseflies in particular were a vicious menace. I was drinking three or four litres of water a day and still woke up with dehydration headaches. Everything was starting to smell bad. I was sick of eating trail mix.

I was walking to have fun, I was walking to raise money for charity and I was walking to tell women about the symptoms of ovarian cancer.

But when, for the hundredth day in a row, I'd sit down for a midday break that couldn't last longer than forty-five minutes before pushing myself up off the ground, heaving up my heavy, smelly rucksack and walking on I thought, *Why the hell am I doing this?* Had I really thought this through? Did I really realise what my plan entailed? When I thought, *oh yes, I'll walk the length of nine rivers and five long distance trails in one continuous journey*, I really didn't consider the amount of steps, the sheer time, effort and strain involved.

Sometimes people would stare at me as if they'd never seen a sweaty woman wearing a gigantic rucksack before. Sometimes the idea of someone walking thousands of miles for charity was odd enough to someone that they would call me mad or crazy. It was undermining and irritating. I felt insulted, wanted to tell people they had no imagination.

There were always moments of splendour, though, that underlined why I was doing this. Sleeping one night in a public park, a small triangle of ancient trees and rhododendron bushes, I heard a noise as I was drifting off to sleep and turned my head to see a deer disappearing into the nearby bushes, rabbits lolloping on the grass.

I walked around the abbey, taking time to go in and admire the ruins and set off south, taking the Stony Way, a 900-year-old path that obviously wasn't walked often. It was part rocky pathway and part riverbed, crumpled stones moved by water and gravity. This was the path the monks walked to get to their grange farms at the top of the hill, up on the flat lands, in the good daylight. I felt very pleased to be following such an ancient path, imagining the footwear they might have worn, hooves of cart animals slipping and catching on the same stones I trod.

Spending a night above the Bristol Channel on the edge of a wheatfield, I heard the tinny noise of a Tom Jones concert coming up from Chepstow racecourse, waves of cheers a few miles distant. The late summer night turned the post-sunset sky a pale lilac, and I sat content with the rustling wheat as the pale yellow moon rose over England and the Severn Bridges. The next time I'd see these bridges I'd be crossing them to Bristol, after another few thousand miles of walking.

The Cistercian Way was a pain to follow – the route was badly described, there were no waymarks and the paths were overgrown – but I really loved the places it was taking me.

I took another week away to go and work at a festival. In the planning of the walk I felt it would be a good idea to take the odd break when opportunities arose, help me to maintain connections to a somewhat normal life.

This one felt wrong, though. It had only been two weeks' walking since Glastonbury. I was dirty, aching, tired and yet somehow it still felt as if I should be carrying on. I would surely regret this lost week when it came to November, when the wind was blowing rain into my face and I still had hundreds of miles to go.

On my way back to Cwmbran I stayed with Rebecca and Phil, my mid-Wales walking supporters. They were going to Pembrokeshire and could drop me off en route. Arriving in Cwmbran I put my rucksack on, we said our goodbyes, I waved them off, walked away... and ten minutes later searched for my phone. I knew straight away it was gone, I'd left it on the bonnet and they'd driven away. I walked back and searched the ground around the drop-off point. Nothing. I walked into the shopping-centre that makes up the centre of Cwmbran, found a phone shop, demanded that they let me use their phone and internet, and phoned Rebecca. There was nothing on the bonnet of the van. They pulled over, searched the engine, there was no phone. I cried, closed my eyes, trying not to break down in the middle of the shop. I'd been talking to people over the last few weeks, or rather, they'd been talking to me, telling me I should back up my photos, be careful not to lose it. I hadn't done it. All my pictures from the first four months of the walk were gone. All those memories of little corners, rest breaks on the sides of hills, stiles filled with nettles, inscrutable looks from curious animals, all the silly little things that weren't worth uploading for other people but contained so much of what made this journey wonderful. Gone. It was a real blow. I had a little cry on the phone to my brother Owen. I sorted out a temporary replacement, did my admin things in the town: new maps, post office to send home the old ones and carried on. Nothing to do but walk.

It wasn't much of a distance that day, only down the canal, across a hill to Risca and then another hillside and down to Machen, where a woman called Samantha Minas had offered me a bed through an online comment. I was pretty active on Facebook and Twitter, trying to post something different each day, making sure I didn't bore people or overload them with similar posts. Sometimes it was a beautiful landscape photo, sometimes a quirky report of a stuck sheep or blocked stile, sometimes a photo of a person who'd helped me and a little bit about their story. It was important to keep people interested, engaging in my story of ovarian cancer and a walk would make them more likely to donate or see the importance of symptoms awareness. It also became a support network for me; I wasn't operating in a vacuum, wondering if this was a lunacy-induced trek, I had people remotely cheering me along the whole time.

I walked slowly and steadily, taking a short nap by the side of the road until I was rudely awoken by a shouting motorist. This was a theme of south Wales. Boys shouting from speeding cars to frighten pedestrians, an aggressive noise, timed to appear loudly and suddenly. It was really unpleasant. I stopped in at a pub on the way for some water. It was hot and sunny, as it had been all week and I need to keep topping up. The woman behind the bar, early 60s with beautiful big eyes and nicely cut blonde hair, gave me a jug of water to guzzle and somehow we started talking about good and evil; she told me what she felt about the different facets of evil and how it can be hidden behind beautiful faces. I suddenly felt that she was a witch, in the traditional wise-woman sense. It was a real surprise to meet her behind a bar in a rural pub but then all ordinary people have sparks of greatness within them, it just flashes more brightly in certain people.

I walked on, up the final steep climb and down past the quarry into Machen.

Samantha was lovely: a very calm, beautiful woman, riding the waves of her particular circumstances with a transcendent strength and spirit. She provided good food, a shower, a washing machine, a comfy bed, a packed lunch and a small glimpse into her life – a very grounded person. I had the idea, as we were having breakfast, that I should phone the *Argus* and ask if they wanted to do a story about me. They wanted to send a photographer to meet me at Caerphilly Castle, another five miles along the road. I, in my eager-to-please manner, named a time that was just a bit too early. Damn, now I would have to rush. I gulped my coffee, hugged Samantha and set off along the long, straight main road to Caerphilly. I'd have to walk fast, I was almost definitely going to be late. Well, things happened, I stopped to pat a dog, cars beeped and waved at me (the flags on my walking poles were a great decision) and finally, a silver car pulled up beside me.

"I own an ice-cream parlour about 100 yards down the road. Go in there and tell them that Richard said you could have a free ice cream." When did you ever dream that such a thing would happen?

I rushed into the parlour, ran through my story to the giggling girls behind the counter, met Richard's wife, had my photo taken, gave out some cards and rushed out again. The ice cream was bloody lovely!

My temporary phone rang as I was on the outskirts of Caerphilly; the photographer was at the castle already. I jumped on a bus, met him at the castle, had a few photos taken and got him to drop me back at the same bus-stop on his way back to Newport, so I could finish the walk into Caerphilly. An hour at a café (it was a fast walk and I needed a rest!), an hour in the library, a place to make online updates without a smartphone, and I was ready to head on. My aim for the rest of the day was to walk up to the high hills to the north west and curl around on a long road towards Pontypridd. There was no point walking all the way down into Ponty as it would be too late to go all the way through the town and look for a safe, quiet bed on the other side. Better to walk a slightly shorter day and make myself a nice bed somewhere up in the hills.

I walked along a quiet country road, waving my flag at cars as they came around corners to make sure they slowed down for me in plenty of time. There were two pubs on the way. I called in at both of them, of course, the first one just for water. It was obviously a very friendly, well-loved kind of pub where everyone knows each other, the kind of pub I really enjoy finding in quiet country places. I chatted a bit, filled my water bottle up, received a few donations, set off again. Another hour or so brought me to the common land where sheep wandered across the roads. I made it to another pub – a pint this time and another chat with the locals and the landlord: more donations, more good wishes.

I left close to sundown, wanting to sleep. Unfortunately, it seemed I was wandering into the Pontypridd young couple's prime sunset-watching spot. There were cars every quarter of a mile or so and litter covered the cropped grass. I carefully avoided looking too closely into any of the parked vehicles and carried on, hoping to find somewhere quieter. The road started to curve down towards the town and I started to worry. There would have been a good spot to sleep out in the woods, but first there were fences and then there was another family camping: children's shouting filled the air. I moved on. Finally I discovered a gap in the fence and found myself on the edge of the golf course – perfect. I wasn't on the course itself but at the edge of an adjacent field; the grass had been cropped for silage and I found a level, sheltered spot. A few drops of rain and some threatening murky clouds made me experiment with putting my shelter up; I was still trying to find a good design that I could put up alone without struggling to get the material taut in several places simultaneously.

I was woken by people walking their dogs and it wasn't even 6am. I rolled over and slept again until seven, then packed up and walked down the hill to breakfast on a park bench in Pontypridd. It sounds silly and very obvious, but the big difference between this part of Wales and the rest of the country is the number of people tucked down in the valleys. As I walked across the hill tops I could see the Wales I was familiar with: miles of hills, sheep, wind turbines, beautiful views. But the valley bottoms were different; instead of scattered farmhouses, maybe a small village, they were full of row upon row of terraced houses all looking the same and creeping in lines high up the sides of the valley, each settlement with a fast, dual carriageway splitting it in two, the road running north-south to carry people into the cities of Cardiff, Swansea and Newport with all their shopping and employment opportunities. It was a real shock to see how heavily populated each valley was, all the towns running into one another along the long thin valley floors. The air filled with the constant noise of traffic

That day's walk was meant to be a short forest ramble over the hill to Ynysybwl, but somehow what started as a path turned into a steep-sided riverbed, and I found myself crawling under fallen trees and scrambling through brambles. I'd followed many paths on this

149

journey – human paths, sheep tracks, badger paths through steep woods – and now it was the paths that water makes across a landscape. I found a human path again, and set to following the right direction over to the next town. The woods were criss-crossed with options and I kept randomly choosing left or right, just trying to head in the right direction. Eventually I came to a thin trail between fences which came out at a layby. A layby with a bed in it. A bed on fire...

It was a fresh fire, licking over the bed base. The bed had been carefully piled up, the drawers pulled out and placed on top, along with some empty beer-cans. The fire wasn't really catching, probably thanks to modern fire-resistant fabrics, but just licked along the woven plastic fabric stapled between the wooden uprights, a slow trickle of burning rather than a blaze. I watched the fire and thought about the person who had pulled up, unloaded a bed by the side of the road in the countryside, set fire to it and driven away, imagining that this was a great way to destroy what you didn't want. So much ugliness and stupidity. It was shocking to see such an aberration in the peace of the quietly-growing countryside. The plastics of the bed dripped fire onto the ground. The fire wasn't fierce enough for the wood nearby to ignite, so I just let it smoulder away.

I carried on into Ynysybwl and a woman called to me from her front garden.

"What are you doing? Do you need anything?"

I grabbed the chance to refill my water bottle and have a wee! We had a nice little chat and I moved on again, through the village. I stopped at the furthest edge, a short rest before moving up into the forestry. It'd been so hot all week, I was sweating and sweating and needed to keep stopping to rehydrate. My feet were also unused to walking. Just a week's break meant I needed to break them in all over again. It's a certain kind of pain, the connecting parts complaining as I forced them to stretch out again in a regular walking motion. They'd forgotten what this was like, life at full stretch, and creased and cramped back into their usual positions, set for strolling.

People kept getting off the bus at the stop nearby and enquiring about what I was doing. They'd seen me walking through the village and were curious about me. I gave out more cards, received more donations.

Up in St Gwynno Forest I rescued another sheep, this time with its head stuck in the entrance to a water-trough, which made a total of three stuck sheep rescued thus far. I also got told off, mildly, by a farmer, for going through the wrong field. He was young, about 17, and looked incredibly pleased with himself as he showily pulled up beside me on his massive shiny red steed – I mean quad bike. Direction corrected, I proceeded into the forest where, at the meeting of two roads and surrounded by thickly-crowding trees, there's a small collection of five houses, a church and a thriving pub called the Brynffynon Hotel.

Sitting alone in a pub is a licence to dream, to listen to the gathered old ones at the bar, forever chatting, airing their views, discussing their favourite kind of cheese sandwich for an hour at a time.

The best kind of pub contains:

Music that's quiet and unchallenging;

Freely available, functioning plug-sockets that the landlord is happy for all customers to use;

A bookcase of tired but excellent literature that the customer is free to swap for their own battered and thumbed books;

Tables and booths in tucked away corners where the tired customer can take off her boots and rub her feet without attracting comment;

Good ale of a name that's not freely available in every chain pub outlet.

Public house in the literal meaning of the name: a place for anyone to sit indoors, where it's safe and the weather cannot touch them. A haven: for me, a retreat from the physical effort of walking.

I spent a happy hour there filling up on water and beer. I was bought a dangerous (for 3pm) second pint by the owner, and received a lovely £20 donation from the same. I left, goodbyes slightly slurred, and headed out of the forest towards Tylorstown, another concrete mass of housing.

It was still hot, the sun beating down endlessly. I tired very quickly in the heat, got lost on the way down the steep hillside and found myself on the wrong side of a spur, almost in Wattstown, another clinging, hillside estate. I would have gone along the road but was directed back up the hill by a friendly farm-worker. He, Jeff, also invited me to stay at his house, because of all the hospitality he received when he was travelling in New Zealand, but I had another couple of miles I wanted to do that day. I came down into Tylorstown, stopped to pick up some food and an ice-cream treat and headed out again, up yet another steep valley-side towards Penrhys. Ever since I'd met a biker couple from the Rhondda over in Monmouth, people had been warning me about the Penrhys estate. Apparently a notorious place about twenty years ago, people didn't have much good to say about it.

"If you want to buy drugs, just ask any eight year-old."

"Don't take your donation tin in there, it'll get ripped off in minutes."

"It'll be alright during the day but don't go in there after dark."

Well, guess what. I emptied the notes out of the tin, shoved them in my bra, headed on up the steep, steep hill into the estate and around the edge... and was totally ignored. Well, that's not true actually, I paused for a rest half-way up, turned round to look behind at the view of the two valleys running either side of the Mynydd Troed-y-Rhiw dead ahead, and noticed a group of people sitting in their back garden staring at me, about 50m away. I temporarily forgot that I was in the deadliest, most drug-ridden and violent estate ever in the whole of Wales, lifted my flag and waved at them. They waved back and I carried on, unmolested.

I came up out of the back of the settlement, past a small pine plantation, and out into the long grass of the open, high hillside. The sun was starting to set far away and, nearby, tall wind-turbines continued their slow powerful circuits. I walked about a half mile from the houses, turned away from the path carved by motorbikes, people and vehicles, and into the long grass to find a bed. The grass waved gently in the wind and the sky faded slowly into the pale gold and lilac of a summer evening. I heard voices behind me and realised that a family were making their way home after a walk. Would they see me? I really hoped they wouldn't. If they did, and they were going to come back and bother me later on they'd only find a flattened patch of grass. I lay flat, with my head turned towards the path. First came the sound of the dog, hurrying and panting, then the high calls of the son, excited. Then came the father, I could just see his head and shoulders, slow and ponderous. Then came two women talking together. I couldn't catch the words of their chatter, just the swooping tones of their sing-song south Wales accents. None of them turned their heads or saw me, and their voices faded away down the hillside towards home.

Much later, when the sky was a deep dark blue, a jeep came roaring up through the grass and I lay flat again, hoping the passengers wouldn't turn their heads. They didn't and I nestled down into my comfortable sleeping spot. It was a beautiful night, I remember waking up as I turned over and deciding to lie on my back for a while and look at the stars. It only lasted a few seconds before I faded down into the darkness again, but I remember feeling the deep peace of simply being a body lying on the earth. The grass waved over me, rustling quietly, all night.

I had a big day next day. My brother was coming to join me for a few days. Maesteg would be the best place to park up, so I had to walk right over there to meet him by 5pm. So, down into Pentre in the Rhondda Valley, into a café for a breakfast cup of tea that turned into half an hour of chats with the owner and the customers, as people kept coming in and being told about me and they kept giving money. Just a few coins or even the occasional fiver but it all adds up, and it means a lot, when you're in one of the poorer areas of the country. A pot of tea was 80p in that café and was bigger than the £2.50 mug I was served in the upmarket gastropub near Chester where everyone ignored me.

I hurried on through the town, waylaid by a man who wanted to tell me how much he loved the Rhondda. He'd been working away for years, no jobs here, forced to go over the bridge for employment. But finally, at the age of 50, he was finding work in the valley, installing windows. He felt great about it, and seeing as I wasn't from round here he thought he'd stop and ask what I was doing, tell me the story of his struggles, sharing some of his history in that open South Walian way.

I crossed the railway into Ton Pentre and set off up the steep hillside, heading for a bridleway which would take me over the Mynydd Mendy and across the Bwlch. It was hot, so hot, and my steps slowed as I tottered up the steep pavement. It was a relief when someone called over to me.

"What are you doing? Do you want a cup of tea?"

It was the Cherrys: Mr, Mrs and two daughter Cherrys. I went inside for a quick glass of squash and a chat; they were lovely, trying to force more water and snack bars into my rucksack. It was difficult to leave but I had to get on – somehow it was half eleven already. I trudged up the steep hillside and onto the tops where I could see for miles, turbines waving in the distance, just pine plantations and sheep covering the land, with houses nestled into the crevices of the land below. I walked a few miles over to where the mountain road from the Rhondda came up and met up with the Bridgend county boundary. The views were spectacular. I had no idea that what I had thought was such a downtrodden, post-industrial area was so gorgeous. I had a great chat with the jolly man running the ice-cream van at the top; he used to inspect sewers, now he sold ice-cream and couldn't be happier.

On I went, across the road and up another sharp climb to walk along a cliff edge, the land dropping away down to the Ogmore Valley below, the road winding in Alpine horseshoe curves below me. I was making good time. Another couple of miles along a stony track brought me past a collection of radio masts and over to the head of the Pontycymer Valley. The land swelled gently downwards and there was another set of steep cliffs ahead. I had to climb up the side of them and walk along the top into a forestry plantation; this day was really taking it out of me and I was only about two-thirds of the way through it.

Coming down through the forestry I got lost; the trees had been felled, leaving a confusing and ankle-rolling mess of stumps, branches, dips and baby brambles. There was supposed to be a footpath winding its way through this, but I couldn't find it. Instead, I looped around on the forestry roads, always making my way downwards, trying to orientate myself with the houses I could see in the farmland below me. Eventually I made it down through the bracken to the highest farm on the hillside. Now there was just a funny little trapezoid of footpaths before I could get to the straight road and the final three miles to Llangynwyd, where my bro awaited. Well, the OS map said there should be a path there but all I could see was a rusty gate and, on the other side of it, head high brambles.

No Way.

I searched around for another route. On one side there was a stream, on the other a high barbed-wire fence at the top of a steep bank. I decided to cross the stream; maybe the path was on the other side. The bank started out being covered by Himalayan Balsam, not too bad; but eventually, as I climbed higher, thrashing my way forward, the brambles came creeping in until I was struggling in a morass of thorns and scratches.

"I'm going back!" I suddenly shouted, at the end of my tether, and started crying as I picked my way back down the bank. "This is stupid! I hate everything!"

I blubbered like a child. I was back at the gate again, there was no way I could cross it; it was pure brambles on the other side and I would make it no more than a few feet before becoming inextricably entwined. I fought through the trees instead, branches catching my hair and realised I could pull my way up the bank and climb onto a cleared patch, which led towards the house and barns.

"You're going the wrong way," a woman called to me.

"I know, I'm sorry," I called as I came closer. If you're trespassing, always apologise, even if it was the stupid brambles' fault. I wiped away the tears as I came closer but the couple sitting outside having an evening drink could still tell I was in a bit of a state: sweaty, wild hair, scratches all over my hands and arms.

I'd started the day at 400m altitude, dropped to 150, climbed again to 500. Another few drops and climbs of 100 metres meant I'd climbed a bloody mountain that day, as well as walking seventeen miles in the high summer sun, and getting caught in a nest of brambles.

"Let me get you a drink," she said, seeing how frazzled I was, and we had a quick glass of squash and a chat, mostly about footpath permissions and a nearby angry farmer who'd once waved a gun at walkers. This couple had three footpaths crossing their land and didn't want them there; that's why they didn't clear the morass I'd just tried to fight through. We talked politely, sharing our points of view about what a pain it was, them to have people crossing their land, me to see a path on the map but to find it's unwalkable on the ground. I casually dangled my hands over the fence as we talked, caressing the dogs as they leapt and licked. Eventually I realised one of the Rottweilers was gently toothing the pads of my fingers, they were forbidden fruit, dangling meat grapes; and he was teasing himself with the almost-biting of them. It added to the unsettling feeling from this family, politeness covered guarded unfriendliness. I was an intruder; they didn't want people on their patch.

I hurried on, finally coming to the road and there he was, my bro. Come to meet me in his summer holidays, complete with a new smartphone and a great fund of stupid jokes. We covered the last few miles to Llangynwyd. I was really tired by that point; if I hadn't been coming to meet him I would have camped up on the hills. The pub more than made up for all the effort, though. The oldest pub in Wales! There's been a pub on that site in Llangynwyd since 1147.

"Who's this now with the flags?" they were saying as I walked in.

"Long distance walk for charity!" I carolled, the magic words. "I've walked over from Penrhys and I've been thinking about drinking a pint in this pub for hours!"

I really had, the hot sun drying out my mouth as I imagined that first sip of cold lager, sitting down with my feet up.

Well, within two minutes came a wonderful wave of friendship and generosity.

"Have a drink, on my tab", said Lee.

"Have a shower at my house across the road", said Karen.

"There's a caravan in the garden, you can sleep in it if you want", said the landlord.

I sat there a bit stunned, trying to keep up with all the quips and conversation coming my way. There was a really funny man in the corner who just got it when I explained what I was doing and how I was travelling.

"Freedom!" he said.

"Exactly," and we clinked glasses.

"Is it always like this?" said my brother.

"Of course!" I lied. "All the time!"

But it is, in a way – just not usually as concentrated as in that particular pub on that particular night.

I had my shower, we had our pints, Karen and Lee invited us over for breakfast the following morning and we were the last to leave the pub, the poor barmaids sitting and texting as we chatted on unthinkingly, not realising that everyone else had gone home.

Fuzzy-headed, we dragged ourselves out of bed early, yawning extensively as we sat opposite each other in the shaky caravan. We only had to go down to Margam Park, see the abbey and stately home, before almost turning back on ourselves to head up into the forestry to the west of Maesteg and over towards Neath. We were sorry and slow, heads throbbing a little – at least mine was. We came over the hill and found a glorious view of the Bristol Channel and the Port Talbot steelworks, smoke and fire belching into the air. Margam Park turned out to be a bit frustrating; we'd come into it the back way and couldn't find the way out! It was a long, slow walk back to the path and unfortunately the next bit of the route was a steep climb through difficult, tiring reeds and long grass at the end of a farm track, up to the forestry above Margam. The path disappeared and we fought through long bracken before collapsing in the welcome shade of the pine trees to have lunch.

We could have continued up and over one more hill and further north, but decided to cut left and down to the ex-colliery village of Bryn. There was one pub, full of about ten older gentlemen who had clearly been coming and sitting in the same seats for years upon years. The pub didn't do food, but were preparing a meal for the cricket team who'd been playing away, and the barman took pity on us and brought a very welcome bowl of chips into the back room for us. Another few hours passed, feet up, comparing aches and pains. Owen had a blister coming and I had a small hole in the side of my foot where a thorn got into my shoe. We left the pub early that night and walked up into a nature reserve. I looked around at the fresh-grown grass covering the old slag-heaps and realised that these were the faded remnants of the mining industry that used to employ all the men lining the seats of the bar. Tight communities left with a hole at their centre and slowly-fading scars.

We bedded down in the heather as a mist came over the valley. The air was still hot and close, but it felt good to see water going into the ground, keeping the lush green growth around me alive.

The next day we tried to cut across the hillside to join the other side of the forestry at Afan Argoed, but the paths were non-existent. I wanted to give up and go around, fed up of energy-sapping undergrowth thrashing. But my brother was fresh to the fight and we tried to find pathways, Owen forging ahead through brambles and bracken. Eventually we found our way to a bridleway and a route between the hills to the next valley, Cwm Afan. There was a choice between another hillside thrash or a road walk. We chose the road walk, both of us a bit knackered – me from the unexpected extra booze the night before, and my bro from the unexpected toll that long-distance walking takes on your feet.

He went back to Derbyshire that day, catching a train back from Neath to collect his car at Llangynwyd.

We spent our last hour that morning in a cafe, the Tea Cosy. It was lovely. I met a photographer from the local paper there, and he had me posing for a photo holding a cup that the café owner was pouring tea into. It prompted a surge of interest and donations, people coming to me to tell their stories.

Otherwise, Neath was a bit smelly and lots of men kept staring at my chest. There was a sexually aggressive air about the town. Once Owen left, I tucked down in the corner of a Wetherspoons to write for a while, and had to run the gauntlet of groups of men making sexual comments about me whenever I walked past them to the bar or toilet, talking amongst themselves about what they'd do to me. I felt angry and intimidated, dropping my head and hoping I wouldn't get noticed.

Neath redeemed itself on my way out, though. First, as I left the pub, a young guy sitting in a doorway lifted his head up from his arms as I passed. His eyes were bleary, his clothes filthy and he wore a badge that said *On The Prowl*.

I expected him to ask me for change but instead he said, "What are you doing? I saw you in town all day."

"Long-distance walk, charity, blah blah."

"Oh, that's brilliant that is, I really like what you're doing. Well done."

I smiled, he smiled. I asked him how to cross the train line and he gave me directions. "Cheers, love, nice one."

Next, I walked down the side of the canal looking for the Cistercian abbey ruins. It was shabby and industrial, and I didn't see anyone until I came towards a chunky metal railway bridge.

Under it were about five or six shadowy figures. I felt vulnerable as I walked towards them, and braced myself for danger. I came closer and saw it was a bunch of kids, maybe early teens.

"Nice flag, can I have it?"

"No, I need it."

"What for? What you doing?"

"Long-distance walk, charity, blah, blah..."

"Oh, wow, I really respect you for doing that."

And they clustered around me, asking questions. Turned out they were hostile at first because they'd seen me talking to a policeman. They didn't have any money until two more boys turned up and they could put a pound into the tin. I took their photo; one of the boys insisting on posing with his shirt off, and we left with smiles and waves and a promise to put the photo on Facebook.

One of the things that's happening to me on this walk is being forced to question the judgements I make about people. It's easy to view the unknown through a prism of fear, mistrust and misinformation.

"Just keep moving forward in peace and love," a friend once said. Would I ever learn to let go and wholeheartedly do that?

I could no longer tell exactly how many miles I'd walked. I could measure the amount up until Holywell, when I'd come inland, but the Cistercian Way had no handy guidebook to give section distances, so if I wanted to work it out for myself I'd have to do that annoying thing where I measured the wiggly line on a map with a bit of string. I decided not to: it didn't matter anymore, I was just walking. When I reached Holywell again in what could be a few months' time, I'd add another definite 602 miles to the 754 I knew I'd covered to that point. Until then it was kind of a haze.

I felt like I was starting to confuse my online followers, with all the unexpected turns to follow new paths. I realised they were starting not to know where I was any more, weren't able to anticipate my route or to comprehend my journey. To me I was following a sequential list of paths; the way I incorporated routes meant I never had to stop in one place and start again in another. My walk flowed, for me, from coast to mountains to rivers. It made perfect sense to me, but not to anyone else; to them it had morphed into walking Wales. I'd created a journey where people didn't have a good understanding of exactly where I was or where I was going next. It was good for my security – it meant that no-one could come and surprise me en route – but people weren't able to plan ahead and come and walk with me. Friends tried, saying they'd come and walk with me in Pembrokeshire or the Dyfi Valley, but because they were unable to see dates in advance, when it came to it they'd made other plans.

Neath to Carmarthen was, well, boring to be honest. The Cistercian Way route description seemed to melt away in this area, I couldn't find useful connecting footpaths either and resorted to the unpleasant trudge of a couple of full days road-walking. The land levelled out; I had the pleasure of coming to a trig point one day, sun blaring in the sky, and realising that this was the highest point for miles in front of me. Everything rippled away from me in waves of gentle hills and I was overjoyed. Carmarthenshire was flat! As flat as Wales gets, anyway.

I met a woman in a pub one night. It was a small pub that wasn't noted on the OS map; I walked through the quiet village planning to knock on the door of a house to ask for water, swerving into a U-turn as I spotted the pub sign. It was the kind of rural place where the conversation of about ten people stopped completely as I walked through the door, not in a hostile way but just to wonder what the hell was going on with the flags, the sweat, the big rucksack. I sat down, puffed a bit and explained what I was doing. They were all very nice, if slightly bemused at this alien presence, and I handed a few symptom-cards out and received about £20 in donations. One woman was really impressed.

"That's a cause very close to my heart," she said. "And other parts of my body."

Her sentence trailed off into the inferred meaning, the things she wasn't telling me.

She was coming back into the pub as I left, having been out for a cigarette, she gave me a piece of paper with the address of the café she worked in, inviting me for breakfast the next morning.

"What you're doing is brilliant," she said, touching my arm. Suddenly tears were in her eyes, and I realised that this was a woman hiding pain beneath a layer of bustle and joviality.

I walked away from the village, up a bridleway to a field full of sheep where I lay down to sleep and thought about this journey and all the tales of ovarian cancer I've heard, other cancers too. Somehow it seems that by my standing up to say *I have had this cancer*, it draws other people to tell me their stories in return.

There was a man, dealing with me in a professional capacity, who leant forward and said in a low voice, "My mother has it."

We exchanged a glance and no more words; it wasn't his time to speak about it.

One woman recognised me as 'the walking lady' while we were both in the waiting-room of the hospital, her head wrapped in a colourful scarf. Her cancer was advanced; she was seeing the doctor to decide on a second course of chemotherapy. She was bright and cheerful but incredibly brittle, her smile quick to droop.

A woman at the next table in a café suddenly started telling me about how she was waiting for the results of genetic testing, how her mother had died of ovarian cancer and she was being tested for the BRCA1 gene. She'd been waiting for her results for eight weeks, her future hanging on the receipt of a letter.

The festival electrician, a well-loved character who'd banter with anyone, bustling and funny with his Scouse accent, had taken his wife for tests that day, suspected ovarian tumour. No jokes in that face as he spoke to me, tears not far away.

The woman in Lidl who asked me, "What are you doing?"

I'd leaned my flags against the fruit display to put some bananas in a plastic bag.

"I was meant to meet you today. My sister-in-law has just been diagnosed and she's waiting for surgery…" We talked for a while about encapsulated tumours.

There was the woman in the beer-tent at a festival who called me back to the table after I put some symptoms-cards into the centre, her eyes large in sudden emotion. She only said that she'd had recent abdominal surgery, not what was removed, and we talked and talked and talked in whispers about the ways we'd found to recover from pain and trauma, people shushing us as the fiddle played nearby.

In a café in the Rhondda valley, and in a pub in Connah's Quay the regulars said, "Someone died of that quite recently."

I was helped a great deal by a woman whose mother and best friend had died from ovarian cancer, who'd driven her friend to all her chemotherapy sessions, who was doing what she could to help me in their memory.

I was met by a woman in Welshpool whose mother died of ovarian cancer and now speaks for the charity Ovarian Cancer Action in Wales, trying to do the same thing I'm doing; raise awareness, raise awareness. Tell women about the symptoms so maybe they don't die so soon.

There are so, so, many more than this; my memory was becoming too full to hold all the people that I met.

They're all so hidden, these personal stories – just an ordinary person going about their business until the moment when they walk up to me and speak.

It gives me a sense of the multitudes of people carrying pain or fear or trauma, past and present. I don't mean this to be negative or depressing, but just the way that this forms a part of what life is. That an inescapable part of this glorious, incredible life is dealing with illness and death and that's OK because life is wonderful, overall.

I do what I can in these moments, I say, *That sounds hard* or, *Are you OK now?* and hear as much of their story as they want to tell me. I try and hold just a little of bit of their troubles for them, by being a person who listens.

I walked from Carmarthen to Tenby and back again, poking myself out on the little tip of the Cistercian path that detoured out to Caldey Island, to visit the monks' abbey on the little rock, a mile offshore from Giltar Point. Monks have been living on the island for 1500 years – the Cistercian inhabitants for eighty-five, keeping cattle, making chocolate and soap, accepting visitors, except on Sundays. It took four days and I was hosted all the way. After over a week of wild camping it felt wonderful to be so nicely treated. I stayed with Melissa near St Clears, then over to Matt and Charissa near Tenby for two nights before back to Mel, so closely did my steps retrace themselves on the way back up north. I came to walk by the sea, following the coastal path for a few miles around Tenby. Annoyingly, I reached Tenby on a Sunday, so I couldn't actually go and visit the monks, the whole point of my path thus far.

It was a visceral shock to see the sea again; it had been at least two months since I'd walked a shoreline, and the weather and coast had changed completely. This was my first taste of the turquoise sea of Pembrokeshire. It was early August and felt like the Mediterranean, bracken bobbing like humid jungle-ferns, small power-boats turning circles in the big bay below Monkstone Point, their white wash rippling in widening geometries.

I walked up from Tenby and towards Brechfa, camping one night and then, after a day spent walking though the peaceful Brechfa Forest surrounded by many bright butterflies, arriving at Juliet's farm, where she'd said I could take a day off, my first in over a month where I had nothing to do. I had a bed and a TV and a day to myself, a day to rub my feet, stretch luxuriously and move around as little as possible. The last thing I did before arriving at the farm was hitch back to the nearest village to buy food for the rest day. I was picked up on my way back by a big bald-headed Polish man, kindly looking, who worked at the local anti-venom factory, a big local employer. When I mentioned I was walking between Cistercian abbeys, following ancient trackways and pilgrimage routes he turned to look at me, surprised.

"There's a Catholic pilgrimage happening in my country right now and I really wish I could be part of it."

I invited him to walk with me, in the easy way that I made arrangements then, unsurprised at the latest magical coincidence, which had brought a seeker and a provider so easily together. We swapped numbers and he came out with me a couple of days later, as I walked from Tregaron to Cwmystwyth. I was glad to have company that day; it was a tough fifteen miles climbing up from pasture into high wet pathless moorland and back down again, skirting the edges of the untamed Cambrian mountain range. Greg wasn't so experienced, getting nervous as we left the road and started squelching down towards the thin river, exclaiming that we couldn't do this, this was too much, too wild. But we faced the endless blowing grasses together, and he was an easy companion. I navigated us through the mostly featureless land, matching the land shapes around us to the swoops of contour lines on my map, walking from lake to lake, sometimes tiny puddles of water, unseen until we were almost next to them. He gave me a bible and a fifty-pound donation and we parted with a big squeeze of a hug. My friend Anna came to pick me up and take me to her house, dropping him back at his car on the way.

There was a sense, during this period, of feeling a bit fed up with walking. It'd been a bit of a trudge over the previous couple of weeks through south Wales. The novelty of beautiful countryside had worn off a bit, and I no longer felt amazed each time I reached the top of a hill. Rolling farmland? Wind turbines? Seen it – many times over. I wasn't miserable; it had just become mundane, the norm. I wondered, when I felt faintly underwhelmed by the relentless parade of greenery in front of me – is it going to be like this for the rest of the walk? There was a sense of simply trudging the miles away, battling the pain and plod, plod, plodding to the end.

My body, most of it, was bearing up pretty well. No pain in my neck, shoulders or back. My legs could go on for miles and miles; it was just my feet that were letting me down. They were painful every day, the tendons and ligaments strained. I hobbled every evening once I'd cooled down and in the morning too, before I got into my stride and the rest of my muscles began working properly. I was even starting to get pains in my legs, ankles and feet at night, shooting pains in the bones and joints. My legs twitched and I experimented with taking painkillers to sleep. I was reasonably sure I could carry on and finish, but it hurt and I didn't know how I could make it hurt less.

I thought the main foot-problem was my recent change of shoes. Every small thing that I did to my feet – new shoes, different insoles, taping them up, even a different pair of socks – affected them in a new way and took time, and days of new pain, to adjust to. It's as if I was experimenting to try and find a system that didn't make my feet hurt, but everything might make the pain much worse.

I'd changed my shoes two weeks before, the same style I'd been wearing for the last 800 miles but half a size smaller; we're talking a men's size 7.5 instead of an 8 (normally I wear a women's size 6). I had a blue-foam wedge under the left heel and a disintegrating pair of gel insoles, which were all discarded with the old pair. First I wore the new shoes with no insoles, then a pair of foam ones and then, after I realised that the pain in my feet was becoming severe, a pair of gel insoles with an extra gel wedge under my left heel. Fine; foot pain was diminished but now my shoes felt too small with all the layers of insoles in there. Should I have gone for the bigger shoes I was used to? Even though they had a good inch extra at the end of the shoe? And what did I do now? Did I change again? More money on shoes and more stress trying to find an address I could have the shoes posted to. It was very hard doing this by myself. The shops I encountered en route dictated what quality of insoles I bought. The crap foam ones were from a fishing-tackle shop in Caerphilly; the better gel ones were in an outdoor shop in Tenby.

I so wished there was a magic support-fairy I could just turn to at the end of the day and have them fix all my problems for me, *I'll buy maps for you, Ursula, now sit and eat this delicious food, and would you like a foot rub afterwards?*

My mood changed as I moved further into mid-Wales. The last few weeks across South Wales and Carmarthenshire had involved a lot of road-walking, sometimes the entire day on tarmac, my feet slapping down on the unyielding surface over and over again in a way that made them throb and ache. As I moved off the road and my path took me into forest and field once again, my feet could twist and bend to take account of the ever-changing surface they found themselves upon. It really helped reduce my, by now, constant plantar tendon pain.

As I moved north I also found myself again in the place I call home, moving into the orbit of my scattered friends, able to be picked up by them and taken home for huge hugs and relaxation.

As I moved into the landscape of high moorland and quiet pine forestry, I found the land familiar to me. Where the farms are more spread out and up on the high lands there's heather, bracken and bilberries, miles of waving yellow grasses and squelchy peat-bog. Where unprofitable small farms have been handed down, amalgamated into large stretches of mountain-sheep territory, the houses are empty, abandoned, heaps of stones and wavering, solitary chimneys, maybe a rusting bedstead.

The day I walked from Cwmystwyth I came into my real home territory: the wildness of Plynlimon and the Nant-y-moch reservoir, leading north down to Machynlleth. I'd left my home there more than five months ago, packed up, given notice and set off to walk to hospital. I'd walked away from Mach, up the single-track road towards my house at the head of the Uwchygarreg valley and past it, up to the highlands of Hyddgen and the slopes of Plynlimon where Glyndŵr's army defeated Henry's soldiers so many years ago. I'd walked to the bridge across the small river trickling down towards the reservoir where it became the River Rheidol, and turned left to go up the mountain. It was the start of my journey to hospital. I had to walk up Plynlimon, find the source of the River Severn and follow it all the way to Bristol.

I gave a gasp of shock as I saw the clump of pine trees by the bridge, remembering that cold March morning when I struggled slowly through the boggy ground and up the mountain, my feet in too tight boots that would give me blisters by the end of the day, my plump body in no condition for physical work. All that propelled me onwards was an idea, the belief that I could do this, that I could simply put one foot in front of the other for months at a time until the small steps grew into a journey stretching for thousands of miles. Now, I was returning having walked for five months and covered almost 1300 miles. The belief had become reality.

I might not have been in the best state, but I was doing it all the same. I walked down through the Uwchygarreg valley as the light dimmed, seeing the familiar waterfall, the forestry plantations lining the steep sides. I came down through the field that farmer Gareth used for silage, past Talbontdrain, the place I'd retreated to in the aftermath of cancer, the small house where I curled, alone, and healed.

The barns were still falling down, the fields hadn't changed, the cars in the driveways belonged to the same people. There were new windows on a house, a replaced gatepost. Here was the road I walked two or three times a week to go down into Machynlleth: the familiar dips, the views of Cader Idris, the same chapel, corners and trees. It was still the same – just me who was different, turning up at old friends' houses, door slamming open with the wind to reveal a rain-dripping, rugged wanderer, seeking shelter. I felt as if I'd been gone for years, so much had I lived over the last five months, and it was a surprise to find James and Vicky still the same, the baby a few months older, walking now, bread being baked, vegetables grown and good meals cooked, raspberries infusing into a bottle of gin.

My feet were fine for a few days of walking and then suddenly, on a day off, came an excess of shooting pains through the heels. It's hard to say what the problem was, so sensitive were they to small changes. It could be that I hadn't stretched for a couple of days, or perhaps that I didn't rest on the final day's walk, simply striding out for twelve miles. Or it could be that the previous four days' walking, fifty-five miles in total, was a little too intensive. I felt as if I was teetering on the brink of serious injury, just a little more over-forcing of my body would break it.

I started trying to limit my speed again, as I had done in the Conwy valley. Having taken two full weeks off over June and July it felt too soon, in late August, to take another break. I was sensitive to the end of the summer too, wanting to continue through the summer to reduce the winter miles that would otherwise come later.

It was harder, in a way, to keep my pace slow. I had to consciously take smaller steps, ease back when the rest of my body wanted to stride out on a lovely, flat, forestry track. I became very aware of the number of hours I spent walking each day. I didn't use any distractions like music or radio; a lot of long-distance walkers write of the poetry they recited as they strode, modern blogging walkers write of podcasts and audio books. Patrick Leigh Fermor would re-enact great swathes of Shakespeare as his nimble, great-coated, 19-year-old self made his cheerful, optimistic way across pre-WWII Europe. Instead, I would sing snatches of songs as they came to mind, usually just one or two lines that I repeated over and over.

Ain't nothing going to break my stride
Nobody going to slow me down
Oh no, I've got to keep on moving...

I'm not sure what I did all day – just think, it seems. I'm not even sure what about. I wasn't bored, never bored and I wasn't lonely, although I greatly appreciated company. I suppose walking slowly made me more aware of the great distance I had still to cover; a whole day passed and I only covered eight miles. Eight miles! And I am trying to walk 3300!!! I felt like a tiny ant who'd unknowingly set out to cross a mountain, toiling over one tiny pebble at a time, only indirectly sensing the great hovering mass to come.

Never mind how slow I felt; it was good for my feet. The reduced mileage helped, and some magical stuff called Muscle Oil, which I picked up in my local healthfood shop. The bottle showed the name of the maker (*Richard Evans, Bonesetter, Pwllheli*) the date (*est. 1800*) and the picture of said Mr Evans, a respectable gentleman in a suit, white hair and round glasses. The curiosity of such a substance was enough to satisfy me. I'd rub it on my feet and calves at night, and the shooting pains diminished. I'd do whatever enabled me to crawl towards and *complete* this 3000+ mile challenge, even if I had to mentally chafe at a ten-mile-daily pace for the whole of the remaining 2000 miles.

I walked very slowly from Dolgellau to Trawsfynydd to Blaenau Ffestiniog, and then to Capel Curig. It took four days, something that would take most walkers two at most. But I'm not comparing; I never do that (yeah right). I wild camped all three nights, first against a stone wall about half a mile out of Coed y Brenin where my rudimentary shelter failed to keep out the rain, and I woke up soggy round the edges.

It was a plain and pleasant day's walk through farmland into Trawsfynydd and out again. I was in search of a café and a sit-down but the two village cafés had closed down. The kind people in the shop offered me a cup of tea and brought a stool outside for me to sit down for a while. It started to rain again as I sat working out my onward journey on the map, small droplets blowing against me as I sat on my high stool, wedged back against the shop window where only the windblown edges of wetness could reach me. I didn't mind; getting slightly wet was going to be the norm from now on. I could already feel my reaction to mild rain getting to be the same as to no rain at all.

The path provided me with symbolic items that day: a pair of rusting nail-scissors hanging provocatively on a mossy tree-root alongside a babbling stream, a scratched and battered disposable camera on a rubble forest road, a button badge that contained the single, solemn affirmation *OK*. I collected them, tucking them into my rucksack's net pockets, alongside my water bottle, imagining what they might turn into if I threw them behind me in a time of need. They could transform into blinding flashes of light or towering, jagged shards of rock. My walk became a quest for a few hours, with monsters and benefactors tracking my progress, hidden and watchful, generous and malevolent.

That night I slept in a beautiful field, a wide, open slope easing gently down towards the River Cynfal. I lay on the remnants of a Roman road and read *The Mabinogion*, finally coming to the story of Lleu Llaw Gyffes, the climax of which took place by the river I was lying near. It rained overnight but I didn't mind. I'd made a great, if slightly sagging shelter, and I was happy and cosy, even sleeping well enough to get up before 8am.

The next day was a short five-mile stroll into Blaenau Ffestiniog, where I could shower, shop and recharge my phone.

I came up the sharp climb of Blaenau Ffestiniog quarry, stopping to admire my final view of the Trawsfynydd power-station towers before continuing to...the end of the footpath! I could see on the map that there was a gap between the path which climbed through the quarry, and the next one I wanted, which snaked its way around the highland lakes and down to Dolwyddelan. I thought there'd be a way through somehow, I didn't expect a dead end.

There, a hundred metres above the quarry, surrounded by rusty machinery and slate piles was a sign saying, *Public footpath ends here. Please return along footpath.* Yeah, right, as if I was going back on myself. I dropped my rucksack and had a scout around. There were a couple of ways up the final slopes of slate and shale, none seeming too attractive. The steepness of the climb and loose rock underfoot made it a dangerous possibility, especially with the 200m drop behind me into the quarry. But I spotted a way to climb onto a bank of grass leaving just a ten-metre scramble up the shale and rock, with only a small drop and a flat bit below it reducing further the very small chance of my rolling down the hill in a flurry of rock.

Holding my breath I moved slowly from footstep to footstep. The heavy rucksack on my back changes my balance in a way that makes it very difficult to go up steep slopes. I resorted to using my hands to pull me up the final few steps and finally I was out on grassland again, above the quarry and free to walk over the moorland towards the forest and down into the next village. But that was for the next day, first I had to sleep.

I walked through the boggy grass and headed for a slate tower; old mine-workings meant that there'd be a layer of stone between me and the squelchy ground. It was a perfect sleeping spot: a raised platform, long grassed-over and with an incredible view back down over the quarry, the surrounding mountains and even the sea. The weather forecast gave a clear night so I decided to chance it and settled down for a night in the bivvy bag. There was a low stone wall along one side of the platform and it was the windbreak I needed. I snuggled down into my sleeping-bag, hood up and dozed off.

Rain. It rained. Let me tell you that there are not many worse feelings than to be lying in a sleeping-bag in the rain with very little that you can do to avoid an inevitable drenching. It happened when I'd been asleep for a while, maybe around 11pm. I was too close to deep sleep to jump up and take action – there wasn't any action to take anyway – all I could do in that situation would be to lose body-heat and make myself and kit wet as I fumbled in the dark and rain, trying to string up some half-arsed shelter. Nope, better to tuck in and ride it out, take the punishment for my laziness. I stayed warm and dry, the few hours of light drizzle only soaked through to the outside of my sleeping-bag. It was times like this that I was deeply thankful for being hosted so frequently. I never had to suffer the ultimate penalty for my shoddy adventuring skills – to bed down in a wet sleeping bag.

Striding through the forestry on my way over the hill to Dolwyddelan, coming around the base of Moel Siabod, I disturbed a fox on the forestry track. Scrawny and black, it was a shabby little thing with beady eyes and thin, scraggly fur. It pattered away from me on first view but then stopped to turn and look back. I walked closer, didn't stop, and it stayed still for a couple of beats then turned to pad away to a safe distance before turning to stare at me again. It was as if it couldn't work out what it was seeing. I imagined my walking-poles from a fox perspective. Two thin legs and two thick legs, a creature that moves ungainly and misshapen, the two thin legs should break and it should drag on the ground and yet it approaches, this unbalanced creature that is not fluid in its movements. The fox stared until I came close again and finally ran, disappearing back to its hidden life in the undisturbed forest.

Rarely climbed by humans away up here, not a tourist destination, Moel Siabod slumbered away to my left. I heard there was a cave up there, where a Welsh preacher had hidden from the English, his Welsh Bible translation – a treasured contraband. I wanted to summit and find that cave, spend a night in a hideaway, but Siabod was not on my route, this quiet peak with such a strong name.

I descended to Capel Curig and finally met Shân, aunty of neighbour Deri, the woman who'd done so much for me on my way up the Conwy valley many months earlier. She was a whirring, excitable woman, an experienced traveller who immediately set about getting my kit washed and drying, before making me tea. We sat for a few hours as I listened to her talking about whatever subject came to mind: her University employer, women's rights, mountain-climbing holidays, government oppression, international feminism.

I heard someone describe her as a top feminist activist in Wales, a scatty whirlwind of a woman who'd spent her life fighting for her ethics and being friendly and helpful to everyone she valued.

It had been a pretty spectacular day. In only eight miles from Blaenau to Capel Curig I managed to say goodbye to southern Snowdonia, view both the upper waters of Cardigan Bay and the Irish Sea beyond Conwy, walk around Moel Siabod, and get a view of the Glyders. I'd reached the serious mountain territory of north west Wales, and it was a little intimidating to think that in a few weeks' time I wouldn't be skirting round the feet of these mountains but going over the tops of them, one summit after another. It would be a serious test of my capabilities, as if the first 1300 miles had been training! I wasn't sure how well I'd manage but, as usual, all I could do was have a go. I had a map and compass, I was certain of my survival skills and my stamina, and I just had to take it slow and steady. It seems that this was my mantra for this sizeable journey, too big to be devoured in one push. I must take it slow and steady, slow and steady.

I came down from Capel Curig, following the Conwy Valley north towards Llandudno. I was going to walk across the top of Wales from Conwy to Holywell to finish off the Cistercian way, and then immediately follow the coastal path back to Conwy to begin the mountain path. This meant I'd walk around the Great Orme twice in ten days. I relished this beautiful and unusual day's walk – on tarmac, true, but with a wonderful sense of the road dropping away to crashing sea below, the swooping of curves as the road, cut into sheer rock, wound its way around the edges of this huge boulder. This was a road to show off human mastery, no other reason for it to exist than Victorian superiority over the natural environment. I slept out on there too, coming to a shelter by the side of the rising road that overlooked the Conwy estuary, nearby vegetation with that familiar bent and elongated shape, showing it had grown under extremely windblown conditions.

I had a view of Snowdonia, Anglesey and Conwy Bay and watched as the sun set and the sky above the mountains turned gentle lilac, the moon rising luminous in the same view. Did I sit and wonder at the beauty of the world, thinking about how lucky I was to be doing this, how I'd much rather be here than anywhere else? Nope, I read my book, *Rabbit, Run* with a main character who would rather be anywhere than where he was, checked the internet, took some photos, rubbed my feet and, once it got dark, laid down for a tolerable night's sleep on a bench.

I'm not saying I was actively disliking it. When I thought about the alternative, which was to stop, return to Machynlleth and pick up the strings of work and social life again, there was nowhere else I'd rather be, nothing else I'd rather be doing than camping and walking. But the euphoria had gone, the thrill of the new faded, the excitement worn off.

It felt sometimes as if the days were all the same; I woke up somewhere strange, walked all day, stopped to rest my feet, eat, read, stare into space. I reached the end of the day, ate more, rubbed my feet again and slept, trying and always failing to get enough rest to do the same thing the next day without feeling tired.

It was during this time, when everything felt tired and painful and repetitive, that I really faced the fact that I was going to keep walking through the winter. I was originally set to finish the walk in October. 3300 miles in eight months. It was late August now and after almost six months, I'd covered nearly 1400 miles. That was the stark reality of what I was capable of.

I'd told myself I would decide at the end of the summer, but I always knew what I wanted to do. I wanted to finish the target I'd set myself, even if it took a year or more. How could I only walk half of Wales? How could I finish before I'd walked around Anglesey? Or the Pembrokeshire coast? Or to the top of Snowdon? Or explored the South Wales rivers?

But rain was coming, autumn was coming, winter was coming. I needed to plan ahead. I'd had a wonderful summer, the kind where so often I could just put down my tarpaulin and sleeping bag and sleep under the stars. I didn't even own a tent! I'd camped through a night of heavy rain a few weeks previously by setting up my tarpaulin shelter, but I woke up in the morning and found a slug in my hair. Things had to change.

I'd been collecting winter kit: long sleeved, merino wool tops, insulated leggings, gloves. Someone off the internet might give me a tent, otherwise I was going to buy one.

I'd had my boots posted up from Bristol and was trying them out instead of the fell-running shoes I'd been wearing for the last 1000 miles. They were good, much better grip for the oncoming mountains, less pain in some ways, and they definitely helped to support my ankles. I realised my Achilles tendon had swollen while walking in trainers, it made a noticeable lump at the back of my heel.

I stopped, on the way to Holywell, at the house of a woman called Ceri Camino, who'd contacted me and offered to pick me up from the path. We chatted as she made me dinner and gave me a foot bath. She'd walked the *Camino* to Santiago, the traditional Catholic pilgrimage route across the top of Spain, and understood the special world of exhaustion and wonder a long-distance walker enters. She offered me her flat for a rest day; she'd go and stay with her boyfriend so I could relax and pretend the place was my own.

After a lot of stretching, ice baths and self-massage, my feet were almost pain-free when I said goodbye to Ceri. It made me realise just how much they hurt all the time. Given that I wasn't even half-way through and faced another six months of walking, the idea of all that future pain was a bit of a scary prospect.

I felt pretty solemn as I set off to Holywell. I camped one night in a farmer's field, near the house. I was walking through the farm, a criss-cross of footpaths running through the land, and got talking to the man in the farmyard. He asked me where I would sleep and when I told him I'd wild camp somewhere further on, choosing for once to be open about my living style rather than shying away from the chance of him telling me off, he immediately said I could camp on his land. I sat with him and his wife in the house for a while, talking about their prize-winning sheep; he'd won Best in Show at the Royal Welsh and had sold all his spare stock by the very next day.

"Brought us forward by a good few years," he said.

I sensed the idea of a farm being an ongoing business, always with a development plan and ideas for which piece of stock or land or infrastructure to invest in next. I set up my shelter in the nearest paddock and he insisted on bringing a woodburner out to me. Saying he used it in his barn for lambing. Then came a chair to sit on as I toasted myself in the luxurious warmth, rubbing muscle oil into my feet and feeling, as I so often did on this journey, that the world is a wonderful, generous and beautiful place.

The next day I walked into Holywell again, out of the flat dullness of the Vale of Clwyd and over the outstretched finger of the Clwydian Range. There was a convent in Holywell, just up the hill from the holy well itself, where a spring of reputedly miraculous healing properties welled up into an ornate stone housing, centuries old.

I decided to sleep in the town and go to the well the following day. I wanted to go to the convent and ask if they'd give me a bed. I'd just walked 600 miles of a route honouring the history of their religion, and I thought this might be a worthy story to allow me a bed in a cell, and a meal, in the tradition of helping poor pilgrims. But the building was high and shuttered with a blank intercom at one corner, plus there was a nun-run guesthouse next door. I quailed in the face of modern capitalism and rang at the door of the guesthouse, too shy to stammer out a plea for a discounted bed.

I wanted to give symptoms awareness cards to the nuns who came to the door. Women who haven't had children are slightly more at risk of ovarian cancer, but I faltered at that too, embarrassed by their nunliness. They were wearing full habits, head coverings; it created a distance from me, an obvious sign of the difference in how they lived their lives. They asked no questions as they took my details, barely making conversation at all. Their lives were something I didn't understand and I felt too awkward to break through our disconnectedness, impose on their strong beliefs with a passion of my own. If their beliefs could be misguided, maybe mine could too.

It was a strange night in a sparse room, somewhere between bland B&B and religious cell. I ventured down for breakfast in the morning, finding a large, low-ceilinged room, decorated with religious paintings and sculptures. The furniture was conference-hotel style tables, tablecloths and chairs. There was one other woman in the room – middle-aged, grey bobbed hair and glasses – sitting at a table laid for one. Next to her table was another, also laid for one. They were the only tables in the room that had been laid for breakfast. We had been placed parallel to each other, facing ahead. We said a brief hello and ate in silence, together alone. There was an air of meekness.

Apart from the crackle of butter being spread on toast and the tick of a very loud clock, the loudest sound in the room came from behind a closed door where the nuns were having an audibly good time. They were clanking pots and pans, chattering non-stop, giggling, greeting new arrivals and occasionally breaking out into laughter. Occasionally a nun would bring out another piece of food for me or my silent companion, some more toast or a forgotten ramekin of baked beans, her face betraying no hint of the merriment she'd just left. I was glad it seemed nice to be a nun.

Further down the road, once booted and bagged up, I stopped in at the well, entering through the gift shop. I sat by the edge of the water, where a rectangular grey-stone pool had been built out into the courtyard, filling out from the smaller octagonal pool, medieval-built, arched and curlicued, narrow steps leading down into it, too delicate now for the mass of public bathing. This was where people had been coming for healing for centuries, since Winefride had her head cut off by a man who was trying to rape her, water springing from the very place her head came to rest. Her saintly uncle Beuno reattached her head; she lived, became a saint herself, and the well became a place of pilgrimage. There was a museum attached, a wall full of discarded crutches, given by the people who came and bathed and walked straight once more.

It was a subdued and respectful place. People spoke in hushed murmurs, quietly filled up bottles from a spout on the wall, a takeaway to drink in times of trouble. There was a woman who stripped down to a bathing costume, assisted by her husband. She waded down into the water and swam small strokes to and fro before coming out quickly to be wrapped and towelled by her waiting partner. She was crying.

I thought about the desperation of illness, the necessity of something to take away constant pain. I didn't believe in God, or miracles, but I believed in belief. The fact that the particular way a person perceived the world would help to make the world a certain way for them, whether through connectedness, coincidence or confirmation bias. If I had God in my life, then all the generosity I received during this journey would be assigned to the benevolent will of that entity. I wanted to believe that this water would heal me, I wanted to be healed, I wanted to be able to walk without pain, I needed this, my journey was really hard work.

I decided to try it, to believe in the water. I had to be wholehearted about it or it wouldn't work so I took time, sitting on the blotched and roughened grey-stone slabs that edged the pool, and thought about healing, calmed my thoughts until I focused on this place.

I thought about the years of repeated visits to this place of pilgrimage, the belief and the need that brought people here. A place becomes holy when it's sacrosanct, when it has no other function than a centrepoint for belief. The well held silence. People approached it in a pause of breath, the stillness creating an empty gap where hope could spark.

I peeled off my socks, damp with sweat as ever, and rolled up my leggings. The water was deeply, icily cold. It was too great a shock and I wanted to take them out straight away but forced myself to rest them in there for as long as I could bear it, watching my luminous yellow feet magnified underneath the water, bobbing gently. I had to dip them three times, if the healing was to work. I felt deeply moved in doing this, my choosing to join something. By choosing to believe that the water was healing me, I was believing in something greater than myself. That there was a greater spiritual force in the world than my limited senses could realise, whatever the name given to it.

I dressed again, solemn, my feet glowing and tingling from their immersion in the ice cold water.

Within twenty steps from the exit I paused by the roadside, wincing as a sharp ripple of pain seared through both my heels at once, as if healed wounds had broken open once again. I guess mystical healing was no good if I was going to continue with exactly the same harmful behaviour.

I walked along the road from the village, down towards the small concrete-lined launch ramp, cars parked either side. Here I was, back again at the concrete flood-barrier where the grey estuary lapped away from me, lined by the Welsh coastal path running left and right. I stepped onto it, a new route under my feet. Here, walking towards me and saying hello, was the pleasant man I'd said goodbye to four months earlier, moustached and rounded, still wearing the same baseball cap, walking the same dog; my first and last encounter on the Cistercian Way. 602 miles had separated our two meetings, but for him it was just another daily stroll by his local seaside, a nice chat with a tourist. He had no idea of the miles I'd covered, all I'd seen and experienced. I'd passed the summer away following the Cistercian path. Ahead lay autumn and the mountains.

CAMBRIAN WAY

Route description: Pioneered by Tony Drake, this mountain route covers most of the highest mountains of Wales and requires much stamina to complete. From the north coast it crosses over the Carneddau, the Snowdon massif, the Rhinogs, Cader Idris, Plynlimon, Carmarthen Fan, the Brecon Beacons and the Black Mountains before touching down in Cardiff. This is a tough high-level route and should not be underestimated.

Length:	287.1 miles
Total ascent:	20,864m
Maximum height:	1,044m
Dates:	4 September –
	14 October 2014
Time taken:	41 days
Nights camping/nights hosted:	17/41
Days off:	8
Average miles per day:	8.69

I was heading down the dragon's back, from the gnarly shoulders of Snowdon, across the knobbly scatterings of the Rhinogs, the coccyx of Cader Idris, the soft belly of Plynlimon and the Cambrian moorlands, and curving around to the east-west whipped tail of the Beacons and Black Mountains.

The mountain connoisseur's route, it named itself. Twenty per cent of the route took me to heights over 610m and only 17% would be on hard, painful tarmac, the lowest of all my chosen paths.

Coming up from Conwy and climbing to my first view, the surrounding heather fell away in a wide curve, and swooped down to a coast I could no longer see. I knew the road and rocks lay below, but instead I had a view of a perfect clear line of purple heather, then blue sea. The Great Orme peninsula lay comfortable in the distance, like a sleeping beast, head pushed out in full relaxation. Llandudno covered the animal's neck, colonising the flat land, enjoying the luxury of two coastlines.

I was heading into the mountains, excited at the change of scenery and the challenge to come. I was going to cross the highest parts of Wales, turn away from rivers and coast, and climb into the peaks.

I gloried in the sunshine and clear air, admiring the carefully built stone walls that ran dividing lines along long-held boundaries. The route went gently into the beginning hills, dipping and rising but always climbing. As the sun began to set I came to a beautiful sleeping-spot, a small area of flat grass beneath a smooth-faced rocky crag, perfect to sit against in comfort and admire the light dwindling from the sky, the colours of heather and turf, first roared pink in the final tinge of sunset and then faded to muted normalcy. I welcomed my luck in being able to cross the land in this way, no human infrastructure needed, just my ability to take what the land offered, natural shelter for a living body overnight whether it was prostrate human or curled, comfortable sheep.

In the morning I reached my fingers up from the gentle comfort of my feathered nest, and pulled aside the clammy plastic hood that covered my face. The hood shielded me from the fierce chilling of the cold September air, but in return it condensed the captured heat of my breath, brushing back damp and unpleasant against my skin. A short time ago, the light on the bristles of wiry grass was pale orange-pink in the first flashing exultation of the sun but now, in the blinking of eyes into unconsciousness and back again, it had dissolved to an ordinary grey. The clouds were thin and wispy and I knew that they would burn away to thin yellow sunshine later.

I levered myself to sitting, slow movements, stiff and aching from the hard ground, leant back against the huge grey rock, furry with lichen, and came slowly to the world. Small birds flew peeping above the thrusts of heather. They were the only animals I saw, apart from the thick black contented slugs.

I walked from sunrise until sunset that day, looking out at a range of peaks and calculating the crossing of gigantic pieces of land, defining the swoop and rise of a peak in minutes and hours. There was clambering, my knees began to ache again and my thigh muscles screamed as I pushed myself further, physically, than I had managed before on this walk.

The Carneddau were huge and gentle mountains, the heights wriggling around on the way south, always another rise ahead in the distance: first Foel Fras, then Carnedd Gwenllian, then Foel Grach, Carnedd Llewelyn, Carnedd Dafydd, each with two or three miles of high and wide ground between them, sometimes short grasses and sometimes rocky stumbles.

The weather didn't lift and there were wisps of mist everywhere around, semi-cloaking the surrounding peaks, blowing on and off like a fluttering scarf.

I saw the final summit far ahead around the horseshoe curve of steep, gravel-sided Cwm Lloer. The cairn that marked the summit was seemingly only a couple of metres higher than the surrounding expanse of thin turf, sparse grass growing in inch-thick soil.

I was passed, as I strode slowly towards my goal, by a thin man running in a neon orange T-shirt, glowing bright and unnatural in the dull outlook. He clip-clopped towards me, streaming sweat and with a huge happy grin.

I'd seen him from hundreds of metres away, marvelled at his endurance to run up mountains, his bravery in being up here. With so little clothing to retain heat only his constant speed could maintain a safe body-temperature,.

I had the wonderful anticipation of watching him approach around the whole horseshoe, growing in size as he came closer. We had just a few seconds to smile and exchange hellos before he was gone behind me, the heavy breaths fading away, his brightness a flash that disappeared, leaving no trace but retinal memory.

Sitting on the rubble of rocks that heaped around the base of the low cairn, I consulted the map. The Cambrian Way went off to the east, winding a long way over as it descended off a spur of the mountain, passing behind the long lake at the valley bottom, before doubling back on itself to go west again and reach an easy entry point to the Glyders range. There was another footpath leading directly south off the face of Pen Yr Ole Wen. It was a much shorter distance away, and with the sun setting in an hour or two I was pushed for time. The contour lines looked very close together, but I'd rather a steep descent than a long detour. I didn't know then that the name of that footpath is the Vertical Mile.

I descended in small steps as the path, inches narrow, wound between huge stone slabs. Sometimes I stepped off tough heather roots, sometimes awkwardly lowering myself into rocky clefts, taking a handhold to take weight from my knees, bracing my sticks below me for balance.

Every pace was calculated, no movement made without thinking; any slip would be a fall of hundreds of metres, slipping and bouncing, tangling myself in a crevice at best. Llyn Ogwen lay below me, a small puddle of water with toy cars zipping alongside it.

I couldn't tell how steep the hill was when I concentrated on the surrounding few metres. It was only when I looked up behind me, to see how far I'd come that I was taken aback; the rocks seemed ready to fall down on top of me, slammingly, impossibly vertical, no visible path.

The path appeared and disappeared, melting into rocky tumbles for me to pick over, searching amongst the heather below for the resumption of the trail. The poles were mostly a hindrance at this close-quarters tangle; I needed free hands to grasp and clutch the rocks for balance.

I started to feel in the grip of madness, regretting my unavoidable commitment to an increasingly difficult path, tiptoeing, pick pick, lumbering and descending, gripping and hefting, bulbous looming crags above me. The light left the valley, turning to pale purple to grey to black as I slowly, awkwardly lowered myself, my rucksack and my stupid bamboo poles, down steps and slides and drops. My water had run out hours earlier, I'd been on such flat high ground that there'd not even been a trickle to stoop and fill up at.

In the darkness I came to a cleft, the path lost long ago, and realised I'd have to lower myself down the rock to a ledge. I peered over it with my torch and saw another ledge more than six feet below. I'd have to drop down by twisting around the edge of the split rock and let myself gently lower until my feet touched a facing outcrop, and I could change handholds to lower myself further. I couldn't do it with my bag – too heavy and off balance – so I thought about it and let it drop down: a tired and angry decision.

The bag went somersaulting about twenty metres down the hill in the circle of torchlight, contents flying out of the pockets in the whirl of turning. I paused in shock; there was no going back now, I had to descend and retrieve it. The poles tucked safely into the cleft and, as I searched for the second handhold I needed to lower myself down to where my feet would touch the rock, holding my torch in my teeth, I thought, *This isn't walking. I'm a walker, not a climber*. I picked my way to the bag, gathering scattered belongings, and continued the descent: the worst was over. I noticed I was shaking as I tumbled awkwardly to my knees among the bouldered edge of the rushing river that was almost safety – gulping longed-for water, cupping it into my hands and slurping.

There were flagstones laid for a sturdy trail alongside the river, leading me to a road with Idwal Cottage YHA at the corner, where the valley turned to run alongside Llyn Ogwen and east towards Capel Curig. Walking along the road in darkness, no energy left to search for a flat and private piece of ground, I walked into the glossy wood-panelled reception and unexpectedly burst into tears, the aftermath of a fear that had been camouflaged by adrenalin. I'd planned to go to the hostel for water but suddenly I really needed a bed. I got a cup of tea dashed with whiskey, my bamboo walking-pole bound and strengthened where it had split on the rocky descent, and a bed in a shared room for £30. The manager was calm and kind: nothing new to her in a shattered roamer coming in late with tales of a near-death experience.

The following day I came up and over the shoulder of the Glyders, the path taking me over a wide grassy area with no discernible path; seemingly well-trodden marks petered out in a bog or rocks, or turned out to be winding sheep-tracks. I was still wobbly from the night before and decided to skip the ascent to the summits, keeping on the gentle walk that day. I had Snowdon to face the next day and didn't want to exhaust myself.

I descended into the valley, heading for Llyn Pen-y-Gwryd, reached the Pen-y-Pass hostel before sunset and had a quick pint, not really wanting to stay in this busy, anonymous building, people wandering everywhere in expensive, branded outdoor clothing. I was turned off by its blandness, the shiny new bar creating a gastropub atmosphere. I decided to wander along the path towards Snowdon and find somewhere to sleep, save myself a bit of effort the next day.

Never having climbed Snowdon this way, I missed the car park corner entrance to the Pyg Track and found myself on the Miners' Track, the route that Snowdon summiteers usually descend on. It was wide and flat, to begin with; the path had been laid in stone to counteract the scraping and degrading of many thousands of pairs of boots. I walked on a cobbled road, levelled and laid by man. It felt totally unnatural, the Snowdon travelator. Even as the light left the sky there were still plenty of people around, a steady trickle of descending walkers coming towards me, the last of the hundreds to climb the mountain that day. I felt this mountain was crawling with people, a steady ant-stream climbing and descending, following each other in marked trails, ants using scent, us laying stones.

I settled for the night beside the first lake, Llyn Llydaw. There was an electrical building a short distance from the path, signs warning against entry, and I could lie on the flat space in front of the door, shielded from the strong wind that whistled against the building sides and rattled loose pieces of sheet metal. Even in the night hours – groups of walkers passed by, night-time mountain marauders, talking in loud, excited voices, flashing their torchlight over me, flicking away. It didn't matter how many people were asleep or awake; the mountain dwarfs us, the beauty subdues us, we can't tame this rock, only swarm over it. The peak of Snowdon remained serene, triangular above me, unaffected, singing its own song in vibrations too deep for human ear.

At the point where the Pyg Track met the Miners', where I climbed up the very steep rocky clamber to join the stony track to the summit, I stopped to rest for a while and take in the view behind me. I realised there was a girl sitting against a rock not far away, snuffling and weeping to herself, not quite loudly enough to distract the stream of passing walkers. I edged over to her and asked if she was OK. She was on the final summit of the three-peaks challenge – climbing the three main mountains of Britain in twenty-four hours – and had dropped behind the main group, losing their team mania and therefore her energy. She was feeling dizzy and tired, overwhelmed by the mountain.

I urged her to eat but she refused, saying she felt sick. I couldn't force in the thing that would almost immediately make her feel better so I just sat with her for a while, trying to calm her, asking small questions to bring her out of panic, getting her to tell me about her journey, about swaying in the minibus overnight, about almost no sleep and only a tuna sandwich for food. *Come on, girl,* I wanted to say, *stop consciously consuming less, now's not the time. Surviving on a small amount isn't impressive, not on a mountain. Your energy directly depends on what you put in your mouth! No food equals no fuel!* I dug in my bag and offered her some small things. Trail mix, then Skittles. She accepted them but didn't eat, just holding them in her hand, not quite ready yet. I urged her to drink and she did, taking small sips of water.

"The best thing you can do for yourself right now is to eat something," I told her, and left her resting, sitting and looking out at the summit of Garnedd Ugain curving out to the left, and the two small lakes: sun-gilded metal cupped in the hands of the surrounding peaks. I clambered on upwards, coming to the final gentle rise alongside the metal café roof, almost at the flat point before the concrete summit. The girl came up alongside me.

"Hey! It's you! What happened?" I asked, surprised to see her energy.

"You happened," she said.

I smiled, pleased. We climbed to the summit together. The trig point itself was concrete-footed, an artificial summit with a wide flat circle for people to gather and gasp and take selfies. We took photographs of each other and then went to the café for a beer. There were plenty of people milling around, those from the train and those from the climb, all quietly mingling in the huge single-roomed building, looking at the view and at the displays of keyrings and postcards. I asked the café worker for tap water but he refused – the only place in Wales that refused me water. I had to buy some instead, to cover the cost of bringing it up on the train. I also bought a beer and a pie, celebrating my own highest-peak challenge.

Drinking my celebratory bottle of Purple Moose, I sat with the girl and some of her team leaders, jolly and alpha. I realised I'd become the experienced one, unconsciously learning how to do the right things to keep me safe, to keep me going. The monitoring of energy, of body temperature, of nutrition, of hydration had become second nature. I wasn't always doing this efficiently, or making the best journey I could – I still felt overweight and unathletic – but I'd taught myself how to cope, how to survive this challenge. I was doing this.

I came down from the mountain via the Watkins path, a steep gravelly descent from a short way off the summit, levelling out later into the usual, human-smoothed path. It finished by going through a beautiful oak copse, where I was plunged into the very different sensory experience of tree cover, the smell of leaves, kaleidoscopes of sunlight, the gentle cooling of branches above; I hadn't realised the starkness of the bare and rocky mountain until I was bathed in tree shade. The delightful oaks formed my final few hundred metres before I reached the road and stuck my thumb out. A car stopped within seconds, a Barmouth farmer and his son, going home from their own day in the mountains. They took me all the way to Machynlleth, where I had four days of resting at a friend's cottage; I'd arranged to feed their cat in return for solitude and sleep. It was the first time in more than four months that I'd taken more than one day at a time to do absolutely nothing.

I wanted to write more during this rest break, try and spin a few threads of story from the wisps of memories that were layering down, day upon day. It felt as if all the times I sat down on sheep-nibbled turf to eat handfuls of trail mix from a battered plastic bag were running into one. But somehow I never wrote, didn't have the energy to do much at all, just lazed on my friend's sofa, eating good food and watching their crappy film collection. My body shifted into neutral and I slept a lot, dazed and heavy. Did it matter about the sequence of things? If the feeling of the wind tickling hair across my face, or time spent watching the dapple of sunlight through leaves could come from any day at all, maybe I didn't need to separate them into date-specific memories.

These are the things that I bought for four days alone: a fine sirloin steak, two chicken breasts, cabbage, broccoli, kale, potatoes, garlic, butter, a box of sugary cereal, milk, yoghurt, cheese, bread for toast, eight scones, clotted cream, raspberry jam, toffee pecan Haagen Dazs ice-cream, crisps and mayonnaise-saturated creamy dips. I bought the food and slowly and majestically ate my way through it. It was almost a problem; hunger ravaged my stomach as I planned for my downtime, so I voraciously bought food in anticipation and then had to eat it all, almost unwillingly, timing my intake so as to eat every last piece. It was an orgy of gluttony, my body craving fullness and nutrition.

I could carry just enough food to keep hunger away while walking, but if I ate camping rations for more than a few days then a hunger would grow, vast and deep, and I could eat and eat when I finally arrived at a generous home, where people had prepared beef stew or a roast dinner, taking multiple helpings and lashings of gravy. I would take the leftover pieces, the final chicken leg, the extra potatoes, adding extra salt to replace all the lost sweat, until I was finally satisfied.

When I returned to the walk it would be to the hardest bit of territory so far. My old mate Stu came up from Aberystwyth. I skipped ahead of myself to walk the Rhinogs with him on his available weekend, missing out the Moelwyns that connected the route between Snowdon and the Mawddach estuary. I'd go back to that bit after he left.

The Rhinogs, a set of four peaks and assorted rocky foothills, are definitely the toughest and wildest territory I'd passed through so far in Wales. It would have been a lonely and intimidating time if I'd navigated those mountains alone. But fortunately I had company: someone to discuss maps with, to take lunch breaks with, to share fruit pastilles and keep my spirits up on this tricky terrain.

Stu was a good guy, coming prepared with a stove and tea-bags and packets of dried food. Always cheery and amenable; I read the maps, he made the tea, we both admired the views. It was a fun weekend.

When I saw my friend hopping nimbly from rock to rock while I paced behind him I was stunned. How can he *do* that? He's 38! That's older than me! I compared his mountain-goat prancing to my packhorse plod and wrinkled my nose with jealousy. My calves were burning, as I stepped my way laboriously up and down, seriously hampered by my heavy rucksack, having to haul myself up each step, bracing my poles to pull my weight up with my arms rather than burden my weak knees. I felt as if this journey had walked all the bounce out of my knees. They were creaking and clicking to begin with, the result of years of being overweight I suppose, but I was starting to feel as if there was no possible way I could jump off something and have my knees absorb the shock of the landing. I was definitely not a lithe, spontaneous kind of a walker. No, no, I had to lower myself gently, using a tripod of walking poles, carefully avoiding any drop, jolt or jar that might damage my fragile shock-absorbers.

We started in Maentwrog late on Friday after Stu had finished work and, after a short walk around the far corner of Trawsfynydd lake, we camped by the dam there. There was a day of walking over broken land, split by small rocky gorges that crossed our path; we were forever climbing and descending in small 30m increments – this was the stony tableland leading slowly upwards to the first peak of Moel Ysgyfarnogod. We took a long and arduous route down to Cwm Bychan, a seemingly easy descent that was actually a morass of bracken and heather, a green scramble that grabbed and tangled at us. There weren't many footpaths apparent in this land, it wasn't a place where many people came. We saw almost no-one in our fifty-six hours crossing these wild and remote mountains: such a strong contrast to the crowded peaks further north. It was a thin sliver of remoteness, however, almost an illusion. To our right the land dropped down to the coast, a line of settlements along it, farms scattering up higher and higher until the land was too rough to build on. To our left was a stranger place, the plains of Trawsfynydd, a very sparsely populated area surrounding a man-made lake, created to service first a hydro-electric and then a nuclear power station, one that ran for twenty-six years and which, now dead, would take a century to decommission and make safe.

Rhinog Fawr was the real challenge: first a rocky scramble up the face of it, catching our breaths on small plateaux before continuing the climb. Then there was a long descent down the other side, stopping for lunch at the bottom, mixing Stu's boiled pasta and my tinned mackerel, before the next climb around tiny lakes to Rhinog Fach, dumping our bags to make the last scramble to the top, then dipping back down before the next steep climb to Y Llethr, this one a dangerous gravel slide: more a sheer eroded slope than an actual footpath.

We filled our water-bottles where we could, in small pools, at plant-filled edges, checking for eddies of water movement to make sure it was fresh. There were goats in these mountains – wild, stinking goats, triumphantly horned. We would walk past a series of rustles in bracken, their scent coming to us either long before or afterwards, depending on which way the wind was blowing.

We spent the last night aligned behind a long, high, stone wall that blocked the chill wind coming up from the Mawddach estuary, only leaving small spools of cold air that spun through the gaps in the stones placed by long dead, gnarled hands. Sheep had trotted a path along the extent of their boundary, leading to a thin compressed track alongside the wall where we could find flat places to make our beds. Stone walls were a beautiful feature of the Rhinogs, seen from great distances, swooping lengths across the land, carefully following the exact contours of the land boundaries. We'd followed a wall for most of that day, making a useful route-guide as it split the land at the highest point, all the way from Y Llethr to Diffwys, the final southern peak in the Rhinog range before the descent to Barmouth. We discussed the difficulty of building these walls: the effort of scrambling and struggling up to the heights, spending the day piling stone on stone, matching edges, weighting them carefully, piling in infinite balance. There was the pulling of the stone from the earth to build the snaking walls, the food these men would have had, bread and cheese, knobbled baked pasties, the clothes, worn woven cotton or woollen waistcoats, patched and mended, greasy caps to keep the wind away, each thread touched by human hand, brought from plant and animal by trial and error to make covering for bare skin. We laid there in our plastic coatings, carefully wrought by machine and computer design and thought of them, the hardy and determined men that built these walls.

The next morning I scrambled out of bed early and climbed closer to the peak of Diffwys for a wonderful view of the sunrise, Stu following blearily behind me. Grey mist billowed low over the land beyond us, only a few high wisps of clouds glowed pink to herald the sun's arrival, and we cheered at the entrance of the golden globe, welcoming life to the earth for another day.

We rushed down over the wide tranche of land descending to Barmouth. Stu had already stepped half-way back into his own world of appointments and house renovations and as he drove away, back to his life in Aberystwyth, I felt a little sense of sadness. *I have to carry on doing this? All alone? For another 2000 miles? Through the winter?*

Maybe it was the shock of returning to walk after a five-day holiday, or losing the comfort of walking with a friend, but I suddenly felt like this was all very hard going. The thought of all the hardship yet to come was hovering above me, my own personal doom cloud. During the five days off I'd added a tent to my kit; someone had emailed and offered to post me one from Scotland. I'd said yes without asking about its type or weight. I'd also added a few extra pieces of winter gear – waterproof trousers, gloves, handwarmer – to my pack. Things I'd happily discarded during the spring were reclaimed in anticipation of the wet and cold weather I knew was to come.

Along with the food I'd added for a few days of wilderness, plus the thick wedge of maps I needed, the weight of my rucksack rose to a staggering 17-18kg. The tent weighed 2.5kg, was a double-skinned, two person, four-season tent. Total overkill. I hadn't noticed the weight while walking with Stu as we'd shared out my kit between us, but it began to tell on me as I headed away from Beddgelert alone.

It's a short day's walk according to the guidebook, thirteen miles up over Cnicht, curl around behind it through the moorland, over Moelwyn Mawr, down through the foothills and along the side of the steam-railway line towards Maentwrog. It took me two full days of aching shoulders and painful knees, lots of rests and plenty of cursing as I humped my heavy bag over two peaks and through endless boggy foothills. By the time I came to terms with the truth – that the bag was horribly overloaded, that I'd borrowed the wrong, far too heavy tent and would have to take kit out again and send it home – I was far up in the hills with nowhere to dump anything. Sitting puffed out and irritated on a boulder, considering the reduced lifespan of my knee joints, I grumpily ate sandwiches, thinking of every mouthful as taking grams away from the strain on my shoulders.

The next day was a lesson in the merits of spontaneous wild camping versus advance arrangements with hosts. At about 5.30pm, as I'd been stumbling my way down the side of Moelwyn Fach for a couple of hours, losing my way and having to scramble down a sheer slope, recklessly throwing my rucksack down ahead for the second time, I came to flatter land, softer grass and the treeline began with a grove of autumnal oak. I could sleep here, I thought. Why am I battling and pushing to get to a bed? What is so wrong with wild camping, because right now I'd love to stop here for the night: it's only because I've arranged this bed in advance that I feel I have to get to it at all costs.

After all that, I reached Maentwrog at 8pm, too late to be able to hitch to Barmouth where a bed and a friendly host awaited me. They didn't answer their phone so I couldn't get them to come and pick me up. Instead, I slept in a bus-shelter in a faintly grumpy and sorry-for-myself kind of way, occasional car lights flashing over me. I'd shone my torch through the darkness to illuminate a nearby footpath but decided against the uncertainty. Who knew how far I'd have to walk along the dark path to find a useful sleeping spot. I was going to catch the early bus to Barmouth the following morning, back to the end of the Rhinog path I'd followed with Stu a few days previously, jumping back to the normal order of things.

I passed through Barmouth, a shoddy, crumbling seaside town. I'd come here for a couple of months during my walk preparation, caring for a woman in the final stages of dementia, her personality degraded to mild smiles and enjoyment of the food I made her, sentences trailing into fragments, a verbal mirror of her fractured neural network. She was a stranger in her own history, sitting amongst her collected ornaments, surrounded by the proof of her life without knowing it at all.

Never a Victorian parade of a town like Aberystwyth, without the class of Tenby, just a place I came to when I was a child, to stay in huddled trailers, parallel boxes lined along the coast where we could cram in, a mess of children scattering knickers and shoes and supersoakers wherever we ran. Barmouth was a place to eat sweets and play in the sand, gritty between toes, clinging to wet clothing, wind whipping hair against my face and never allowed to go into the amusements, except occasionally the trays of 2p machines. I'm sure they never had gaps at the sides when I was young, holes to swallow your chances in the most blatant way.

I remembered a rock shop where they had that most glamorous

of things, a fried breakfast made out of rock, sweets that were souvenirs, precious riches that you could take home to show you'd been to the sea. We came as a two-parent family, to a rich friend's holiday home, we came with single parents, always running down past the rock shop and over the railway line, alarm beeping and the barriers closing to allow a train to roll high and gentle across the road itself, metal rails set directly into the tarmac.

The sweetshop was still there, as was the mystical remembered talisman, the fried breakfast: pale yellow yolk of fried egg sitting uncomfortably on a blob of white, an insipid grey pink sausage and a mass of orange lumps that were baked beans. I couldn't believe that I'd ever thought this magical. There were other 'foods' too; fish and chips, cupcakes, bananas, apples – all solid sugar lumps that didn't interest me at all. I bypassed the chocolate willies and boobs, lurid neon marshmallows, tins of toffee and fudge, and settled on five sugar mice aligned in a packet, each a different pastel colour with black dotted eyes. They no longer had a string tail trailing behind them but a hygienic paper stick protruding uncomfortably. I spoke to the man behind the counter, grey hair and round glasses, told him that I used to come here when I was a child.

"Then it was probably me that served you," he said, smiling, and told me that his family had owned this shop since the 60s.

I wanted to cry for a benevolent lifetime spent selling sweets to tourists, giving them their tacky take-home souvenirs with his kind eyes, taking pride in his history of this place. Sun-reddened customers, mildly drunk. Bare legs and flip-flops, queues outside the chip shop, inappropriate holiday clothing paraded on the north Wales coast. I love Barmouth with its grimy rundown history. It's tacky, the Carousal café, missing the C from the lettered frontage outside, the discount shops and the inflatable dinghies lolling against shop doorways. It's a place I might run away to, go and hunker down in the winter and close down like the shopfronts, give up on living, be a shell of a person in this empty town that lives on crowds.

I stopped in a cheap café for a couple of hours to write a whinging blog about how hard everything was, surrounded by the whiff of cheap frying oil. I also repacked my rucksack, divesting myself of unwanted weight. It was expensive to post the tent ahead but I simply couldn't walk any further carrying it. This mountain route was feeling like a lot of bloody hard work; no sooner was I over one mountain than I had to walk towards another and climb that one too. It wasn't walking any more, it was almost scrambling, using my hands and feet to haul myself and rucksack to the top of a steep peak. What was my reward? To look at the view for five minutes and then spend a couple of hours picking my way down, lowering myself slowly and ungainly over rocks and boulders, leaning heavily on my walking poles, knees hurting with every single step. My body had power, I could feel the muscles of my legs working hard, but it was all so much fucking effort. Why was I doing this? Why?

My mood got better as I walked up Cader Idris. Maybe it was the place I'd slept in the night before: a small copse of beech trees next to a track leading away from an isolated farmhouse with an incongruously well-kept flower-garden. Box hedges and hollyhocks surrounded by the wildness of high pasture. I hadn't meant to sleep there, I'd crossed the estuary from Barmouth and climbed into the hills but it was still a couple of hours too early to stop. The bouncy grass in the flat spaces between trees was just too inviting, though. A farmer went past me on a quad bike, two sharp-eyed, slinking dogs riding the back of it. He didn't notice me at first but, at the last minute, caught sight of me out of the side of his vision.

"You look exhausted," were his first words to me.

It must have been the way my body slumped against the low stone wall, tucked away from the breeze whipping over the top of it.

"I am," I said, smiling weakly. He drove away after a few friendly words and I decided to settle there, against the wall; perhaps it was a day I didn't need to push myself any more.

There was the threat of thunder coming up from the south of the country, a night of big storms and hard rain for others. But I heard nothing more than the faintest of rumbles in the depths of the night, a tender breath of spotting rain making me snuggle further down inside my warm cocoon, thinking of the tattered edges of the storm blowing by, far above me.

The following morning, Cader had become a cauldron, overflowing with white mist that rippled down the cliff edge, oozing down the sides of the mountain 700 metres above me. I'd never seen it this way before, apparently full of mist on the other side but clear blue sky above me. I came along the valley to the northwest of the mountain. I could have cut across the reedy, high land, climbed the heights of Tyrrau Mawr and come across to the Cader peak from the west but I knew the effort that would take, the picking around wet patches, shaggy clumps of moor grass ready to roll my ankles, the steep slope towering above me waiting to reduce my efforts down to small steps and long rests for breath.

Instead, I took the Pony Path, the easy, steady climb up to the edge of the horseshoe, my favourite mountain, looking from the peak over a bowl of cloud, as far as I could see. It was a slow descent to the car park, the hundreds of steps on the Minffordd Path testing my aching knees, lowering myself awkwardly with the help of my flagpoles. I slept in that car park, hiding myself from the main drag behind a line of trees, too tired to walk any further.

The next day's trek was long but easier, somehow: across a set of high hills that curled around the northern edge of the Dyfi Forest, the great basin of pine trees dropping away to my right. I'd walk from gentle peak to gentle peak before dropping down to spend the night in Dinas Mawddwy. I realised that the land had changed, these weren't rocky steep mountains any more but peaty hills, gentler and easier to traverse. I'd made it over the highest points of Snowdonia and nothing would be so difficult again.

During a break that day, I found myself chanting *Shu-Gar-Mouse, Shu-Gar-Mouse* as I rummaged, elbow-deep in my rucksack, feeling my way around the odd shapes I knew so intimately; there was my book, my socks, my first aid kit. And there were the mice, snuggled down at the bottom, three left in the packet. I stopped the chant, laughing at myself but also a little shocked as I realised how much I was relying on this sweetness. It was something I was starting to need, a boost to get me through the late afternoon energy-dip. Was I becoming an addict without realising it?

At times, I'd go to sit in a café for a while, pot of tea, extra hot water to eke it out, palming handfuls of peanuts or the trail mix that I could chew endlessly but never to satisfaction. Having denied myself a sandwich or toast or a slice of cake, thinking of the cost, I'd find myself chewing sugar-lumps, wolfing pure energy, putting anything into my body to satisfy a gnawing urgent hunger, enjoying the sharp sweetness of an entire sugar cube, sucking it against the roof of my mouth until it disintegrated into sweet juice and crystal crunch.

The Cader-Idris good mood remained as I walked further south. As the terrain became easier to cross I could see what I'd come through and understand that maybe I was suffering because this was hard, not because I was weak and rubbish. I'd also walked into the mid-Wales area where my morale-boosting friends were; I could stay with Jackie in Dinas Mawddwy, Annie in Comins

Coch, Heloise in Llanidloes, Anna in Swyddffynnon and then Alice in Tregaron. A neat row of stopping points.

The day after leaving Dinas Mawddwy I came down the side of the hill and onto Annie's land. Grandmother Annie herself came out to meet me, with granddaughter Amma who cried my name, running forward to give me a hug.

Annie was a major source of strength. We'd met during recovery from our respective illnesses and had bonded over life-changing events, talking of how it felt to experience a before and after, two strong and single women, finding their way through a changed world where we were suddenly weak and vulnerable. Now I came to her calm and strong; she'd planted woods and I'd set out walking, we'd both come to the other side of our healing. I sat in the barn with her family and found I couldn't speak. The song of the mountains roared at too low a pitch to ever tingle my insubstantial ears but, after walking in the high places all day, I felt it as a vibration of spirit, an imbalance of self. My senses had extended out of my body while I was high up there, pennants of spirit had fluttered around me, flying out in the wind where the turbines whirled and groaned. I had a distinct sensation of having to pack myself back into my body before I could organise my mouth to make conversation, spirit breathing heavily after a long exercise, like lungs too small to take the air they need. I'd grown, out there, the wind whirling my senses out to the horizons, in sight of the hills calling out to the sky.

Occasionally, for a treat, I'd buy a loaf of bread, some butter, cheese and pâté, maybe chutney or onions or cucumber, and make a stack of sandwiches, folding them carefully back into the loaf wrapper, wobbling with the accumulated fillings. They'd last a couple of days as I rationed them out, two sandwiches twice a day. It was a nice break from the stark repetition of my usual rations but way, way too much weight for my shoulders. A loaf plus cheese and fillings became more than 2kg of sandwich. I'd enjoy eating them, though with decreasing pleasure as the repetition became tedious. The final sandwiches were a bit of a chore, squashed bread sweaty and slimy – although I'd eat them, it was tasty calories and still better than my dried food. I did this at Annie's place, packing sandwiches in her barn kitchen to see me over to the other side of Plynlimon.

The next mountain was barely a mountain at all, my third visit to Plynlimon. I'd cross it from north to south this time and with company: my friend and inspiration, Hannah Englekamp. She'd walked 1000 miles around the border of Wales with a donkey the year before I set off on my walk, combining a hardy, intrepid attitude with great photos and humorous blogging updates. All that plus a donkey made it the perfect public journey. We met for our first coffee in the late-2013 gap between our journeys, and found a shared adventurous spirit: her in the tingling afterglow of a walk successfully completed and me in the nervously twitching, wide-eyed preparatory stage.

It mizzled all day. Low cloud coated the tops of the hills as we walked, first winding through the lower moorlands, around lakes and crossing boggy valleys. Fortunately, at the end of a fairly dry summer, the water was in the air and not the ground, so we could cross the bogs without too much bother. Tufted white grasses burst from cracked brown peat, trodden with sheep hoofprints. Then we climbed into grey drizzle as it whipped diagonally past the thistleheads and dried grasses. It was still a good day, though; we wrapped ourselves in waterproofs, me rolling my flags up to avoid their unpleasant wet flapping against my face. We took silly photos at the summit, dipped our empty water-bottles into the peaty pools of the high places, tasted the brown tinged liquid, and decided the distinctly earthy flavour might make a good whisky mixer but otherwise should definitely be used for survival only. We drank as little as possible until we descended; this wasn't fresh water any more.

We camped in the rain, me using a newly borrowed truly lightweight tent for the first time; it turned out that Hannah had the same model and showed me tricks to get the fabric perfectly taut. We sat in our individual cocoons, chatting through small gaps in our zipped-up doorways, pushing pieces of sandwiches and pork pie through to each other, alternating swigs from a bottle of brandy. Hannah spurned my bag of trail mix after the first handful; I'd been adding varied packets of snacks into it without thinking, so Bombay mix and salted peanuts rubbed dusty shoulders with yoghurt raisins and dried apricots. I was happy to munch at whatever flavour presented itself, enjoying the salt-sweet combination, but sensed she was faintly disgusted!

It was my first day of walking and camping in proper rain for months, and it felt like a foretaste of the difficulties ahead. Hannah was relentlessly cheery in the face of my grumbles and I realised that I was feeling a bit ground down and worn out; the accumulation of so many months of effort revealed in the warm light of her fresh energy. It was good to experience someone else's positive attitude and realise that my own miserable one was just that, an attitude, a state of mind. I could enjoy this more, if I decided to.

Coming down to Cwmystwyth, where I said goodbye to Hannah, I reached Anna's patch and she whisked me home to a place where I could hang my sodden clothing and take a bath. She didn't normally drink, but had a dusty bottle for Christmas recipes so we improvised with Amaretto and milk cocktails, giggling at their deliciousness. My tent was still damp the next morning and

I used it as a thinly-veiled excuse to take a day off. I was groggy and unwilling, preferring to spend the day drinking repeated cups of tea and eating Welsh cakes. I oiled my boots, waiting for the oil to sink into the thirsty leather before reapplying. I oiled a leather satchel of hers too, a small token of gratitude.

The path from Cwmystwyth led upwards, winding from tarmac road to farm track to footpath, up along the edge of a deep wooded valley and into the high places, where trees didn't grow and there were no fences, just a landscape of rippling grasses and rolling land, where the sheep could roam for miles, the land soaked in water, pools and small lakes springing up. Up here the grass was short and coarse with long seed-stalks, silver brown in colour, harder wearing against the colder temperatures and strong winds. A rocky cairn stood high up on a nearby outcropping, ritual monuments built in the Bronze Age, marking death, talking to the gods.

On the way up, where the path took me around a ruined cottage, there was a gate beside a row of hawthorn trees, where, hanging on the fence, was a heavy carrier bag. I'd found it there when I walked this route months earlier with Gregorwicz the Pole but had left it behind in case someone came back for their forgotten booze. I checked inside. Treasure! Four full cans of Strongbow!! They'd been swinging here for weeks. I couldn't resist and washed water over the mouth of the cans, rubbing round the tops with a dirty finger, opened one and drank it down. A light alcohol dizziness made the next few hours mildly more enjoyable than usual.

I reversed the steps I'd taken with Greg, months earlier, eventually swinging right to descend a steep slope, treading carefully down on the bouncy grass to bring me to the only house in the landscape. A curlicue of tarmac far in the distance was the only other mark that humans had lain here. Down in the dip where a stream curved the cottage was a long-abandoned structure now maintained as a bothy for travellers. An open house that I can just walk into and sleep in for free? A long-distance walker's dream. In trepidation, I pressed down the latch and opened the door; inside were a set of dark, empty rooms. It was a cold place, sparse and unclean. I could feel the empty energy, the lack of anyone there to make it a home. A great open fireplace stretched across the side of one room containing an old range, ovens on either side of a small grate. Smoke-marks blackened the beams and plumed out across the once white ceiling. Inexperienced people had made scatty, scavenged fires here, filled the room with smoke many times over, graffitied names covered every wooden surface. It felt like a sad shell of a house, once a wholesome farming cottage, reduced to an anonymous shelter, disrespected.

I had a picnic to eat, courtesy of Anna, who brought my bag to the bothy, children trailing around her, leaving a bag of sandwiches and a tin of gin and tonic. I drank another can of cider and left the gin on a shelf, a gift for another walker. That night I had a proper twelve hours' sleep; without electricity or phone reception there was nothing to keep me awake beyond dusk. It felt strange at first, trying to sleep in a house with unlocked doors. I felt frightened of noises, aware of every creak, thinking of ghosts, intimidated by the dark and empty space surrounding me. I checked under the bed platform before laying out my bed on it. How foolish, I thought, that I would feel more secure lying against a wall outside. Eventually, though, I slept thick and deeply, dawn light failing to wake me, only able to creep through small windows.

The guidebook told me to keep wild, stay on the higher hills and make a straight line south towards Soar y Mynydd, but instead I dropped down into Tregaron to spend a night with Alice and her mother in their tiny terraced weaver's house. I sat down in a low, high-sided chair beside the stove and watched their tall, thin figures moving around the kitchen, stooping over the table to prepare food: the kitchen's coal range forming the warm belly of the tiny cottage. There was something very ancient about the close darkness of the warm kitchen, the way houses would have been before insulation allowed warmth to spread beyond a fireside.

I headed out of Tregaron with a newly heavy rucksack, adding in a couple of parcels I'd sent ahead of myself: such essentials as waterproof trousers and a new set of maps. I'd taken the trousers out at Barmouth and then added them in again. I had to admit that I needed them, even though they were heavy and I still hated wearing them. Then a couple more days' food made it up to a heavy load. At the last minute, feeling foolish, I slipped in a massive book that Alice wanted to lend me. *The Goldfinch* by Donna Tartt. I just couldn't seem to stop loading myself up, everything seemed either essential or insignificant. Each small item was so trivial in weight and volume, but together they were adding up to a load that was hurting me and restricting my ability to walk. I just couldn't seem to stop carrying stuff.

I trudged up the hills east towards the Cwm Berwyn forest, sun rippling on the hills, bringing out the colours of the browning bracken. There were two birds fighting in the sky above me; squealing and flapping they flew hard to get above one another and claw in, talons first. They flew out of sight, above the trees, but they continued to call in anger until a single bird flew silently back to the rocks, his peace defended.

At the top of the forest I turned right into a stretch of about three miles of pathless bog. It took longer than the five miles of road to negotiate, stepping my way carefully between clumps of grass, feeling ahead with my sticks, pushing through sometimes chest-high reeds. Not impossible, just tiring. I fell over once, clumsily sinking backwards as one of my poles unexpectedly pushed deep into the water and I wasn't balanced enough to keep upright. There was panic as my big rucksack weighted me down and I was unable to right myself, flailing like an upturned beetle. Fortunately I was cushioned on the reeds and didn't get wet, just slowly turned over with my big shell on my back and pushed myself upright. There's an alien feeling about bog-walking, it's a place humans are truly unsuited to; the ground is tough to manoeuvre over, treacherous, it's difficult to find safe places to step, water is always sucking at your feet. Every step could find deep or shallow water, it's impossible to tell. I struggled and pushed along, the forest running alongside me behind a fence, ground rising to the left of me. I was descending into a wide-bottomed dip, where water collected and began to make a stream.

My walking pole, searching and poking for hard support amongst the water-pockets and slurping mosses, brushed aside the hanging reeds to reveal a frog, small and squat and perfectly at home on the root-riven wetness. I had a very strong feeling of his rightness here, the place where he could live comfortably, being here in the wetness, his skin balanced inside and out. I felt our contradiction as I passed over this ground, clothed in protective material, seeking safety elsewhere.

There was a hostel ahead, Ty'n Cornel. I thought it might be a bit early to stop and didn't want to spend money on a bed when I could camp. On the other hand, it's one of two independently-run hostels in the area, sold on as unprofitable by the YHA and kept going by the love and dedication of volunteers. I wanted to at least stop in and see what was there.

It was raining again as I came towards the small farmhouse, and the forecast told me it would rain all night. The door was opened by Russ, the friendly volunteer warden who led me into the dark hallway, where I could see through to a front room with open fireplace and rocking chairs. I knew I had to stay there for the night and learn more about the place: its history as a farmhouse and hostel, last lived in in 1953, sold to the YHA by the farmer in the late 60s on condition that he remained as warden.

One bad thing happened at Ty'n Cornel and it was pretty awful. I was issued with a sheet sleeping-bag that had a panel to stuff a pillow into at the top, it pulled taut between the pillow and the bed and I woke up in the middle of the night with the muscles of my neck in solid spasm.

Whenever I camped I would bundle my clothing under my head as a makeshift pillow; it was never quite right and would condense into a hard and low lump that I was forever trying to mound and mash high enough to relax onto. I'd regularly wake up with a stiff neck from my poor pillow-substitute but that morning in the hostel was even worse. I couldn't raise my arms above my head or even pull a hat on without neck pain. I could still walk but I felt awful – further pain on top of my existing struggles was too much to handle. I set off – I had to – stopping every so often to work the muscles of my neck and shoulders with my fingers, trying to soften away the tension. Fortunately I could still wear my rucksack; the thick straps bore down on my shoulders, stretching my inflexible neck into discomfort, but it was a manageable burden.

I walked from Ty'n Cornel down the Doethie Valley. The grey skies tamped down the beauty of the place, but it was wonderful even without gilding sunshine. The valley wove south, hills sliding together like interlaced fingers, steep sides covered with bracken and moss, trees growing in the cracks made by the descent of water to the river. No road, just a well-worn path winding around each curve and turn of the river, deciduous trees everywhere. I only saw looming pine forest at the top of a single rise. Eventually I came down into woodland covering both sides of the river and it was a rare pleasure to see the entire side of a hill covered in deciduous trees, so different in their natural bumps and rises to the ranks of pine which spread, rigid and silent, in their man-made rows.

Arriving in a stone church porch in a drizzle of rain, I decided to read my book there for a while and decide whether I wanted to go any further. I could search for a hospitable field, quiet, not overlooked, free of animals, with a clean, flat, grassy covering, and put my tent up to shelter from the rain, or I could nestle into the stone floor here and be uncomfortable but very definitely dry. The very fact that I'd stopped at the church was a sign, really. I definitely didn't want to go any further, just had to run the gauntlet of the warden coming to lock up. I wanted to completely and utterly stop, make no more movement; it was a familiar end of day blankness.

Eventually I heard someone inside the church and as they came towards the front door I worried that I'd scare them, anyone would be scared to open the door and find a silent figure in a darkening stone porch. The little lady took it well, not jumping too much, and we had a conversation about what I was doing.

"Do you want to sleep in the church," she asked and I said, "Yes". I could tell she felt sorry for me and I politely fended off offers of a heater and food, I didn't really need those things in that moment, plus my pride wouldn't allow me to appear too needy.

I lay down to sleep on the luscious red carpet, bats squeaking and flapping above me, rattling plaster down from the walls. I managed to knead some more of the tension out of my neck and slept in fragments, waking up every so often to ease myself into a new position, pain in hips, pain in back, pain in neck. My body was too tense to relax into deep sleep.

There was a rustling at the door the next morning, and a note slipped underneath, near my head. *Dear OWWW. Hope you slept well! Please call in to 'freshen up' and have some breakfast. Sue.*

A lovely, kind woman, she said I'd looked exhausted the night before so she had to help me. I sat in her clean, simple kitchen and chatted about her grown children, living in nearby villages. She asked what else she could do to help and I allowed it, choosing not to brush her away with an *I'm fine.* She could do something, she could take my bag ahead for me. I hated asking, I hated needing help, I hated people going out of their way for me but it would be so nice to walk without my bag for a few hours and reduce the strain on my body. We arranged that she would leave it at a hotel in the centre of Llandovery, and I watched her pack lunch into the pockets, squirming under all this tenderness but staying quiet.

I left. I can't remember if we hugged or not but I took a photo of this mild and generous woman, just one of so many people who were giving to me, lifting me up. When I reached the hotel – a wide-roomed, traditional town hotel, the dark wood and wide floorboards evidence that this had been a place of eating and meeting for a few centuries – I retrieved my bag and discovered a card and £20 note in the top pocket. *For you, towards your new boots or whatever you need.*

I sat in the corner of the bar behind the door, against a wide light window and cried quietly, gentle slow tears trickling down my face. I was trying to keep my spirits up but I was so often tired and in pain. This all seemed like very hard work, especially with the added neck-pain and mountains of recent weeks, and it was when people were kind to me that I collapsed a bit, able to let some of the tension go.

The hotel had a lunch menu and I decided that, rather than put

Sue's money into my normal budget and let it slip away piecemeal on ordinary things like peanuts or mackerel, I'd treat myself to a whole lunch at the pub. Cafés were for pots of tea that I could magic into an hour's sit down, eke out with hot water, occasionally with the additional treat of pieces of toast. I didn't have enough money saved to eat meals out all the time. But today I'd enjoy it, worry-free. I had a cheese sandwich and chips, followed by coffee and an ice-cream sundae. It was simple food but excellent quality; the chips were cooked in beef dripping and they were incredibly delicious, a short, thick, juicy kind of chip, each one savoured and crunched. The cheese was proper mature cheddar, in good healthy bread. It was real food, I was so glad I'd chosen to do this, give myself a haven for a couple of hours.

On the way out of the town I stopped to buy some magnesium tablets. I'd read online that they were a help in energy release; I knew that months of a broadly similar diet would inevitably affect my nutritional balance and already took a multi-vitamin to try and keep myself healthy. I'd added in cod liver oil for my joints, then glucosamine sulphate to try and help my knees; now I wanted magnesium, an essential chemical component of the release of energy from food and commonly found in green vegetables; I definitely wasn't eating enough of those.

I walked away from the town and out to the beginning of farms and pastureland. Then came a sunken green lane for me to ascend, ancient hawthorn writhing and bowing, marking the edges of the ancient thoroughfare. This was wealthy and fertile Carmarthenshire: no major hills, just rolling pasture. I passed outlying farms and came to a small wood where I decided I'd sleep, finding the place where fields marked the beginning of the farm, as if I'd walked out of reach of one village and into the next, the woodland acting as a barrier between the two communities.

I found a perfect spot at the beginning of a ditch, barbed wire protecting me from curious beasts and a tree standing sentinel above me, its roots parting to run either side of my head. It was a dry night so I could camp out and lie down to sleep early: 6pm, and there were at least twelve hours before sunrise. I dreamed, despite waking regularly to change position, the usual pain of hips crushed against hard ground keeping me from sleeping too deeply.

In the night a cow cropped grass close to me, munching and swishing her thick tongue around the blades. I woke with her movement and lay safe and comfortable in my cocoon as the full moon sailed overhead, lighting the cow and the trees in shadows and gilding. A fox bark struck the air; the animal circled through the woods, first near the farm buildings and then closer to me, each call a jagged streak in the deep night silence. I imagined hens nestled warm and fluffed behind closed doors, the slumber of the man in his sheltered bed; here I was with the cow and the fox, one of the animals, happy and living in the darkness. Part of me knew I should be afraid of this calling from the wild night, this shriek to make settled beasts shiver, but I was calm in the moonlit tableau, happy to be part of it. We were united, roaming with impunity in the freedom of the dark.

The next day I felt rested and happy after twelve hours lying down. I'd obviously really needed it. I plodded through the village of Myddfai and onwards, up a hill and out to rest against a tree. I leant my back against the trunk and looked out at the view: the Black Mountains and the Brecon Beacons lifting from the wide Usk valley, a first and last barrier between north and south Wales. I was coming at them from the west so these great, flat-topped heaps of earth rippled away in front of me, one after another, like piped cream on a birthday cake, made mountains by height above sea level, not their crags or peaks.

The pain that comes at the end of strength is blunt and blocky. It is muscles that have set solid and have nothing more to offer. Legs burning, body heavy, I'd struggled up yet another hill carrying my weighty load along with the exertion of all the mountains gone before, the weak focus of tiredness, the rarity of private resting-places nibbling away my concentration. And yet I looked ahead at those steep climbs to come and thought, *That's where I'm going.* No questions, no uncertainty, no fear of the pain and effort involved, just the simple fact. That was where I was going. All the chattering uncertainty of my fearful brain was silenced by this solid statement. I looked at the hills and knew that I'd walk over them, that I wouldn't give up or stop, no matter how long it took me.

I didn't realise I had this blunt certainty within me; a summer of pain and shuffling had ground me down, reducing my reserves to the point where, when my paths took me over the mountains, up each slope and down again, I didn't know how much deeper I could dip. But here it was, I'd scraped through to bare bone, broken myself open, and the revealed core still had tenacity and achievement all the way through it. There they were, those hills, and that was where I was going. I laughed aloud in relief and happiness; the uncertainty, the creeping doubt had vanished.

I came over the first of the southern mountains following a windy night in a rescue-shelter alongside dingy Llyn y Fan Fach, water tainted by rusting, disused machinery. Three sheep munched disconsolately at the greening edges of the waterline as the wind boomed at the shelter roof. I expected expressions of discomfort, half-shut eyes perhaps or bodies huddling together, leaning against walls, but there was nothing. These steadfast animals lay relaxed on the cropped grass, streaks of mist blowing between them, content, as if the sun was shining. I lay for the night in the tin-roofed shelter, wind banging and blowing so hard I thought the building must surely collapse.

I was starting to feel exhausted and blank. The walking had become much harder with this mountain route and so the breaks became longer, more frequent. When I stopped, I'd slump against something: a tree, a pile of rocks, a stone wall. I stared around me palming handfuls of trail mix into my mouth, gulping and swilling cold wild water from my shiny blue bottle.

On this high level route there were no houses to fill from, just hills. I drank water from streams, checking maps for blue lines crossing the path, gulping litres from the final source before I went high. Filling my belly with a litre and a half, ballooning it with liquid then taking a litre up to the drier mountain peak. I didn't realise how chemically flattened tap-water tasted until I returned to it. Water from the mountain was full and fresh, sharp and clear in my mouth, bringing the earth with it, not in its floating particles but in the absence of human interference: pipeline tampering, filter it, dull it, kill the essence, kill the life.

The water lives and I drink it straight from the mountain as I walk across the ground. I've taken water from streams, from springs, from lakes – even, in dry-mouthed desperation, from puddles of brown oozing bog. Only at the tops of the mountains though, where humans can't drag their polluting machinery or the sheep piss and taint the peaceful flow. Just the algae, the fish eggs and the small water creatures, shelled and jointed, swim in my water bottle; you'd never know though, it's clear when I hold it to the light.

The morning after the windy night, I sat in a semi-circle of built-up stones up on Picws Du. The shelter was the accumulated sum of travellers' contributions, placed there rock by rock to build a retreat from the mountain. Ducking down into quiet air gave a place to pause, the constant abrading of wind and weather was as exhausting as the physical effort required to traverse these rocky high places. A tall figure loomed into view, thin and grizzled; he said my name and proffered a chocolate bar. Hooded and suited in waterproofing, lumbered with a gigantic bag, the man had large, kindly eyes and a gentle air about him. Turned out he'd been following my tracks along the Cambrian Way for days, drinking the gin I left in the bothy, seeing my symptoms-awareness card in Strata Florida, talking about me to Russ in the hostel. Another long-distance walker, going my way. I was intrigued.

We talked, circling each other for a day or so, meeting at odd points, not wanting to commit to a shared walk, both admitting that we were aiming for the same hostel but taking different routes to get there. Finally we shared a day or two walking together. He was searching; I recognise that in people sometimes. There's a sense of people who need to unburden themselves, who carry hidden pain that can be brought out, flooding from within.

Finding someone to walk with was a joy, I had some inspiration and entertainment. However, Olivier was interesting and irritating in equal measures. I wanted a companion, someone to walk with and share the experience, share the hardship. My solitary experience was both a support and a cage, both bolstering and limitating. It was great to hear Olivier's stories: chatting together made time and miles pass so much more quickly. It was so rare to find someone else who was driven to do what I was doing, to walk a challenging path, wild camping, carrying all you need for longer than a weekend. He was only walking for three weeks but it still felt like a similar journey.

The problem was that he walked faster than me and I couldn't keep up; irritation came quickly as I forced my body into more pain just to match his pace, prioritising a companion over my own capabilities. By the end of the second day I was trailing way behind him, thin slivers of pain shooting from my ankles up through the bony front of my calves. I was frustrated at myself for not articulating that I couldn't walk the daily distances he was set on covering. Over a summer of walking 1500 miles I'd learned to balance my body's limitations with the demands I put on myself and I couldn't change it to match another's physical capabilities, especially not a tall thin man who strode longer than me and covered ground so easily. He had his own path too, his own reasons for walking and his own adventure to discover, his own wet feet, leaking boots, challenges of weighty kit and his own peace to come to from the life history that followed him. It's hard to mix adventures when you meet half-way through. I missed him and yet was glad to say goodbye.

I sat by the canal outside Crickhowell and checked my phone. There was a voicemail from my work, the care agency, wanting to know if I could come back to cover holiday for two weeks. I didn't want to break the walk for this, I needed to stay in this journey, not keep stopping, prolonging it over and over. Part of me felt that stopping would break the spell that held me in this constant movement, show me the reality that all this pain and effort was optional. Plus, I didn't want to return to normal life; the magic of fresh air and freedom was intoxicating, the spirit-lifting life of constant outdoors, sunlight gilding, dew blanketing, steam from breath and bird calls echoing. The fairy-space of moss forests and stream-gurgle waterfalls, the spell cast by a charity walk meant a dreamtime where every person I met was incredibly nice to me. I didn't want to return to a tight schedule, rushing between houses containing waiting elderly people, making the same small conversations over and over, completing the same small tasks, keeping people alive, fed, warm, safe so that they could repeat the same again the next day. It's a life of stasis, of slow decline, creams and medications, television, microwaved meals and a background drone of minor ailments.

My walking life was fulfilment and freedom and I wanted it to go on indefinitely. But I'd told my employers I'd be away for eight months and here it was: eight months passed and I was only just coming close to half-way. Going back to cover might win me the goodwill to postpone my eventual return. I wanted to keep the possibility of a job to return to, income to pick up immediately after I'd dug to the bottom of my savings and through into debt in the name of this journey.

Maybe I should accept this unexpected two weeks of wages, top up my meagre balance. I phoned back and said yes. Once the decision was made I felt relieved; it was the right thing to do and I really needed a break. I was beyond tired, slipping into blankness. First, though, I'd walk to Cardiff, just another week to get to 1660 miles and the half-way point.

I'd been waiting for half-way for months, looking forward to the next milestone for far too long in advance. Almost half-way felt no way at all, the photos and fizz of the previous 1000-mile landmark was long trodden away. It had been a needless psychological load, trudging through 600 miles in an aching grind of looming mountains and the chilling, darkening turning of the year.

The wind was strong as I left Crickhowell, driving thin rain against my side. I'd climb that day, head north up to the exposed hilltops, a long, amorphous range of hills, the contours wide and clear once I reached the heights. It meant nowhere to shelter. I couldn't sleep up there, the wind would continue all night; I'd have to walk the entire length of the hill route before I could drop down into the Cwmyoy Valley and find somewhere to sleep. It was going to be a long hard day and I braced myself for a tough time.

The weather became grimmer. I walked upwards into a thick layer of cloud which completely obscured any view and, more importantly, hid any hint of my route ahead. I could see about 100m ahead, enough to navigate with the contours of the map. It was a relatively easy piece of map-work, I just had to follow the highest line along the top of hill until it met another, then turn right, cross one valley head and dip down into the next. I found a trig point and crouched down behind it, finding the side that faced away from the biting wind, a bleak sea of trampled peat around me. The clouds cleared for a few seconds to give a view of a sun-dappled mound of a hill half a mile distant, then reformed and I was alone in a blush of white, my clothes sodden with the accumulation of thousands of small droplets. I couldn't fully rest here, the wind was snatching the heat away from my body too quickly, so I took enough time to locate and chew on a sesame snap and gulp some water before heaving myself up from the crouch and lumbering on, back into the blind walk from point to point, the lack of view taking away any real sense of progress.

It took all afternoon to walk the cloud-laden hilltop route, and eventually I came to a crossing point I'd visited before, as I came down the Cistercian Way. To my left lay the path down towards Hay-on-Wye, ahead was the short 100m to summit Lord Hereford's Knob, and to my right was the start of the valley that would lead to Llanthony and Cwmyoy, my route back to Abergavenny. Last time I'd been here in bright sunshine, and I'd lain down in the grass for a long rest when I reached the highest point of the pass. Today there was neither sunshine nor rest. I was tired, but there was still nowhere to shelter. My route was supposed to take me up to the rising point of the lordly outcrop and then retrace back and down into the valley. I was sorely tempted to skip it, just walk straight down into the valley, but couldn't bring myself to cheat. What was the point of putting myself through this entire, painful, exhausting enterprise if I was just going to dodge parts of it?

I climbed the Knob – still in cloud, no view – and came back down the short hill to turn down into the valley. I remembered that the first house on the path was an empty one, a holiday cottage with a barn attached. I'd go there, I decided; the ground was sodden with water and there would be nowhere dry to sleep tonight. It was one more mile. The light became twilight as I walked, stepping over and around the many swollen rushes of water that poured from the hillside and into the stream next to me. Eventually I came to the barn; half was full of rocks from a collapsed wall and the other half was a dirty, uneven surface of packed-down sheep shit, a hay-rack running the centre of it. But I found a flat corner, tucked against a hay bale.

I slept late into the morning, continually waking to turn over, an effort that gave my aching hips a sense of relief, allowing me to slide back into sleep for another half hour before discomfort spread to the new side. I only woke properly when the flutter of a small bird landed on the edge of my sleeping bag hood. It was a barely-sensed experience, the air of its wings against my face, the scratching of tiny talons against the fabric brought me awareness of this small animal as the stirring of my eyelids scared it to immediate flight. I saw myself from the viewpoint of this tiny forager, the stillness of my body in the barn, the sudden appearance of a strange-smelling object, its tentative exploration in search of food.

That night, after an agreeable day of walking a pleasant woodland path on the edge of the descent into Abergavenny, became a terrifying experience as darkness fell. Tree roots became trip hazards, trailing branches became stabbing, scratching obstacles. As the light dwindled, I became eerily aware of the creeping darkness behind me. I was on the edge of a town where humans are, where danger is, where the lapping waters of society jettison the unwanted out into the night: the oddments, the lurkers, the people with no place. If I used a torch for guidance I was clearly defining myself in the dark trees as a target, something to be focused on, followed. The light doesn't illuminate, it blinds, limiting my senses to the small circle at my feet.

If I turned off the torch I'd become part of the wood, another creeping element of shadow, moving silently with the waving branches and the small busy creatures. If I sat still, eventually I'd hear the rustling mice, the gliding owls. I needed the light because I didn't belong there, I needed to move through this wood, not become part of it.

I was relieved when I climbed the final stile to reach the chemical-orange tang of streetlight on tarmac and could once again become an anonymous shadow, seen for a moment slipping past an empty street corner.

I made my way down the steep road, the lights of Abergavenny laid out before me, and waited at the hospital for Jess to come and pick me up. I'd exchanged texts with Olivier; he'd also reached Abergavenny and was in a B&B, drying out his sodden clothing. He was at a turning-point, deciding whether to finish here or take an extra couple of weeks to walk the northern section, buying a new pair of boots on the way.

A day or two later I arrived at the city of Cardiff, coming down via the canals of Cwmbran and Pontypridd, a squat urban kingfisher making a welcome appearance. It was the only highlight of the day, that and the woods around Castell Coch at Tongwynlais. Once I reached Cardiff Bay after a long, draining tramp on concrete, I was done. I'd finished the Cambrian Way, the toughest route of all of them. And I was half-way to my total.

This was my walk and I was doing it my own way. It was hard to fix on just one feeling about the achievement.

There was the happiness of knowing I was half-way through; that I, with my plump little legs that turn in at the ankles, had managed to stride, plod, climb, drag and stumble my way through almost 1700 miles. If I could do this I could do anything; or at least walk another 1600 miles.

There was also the apprehension of only being half-way through: half-way through the effort, the grime, the sleepless nights trying to curl my body around the unyielding ground. There was the same again to come. All the high hills rising in front of me, all the muddy patches, all the gleefully saturating bog, all the pain: foot pain, back pain, neck pain, ankle pain. All the evenings spent hobbling, barely able to put feet to the ground. All the foot rubs, calf stretches, back-bending sun-salutes. All the outdoor shitting. The difficulty of no private space. I had to do the same again. Except the second half would be through the winter.

There was also the anticipation of being just half-way through. I got to walk another 1600 miles before I had to go back to work, had to return to a normal life where people didn't tell me how brilliant and inspiring I was. I had another eight months of freedom, of the wild wind blowing my hair, of hard-won mountains, of turning to look back at the view, of dreamy hours in cafés, of conversations and connections with strangers, of wild flowers and bird calls, talking to animals, waking up at night and watching the moon. The wind could blow my senses out to the horizon for another 1600 miles. There would be rain in my face, frozen red hands, deep, deep exhaustion...and I would savour it all because, despite everything, it makes me deeply, deeply happy.

I went back to work in Machynlleth, borrowing a car to get around. I slept in it for the first night and then was lucky enough to stay at a friend's place while they went to France. I had a fortnight to savour an empty house, time to eat and rest. My leg muscles slowly relaxed, kicking and twitching in the space of the big double bed, shooting pains running through my bones. It wasn't predictable, the way my hurts would manifest. A single small bone in my ankle would suddenly start to throb, spending an entire day sending pulses of pain into the rest of my foot before silencing, returning to obscurity overnight. I stretched and rested, trying to swim as often as possible, allowing my body's tension to float outwards with the ripples from my crabbed and awkward swimming-strokes.

My body was hardened and held, braced against the workload of the previous eight months. Once I let the effort go I felt groggy and tired for almost all the two weeks, allowing my will to stop pushing my body onward meant I could allow it to feel all the lack of energy underneath. There was a friend, Guy, who was also staying in the house while his own was uninhabitable. We watched films and chatted, drank small amounts of booze, cohabited in a gentle and relaxed way. I cooked in the high-ceilinged, slate-floored kitchen, ate chicken and chorizo, buttered toast, pots of rich ice cream. Two weeks of work and then a week to wait for a replacement bank-card, a lost purse conspiring to allow me a final morsel of rest. There were things I could do: write, update my blog, do publicity, make the journey better-known, organise my kit, plan ahead. But doing nothing was equally important. While walking, all my separate pains condensed into a constant, scratching noise that scraped in a high-pitched line across my flow of thought. After all the stimulation of the journey, all the intensity and high bright days, the joy of generosity and the beauty of leaves and sunlight, I needed some nothing to balance it out.

Until the moment I started back out again, the walk felt very far away. I was sophisticated, showered and clean, clothes laundered, nice-smelling hair waving long across my shoulders. Luxuriating in the feeling of stretching out for a lie-in in a clean double bed, I couldn't imagine heaving a rucksack onto my shoulders and walking with it, for months, for miles, over hills and mountains, down to the shore and around the coast where the icy wind would sting gritty droplets across my face, blow my senses out to sea. Salt and grime would taint my possessions, rubbing sweat and slime nightly into my sleeping-bag until eventually everything stinks and I'm a wild-eyed mad woman, staggering into pubs and ranting my story, crying out, shouting of cancer and wilderness hardship, intimidating the normal people who cower behind their safety barriers of just-in-case and what-if, fearing discomfort and the unknown.

That's exactly what I was setting out to do though. I knew what I was heading for.

IRISH SEA

Holyhead
ISLE OF
ANGLESEY
Llangefni
Llandudno
Conwy
Rhyl
Flint
Chester
Bangor
Caernarfon
Betws-y-Coed
Wrexham
SNOWDON
Porthmadog
Pwllheli
Bala
Llangollen
CADAIR
BERWYN
RHINOG
FAWR
ARAN
FAWDDWY
Barmouth
CADAIR
IDRIS
Shrewsbury
Welshpool
Machynlleth
PLYNLIMON
Newtown
CARDIGAN
BAY
Llanidloes
Aberystwyth
ENGLAND
WALES
Tregaron
Elan
Village
Worcester
Cardigan
Builth
Wells
Hay-on-Wye
Hereford
Tewkesbury
Fishguard
St David's
Llandovery
Brecon
Haverford West
Carmarthen
Llandeilo
BLACK
MOUNTAIN
PEN Y
FAN
Abergavenny
Tenby
Llanelli
Merthyr
Tydfil
Neath
Rhossili
Swansea
Pontypridd
Newport
Chepstow
Porthcawl
CARDIFF
Barry
BRISTOL
BRISTOL CHANNEL

SNOWDONIA
CONWY
DEE
CLWYDIANS
DYFI
DYFI MOUNTAINS
SEVERN
SEVERN
WYE
YSTWYTH
CAMBRIAN MOUNTAINS
TEIFI
WYE
TYWI
WYE
BLACK MOUNTAINS
USK
TAFF

N
W   E
S

0 Kilometers   30
0 Miles   20

228

COAST TO COAST PATH
SNOWDONIA TO THE GOWER

Route description: Another high mountain route including the peaks of Snowdonia from the Carneddau to Cader Idris, continuing past the great dams of The Elan Valley from remote moors to beautiful valleys before crossing the Black Mountains to reach the Gower coast.

Length:	207.1 miles
Total ascent:	13,415m
Maximum height:	1,043m
Dates:	10 November – 18 December 2014
Time taken:	39 days
Nights camping/nights hosted:	16/23
Days off:	5
Average miles per day:	9.29

It was only a three-week break but I came back to a tangible difference: darker evenings and a sharp chill in the air. The weather was cold and bright, there were sunny days and the beginnings of frosty nights. When I'd stopped I could kid myself that it might still be late summer, but it was definitely autumn now. Now I watched the wind scatter falling leaves around me. There was no going back.

The forecast told me I was set to walk through a week of gales and rain. First I had to walk west from the end of the Cambrian Way in Cardiff along the coastal path to the tip of the Gower where I'd pick up the tail end of the Dragon's Back, a path that led from the Gower back to Conwy. It was another mountain route, but not quite as challenging as the Cambrian Way. This time I'd miss out the Brecon Beacons and go around the Rhinogs, rather than doggedly over every peak as the Cambrian Way had taken me.

A gale blew as I walked along the clifftops of the coastal path, the crumbling edges scattering drops of earth. There was mud and rain, leaves rattling and scratching. A flock of crows rose and flapped ineffectually at the oncoming force, fighting to stay still. Trees washed themselves in the wind, swaying and swishing, freeing the detritus. Dead dry branches too stiff to flex came down with a crack and thud to start new lives as moist, rotting beetle-homes, delicately disintegrating flake by flake. The time for relaxed walking was ending. Body temperature and waterproof kit were now problems to take seriously.

It was all a bit of a shock, really. I knew it was coming but it was still pretty difficult to cope with. I could still do this but I had to be more regimented about it. It took definite steps to get into bed warm and clean. Before this temperature drop I could stop anywhere, scatter my belongings and slump for a while, mostly sleep safe in the knowledge that no rain would come overnight. Now I had to clamber into the tent, shed wet trousers and jacket in the tiny entrance, keep muddy kit away from the tent walls, climb into bed, tucked up by 7pm, make sure I'm warm enough, no skin left uncovered.

The clocks had changed; sunset came at half past four, total darkness by five-thirty, so I had to stop and make camp by a terribly early hour. I'd been used to nice lazy mornings, a gentle wake-up, sit and stare for a while before lumbering off, as long as it was by 10am I didn't mind. Now I had to revere the daylight hours: there would be only ten of them and I was used to walking for ten hours a day. So I'd set an alarm for 6am and get walking by 7.30. It was enjoyable, once I got past the pain of the first alarm.

The foot pain, which had disappeared while I was working, came glimmering into being once again. I had to stretch religiously; it was the only thing that made it bearable. As the pain returned I wanted to weep in anticipation of the future. This is how torture works, I realised. People don't break under the duress of the suffering but in fear of the many more painful days to come.

I could walk in the rain all day; that was fine. The problem was finding dry places to sleep, and keeping enough of myself free of damp so I could sleep comfortably. I could change into dry clothing, but putting on a damp waterproof, hat and gloves was unpleasant. Packing a wet tent away was awful: pulling out a wet tent to sleep in even worse. Finding a truly waterproof jacket was impossible. Rain soaked through where the straps of my rucksack rubbed at my shoulders, it leaked in at the neck, ran down and dripped onto my legs, and oozed down into my socks. I couldn't find waterproof trousers that weren't incredibly cumbersome and sweaty, so preferred to go without. I'd tried at least three pairs of gloves – Sealskinz, ski gloves, mountaineering mittens – tucking them into my raincoat at the wrists, tucking my raincoat into the gloves. It always ended up with rain gathering in a small pool at the crook of my bent elbows – I could pour water from my sleeves whenever I stopped to rest. I'm not sure if I had bad kit or if it's impossible to find properly waterproof, durable, lightweight clothing that will withstand daily use. I had neither the time nor the money to experiment.

Back in Cardiff, I'd borrowed money from my mum to put towards better equipment. £400 to spend on a new sleeping bag, rucksack and waterproof. I really needed to put money into good-quality kit, not make do with the cheap and readily available alternatives that were actually making my journey harder. The new waterproof I chose from the sale-rail, breathable Gore-Tex and reduced to £90: simple. The other items were more complex to procure.

I searched online for the rucksack, finding one on a discount site that seemed OK. The big excitement was that it weighed 600g less than my current rucksack, mainly by minimising strap padding and the thickness of the material. I'd been galled to discover that while I'd been trying so hard to reduce the weight I was carrying by minimising its contents, the actual rucksack itself weighed a whopping 1.4kg, 10% of my total carry weight. It had to go. The new rucksack was one main pocket inside, instead of two separate ones. Less material to make up the rucksack, but it meant I'd have to remove everything to get at my sleeping bag every night. I took a gamble that this wouldn't matter too much, even in the rain or unpleasant conditions, and ordered it. There were lighter ones available through special order companies, but they were twice as expensive. I'd found lightweight-gear companies through the walking blogs I followed, but I didn't have the time or budget to order everything from them. An expensive sleeping-bag was vital, I had to compromise on the rucksack.

The sleeping-bag was a £300 lightweight bag, made to special order from an online company. The bag I had just wasn't meeting the winter conditions, I could feel the cold cutting through it, a thin sharp blankness of cold, slicing away and stealing my carefully hoarded body-heat. I had to have better if I was going to keep myself safe and alive through winter camping; I couldn't compromise. Four-season bags were available in UK outdoor shops but they weighed so much, up to 2kg. This one was good to -12°C and only weighed a tiny 600g. It was the right decision, but would take almost two weeks to arrive. I'd just have to sleep cold until then.

Coming along the coastal path towards Porthcawl, I found a river blocking my way at Ogmore. It ran wide across the beach, spreading out over the flat sand and carving a wide and shallow path through the washed grains. *Fordable at low tide*, the guidebook said, and here I was, just half an hour past time. It looked possible – the river washing out thin and shallow, a wide stretch of water ruffling up against the sea. Clear blue sky and small clouds scudded as I walked away from the higher grassy dunes, and out over the wide flat sands towards the water barrier. But close up the water was still deep and rushing, ripples in the surface showing the depth further into the centre. I tried but it wasn't possible, getting as far as the thick current reaching up for my ankles and threatening to fill my boots with any further steps. I could have taken them off, waded through but somehow I didn't like it. Didn't want the tape on my feet to get wet; the adhesive was too delicate for the icy water. There was no sense of how deep the water went, or how strongly the current would pull me along. It was too cold. I'm not sure why I stopped and turned away but I didn't try and ford all the way through.

There was a chubby man in a rugby shirt who was turning away from the same challenge and I caught up with him, interested in what he was doing, sensing another searcher, as Olivier had been.

"I wanted to walk from Llantwit Major to Porthcawl," he said, embarrassed. "I don't know why."

I said that there was a way around the river crossing: we just had to make a detour a couple of miles upriver to some stepping stones, and perhaps he'd like to walk together We chatted and walked and he described a life that spoke to me of a cardboard house on an estate of the same, shopping trip on Saturdays, ASDA, Halfords, B&Q, men like rugby and women look after children. He was shy and awkward, nervous of seeming out of the ordinary, obviously used to living a life of conformity. Little did he know how strange the person he was talking to was, or that I didn't care how he lived as long as he was fulfilled. Eventually he revealed that he was a Christian; God had told him to make the walk today. I got a sense that he was dissatisfied with his life, that he didn't know where to go next. He saw a colleague and stutteringly explained that he was out for a walk. I suspected he felt judged for being seen with a woman who was not his wife.

Finally, in the last ten minutes of the detour, he tried to convert me to Christianity, telling me that I should try and see God in my life, that He was sending me messages.

"Maybe I'm a message to you from God", he said.

I pulled away, telling him that his way home was through the sand dunes and onto the beach, where he'd find a straight walk to the town. Maybe I'm *your* message from God, I thought irritably. Didn't I come along at just the right time and show you the way? And aren't I melting away to anonymity, leaving you when you're safely on the path towards home? There was a blinkered sense about him that irritated me: only one way to live life and anything unusual to be avoided, leaving him floundering in dissatisfaction when he wanted more but didn't know how to search for it. I was happy to turn away and head into the forest, leaving him to find his way home through the sand dunes. The ruins of a castle dominated my view, a double-storey broken building, ivy and stones. I was still resisting sleeping in a tent wherever possible and this night was too exciting to resist. I could sleep in a castle!

I was woken out of my moonlit slumber by people talking, coming up the spiral stone stairway to the upper floor where I'd made my bed. I sat up, fumbled my glasses on in time for their bright torch to sweep over me, bringing them to a halt. We paused, something swinging from the boy's hand and two or three dogs flickering in and out of the torchlight. One came up and licked the hand I was holding up against the light and this broke the spell, the boys backed away down the stairs.

"D'you wanna fag," one of them called out. I didn't answer, not wanting to confirm I was a woman, waiting for them to leave. As their lights swept away amongst the trees, I found my hands were trembling.

I hated to be discovered at night. Constrained by energy and budget, I needed to be able to have the flexibility to sleep anywhere, yet I wanted no-one to see where I was sleeping. I preferred it that way because every time I asked permission to camp somewhere, I was pointing to a place and saying, "Look, I, an unaccompanied woman, am going to be unconscious on the floor over there for the whole night." I couldn't do it. Staying hidden, stealthy, untraceable, hiding from other humans, was how I, as a solo female, kept myself safe. Too many years of propositions while hitchhiking, of furtive gropes in nightclubs, of women I knew being assaulted and raped, too many years of having to guard myself against male sexuality aggressively expressed. I didn't experience any negative incidents while I walked, none at all, but maybe that's because I was so careful about hiding myself. There's a deep vulnerability in lapsing into sleep in public, both in an animal sense and as a woman alone.

Leaves skipped and tumbled alongside me, keeping my pace as I walked the length of the seaweed-strewn beach towards Porthcawl. Storms were forecast so I hid in the town centre, waiting out the 50mph winds. First a shower at the gym, then coffee in the ice-cream parlour, watching the ancient Italian vanguard chatting at a back table as their children polished and cleaned their inheritance, serving and nodding with long-practised recognition.

An old man acting confused, army medals pinned to his jacket, out of place anywhere else, but here just 'Dai', known, accepted, even if only with amused tolerance. I imagined the beach out there, battering me with wind and noise, and turned away, heading instead to a cheap, anonymous pub. I folded down into a deep seat with a sigh, attracting the attention of an elderly woman nearby. We chatted a bit and she offered to buy me lunch in memory of her son who had died from cancer long before but hadn't been forgotten. Hers was yet another ordinary face with a heart-felt history. I accepted and began looking at the menu but I wasn't really ready for food yet and began daydreaming, watching the windows from the comfort of my bucket-seat. I could see scraps and papers flying through the air outside, people staggering on street corners as the waiting gusts slapped them, umbrellas turned inside out. Swags of wiring swung like skipping-ropes, wildly careening in the air, way up over the streetlights.

Suddenly the woman came over to the table, coat on. She'd put £20 behind the bar – for someone on my budget it was an incredible amount for just one meal. I stammered my thanks; as usual my gratitude was too huge to express without embarrassment. I stuffed myself with a burger and ice-cream and still had enough credit for two cheese baguettes. The foil-wrapped baguette bullets were still warm as I took them, packing them away carefully for later consumption.

The storm passed over Porthcawl as I ate my gifted meal, and I left the pub to make progress in the couple of hours left before dark. The setting sun reflected on silver sands and I followed flat roads to the edge of town, where I found a small secluded field to put my tent up in, just before the sandy golf course began. I sat in the tented dimness feeling peaceful, knowing that, although it gets incredibly hard and sometimes I'm tired or sad or fed up, there's a part of me that never stops enjoying this.

The following day I walked all the way past Port Talbot, stopping for a while in a pub where violence simmered. It had grubby carpets and peeling wallpaper, warnings against drug-taking papered all the way to the toilets. This was a place where people were careful of eye contact, where people sat and stared into space while others muttered conversations in corners or held court at the bar. I walked around the huge domineering steelworks, the strange steams and smells, the grand pipeworks and chimney. It was an unfriendly place for a long-distance walker, there was nowhere to sit or stop. I had to keep winding on through the long thin line of estates that filled the unpleasant space between the motorway and the works. Eventually I made it to the seaside part of town, a long concrete promenade giving way to high walls of sand dunes, and I could finally feel I was distant enough from people to tent up in the centre of the dunes and sleep.

A long, hard day on tarmac and my feet were throbbing. I'd overstretched myself, walked past my usual ten- or twelve-mile limit, through discomfort and into too much pain. I followed with great care the usual routines of foot-rubs, easing the tension out of my muscles as much as possible, stretching my calves, wiggling my ankles, trying to make sure that they wouldn't hurt again tomorrow.

The final baguette made my tent supper, sitting with the door open watching the sand change colour with the darkening sky. I was sick overnight. I'd waited too long to eat the warm food received in the pub and it had obviously fermented in its foil wrappings. A moonlit tummy upset, scraping sand to cover my unpleasant leavings. I felt weak and shaky the next day, but fortunately it was only six miles to Swansea where I had another place to stay: Neil and Clare, a friendly couple I'd met on the Cistercian Way near Tenby. Months later I was finally here, to accept their offer of a bed. It was mostly a barren roadside trudge along the main motorway turnoff into the city, enlivened by a couple of quiet miles along the Tennant canal. I kept meeting older, weathered men who would walk alongside me for a while and tell me their life-stories in thick Swansea accents, a total pleasure to listen to.

During a few nights camping on my way to the tip of the Gower, I bedded down in a churchyard. That night the chill wind whipped over me straight from the sea and I was way too cold, my sleeping bag was too thin to withstand windy autumn nights. The wild camping had to stop; it was time to retreat inside the tent. I still kept at it though, always looking for a way to avoid the hassle of putting up a tent.

An unsettling experience on my way back to Swansea made me reconsider the ethics of wild camping.

It was getting dark as I came to a thin strip of road lined by a bank of rich houses on one side, an open area of land leading to cliff edge on the other. The Gower is where the rich South Walians escape to. I saw empty houses, second homes, high-class building work being done; blue glass balconies and large windows were clear markers of modern, monied architecture. The ribbon of road led to a farm in a cleft between higher hills and the coastal path turned away over open grassland to follow along the edge of the cliffs. The problem was the cows. They roamed the space between the houses and the sea. There was nowhere to hide from them, just scattered gorse bushes, too spiky and unfriendly to wriggle under. Nowhere to put up a sleeping space without the chance that a cow would come and trample me, its heavy, clumsy hooves thudding onto my tender legs. All the space that was flat and narrow enough to lay a tired body down on had been investigated, churned and opened wide by bovine traffic. I couldn't face trudging off along the cliffs, not knowing for how long the open area would continue, or what would come next. The sun was setting and I'd walked enough, I had to stop soon.

I kept looking into the houses along the left-hand side of the road, hoping for an obviously empty house or a building site open enough for me to sneak into and lie down in a corner. Nothing seemed easy, and I was too timid to venture into the ones that seemed possible, fearing to be seen by neighbours. There was nowhere safe to sleep and it was starting to get dark.

The final house was a bungalow behind a high hedge. Noticeably shabbier than the others, it had a forlorn, abandoned feeling to it, unmown grass and drawn curtains. I walked in through the gate and wondered, could I sleep here? It was the last definitely cow-free place before the open cliffs. There was a quiet orchard beyond the lawn, grass grown long and folded, apples dropped and rotting. I walked to the bungalow and knocked, thinking perhaps I'd ask permission to sleep in the garden but there was no answer. Empty house, I thought, and walked around the back to the orchard, laying out my tarpaulin. But I was wrong.

Boom! My heart jumped in my chest. There was movement inside the house.

"I'm sorry, I needed a safe place to sleep, away from the cows, and I wanted to camp in your garden. I knocked at the door and thought the house was empty."

It was so hard to go back to the door and say these words, but I had to immediately admit my mistake. I was totally in the wrong and had to accept the force of the owner's displeasure.

"Why would I open the door when someone knocks on it?"

The man kept his body behind the door, just his head sticking out, bespectacled and glaring, a mixture of bald pink skin and unkempt hair. He was incredibly angry and frightened. A strong smell of weed came flooding through the doorway; the house was saturated with it.

"No-one answers the door any more. It's all phone-calls nowadays."

This felt very immediately not OK, a situation fraught with unpredictability and therefore potentially dangerous. I judged it

239

best to apologise and back away, hurriedly pack my bag and retreat, head bowed. He was right to be upset, whatever the logic of the world he held close inside his home.

I was sorry that I'd accidentally breached the security of his retreat. Sorry that I had accidentally made a paranoid person's world view worse, their perceptions less trustworthy.

I'd trespassed on that man's property, so fixated on my own needs I forgot that it was all trespassing, every time I bedded down somewhere without permission.

I closed the gate, shamefaced, and returned to the previous problem. Twilight now, and cows still roaming. I walked a short way towards the farm and turned in at the next field. Once I'd climbed over the gate, trespassing again, there was a long tractor-trailer with a single axle, left down on the ground so that its back end lifted high into the air. A diagonal of planks and metal, with enough room for me to wriggle underneath, my head almost under the thick metal axle, positioning my body carefully to avoid a stray coil of wire and the light rain that was starting to fall. I was starting to relax into sleep when a tractor came along the lane and paused, engine rattling, by the entrance to the field. The gate opened and the tractor came through it.

What was happening? All these unexpected people! As the tractor roared into the field and swung around towards the hay bales, I struggled out of my sleeping-bag so as not to be caught vulnerable on the ground. I stood near the trailer for safety, but far enough away that I would be caught in the beam of the headlights as the tractor swung around towards the bales, golden drops of water misting the air. I was the unexpected one, the trespasser, I had to make myself known and await his response. Anger, punishment, whatever that was.

"Oh that's OK," the man said. "Don't worry, I won't tell the boss…"

It was a surprisingly casual response that came so often from the people who worked the land when they found me in barns, sleeping on commons, or under an upended trailer next to a stack of huge black plastic hay-bales. I told the tractor-driver the story of the accidental intrusion next door and he said the guy was dangerous, known for his odd habits, had attacked other locals, wasn't a friendly neighbour. We wound up talking about his time as a security guard in Swansea; he was friendly and relaxed, trotting out his best stories as if we were round a table in a pub, not standing together in a dark field. He was a silhouette in the headlights, the fibrous outline of his woollen cap and clothing glowing bright gold. I don't think I told him of my fundraising heroics, just remained an anonymous, apparently homeless figure.

I returned to Swansea with the promise of another night with Neil and Clare. Could I stay and have a rest day? I tried to take a rest day once a week but really it was when the opportunity manifested; I never spent a whole day in a tent, it was too intimidating to camp for two nights in the same spot, remain where anyone could come back to find me. Instead I took days when a friend's house appeared en route, or if someone offered me an empty place to stay. I was ready to rest all the time; it was never a case of appropriate timing – only an appropriate place.

I was unused to asking and felt nervous in my hidden need. Asking for help brought me closer to the desperation that would follow a refusal.

"Yes, but we're going away for the weekend."

They left me a key and said goodbye half-way through Friday afternoon. I tried to pretend that I really would leave the following morning, but I knew I'd stay for the weekend. An empty flat was too tempting, the chance to wallow in junk food and television. I needed the blankness, the blessed relief of not walking.

I had to give in to the desire to stop, allow myself the rest I needed, but not allow myself to let the journey go by omission. I was afraid that I might keep stopping until I'd quit without ever stating the fact, without ever admitting that I found it too difficult. It was how I did things: how I'd failed my A-levels, how I'd given up on creative projects, how I'd given up on anything I was uncomfortable with. I'd slink away without facing the reality of failure, never admitting out loud that I couldn't do it.

I knew deep down that I had this quality within myself and didn't want to do it with this walk. I couldn't quit, it was too important to me. Ovarian cancer had taken over my life, first through my own illness and then my desire to tell women about the symptoms. I had to finish, to walk back to hospital. I'd set myself this insane target and I wouldn't let it slip away into nothing. I had to guard against my own tendencies but also allow myself the rest my body screamed for. I needed it to keep strong enough to complete this journey.

I prised myself, unwillingly, from the sofa of the Swansea flat on Sunday afternoon and set out north again. This time I headed directly towards Llandovery, and then resumed the mountain paths I'd followed southwards on the Cambrian Way. There were differences, approaching mountains from different faces, walking through different valleys, but the peaks were the same, I was going towards Plynlimon, Cader Idris, the Rhinogs, Cnicht, Snowdon, Glyders, Carneddau and descending again to Conwy.

The weather got colder as I headed inland. I loved the thrill of poking my head out of the tent in the mornings to discover that I'd survived a frosty night, my sleeping spot leaving a wonderful green patch in a crystal-white field corner. I was enjoying myself, despite the soggy tent and painful feet. I'd given up on trail mix, it tasted fine but the idea of eating it repulsed me. Fortunately, the meal repetition of cold couscous and mackerel remained appetising.

Waking up with a cold nose, poking outside my sleeping bag hood to see if it was light yet; pausing as I came down the hill into a silent, peaceful wooded valley and seeing a heron glide below me around the curve of a small river; trudging up a country lane; resting my pack against a fence post while I checked my map; early-morning fog lying low in the valley bottoms; the sun shining suddenly over a hill, lighting the remaining leaves on the trees around me with a pure yellow light; helping stranded worms to cross safely to the other side of the road; my new hat which had a huge bobble on it; copper bracken glowing in the sunlight, muddy farmyards, puddles in lanes... I loved all of this. Late November and if this was winter, I could handle it.

I was irritated to realise I'd planned badly for this section, finding myself without maps to cover my path over the western edge of the Black Mountain. I'd have to go by road instead, climbing up the safe way to cross the moorland between Brynamman and Dyffryn Tywi. This was a time where I sorely missed a support-team. Without help, minor problems grew to the size of a route diversion.

I'd had a great morning in Brynamman, waking up in a misty field, frost just beginning to creep around the edges of leaves and grass. After a few miles on the road I came to the village. Three women were standing at the door of a pharmacy, waving at me.

"Well done!" they said "Keep going! Call in at the Brynamman Community Centre, they're waiting for you."

They gave me packets of energy tablets and a £5 donation. Further up, into the village, there was the Centre. I found myself at the table of the café, bemused, with a huge cooked breakfast in front of me. Someone had recognised me on the road and phoned ahead, told them who I was and that they should treat me. Every pot of tea during that cold walking-time tasted incredible, hot and bitter and smooth. I gorged myself on a full plate of hot meat and oil, beans and bread and felt wonderful.

The day went downhill from there. I'd aimed to stay in the Llanddeusant Youth Hostel; after two nights camping, in freezing or near zero degree conditions, it was time to treat myself to a cheap bed. I'd have to push it a bit but I could do it, I reckoned. Fifteen miles was more than I could usually manage at that time, throbbing foot-pain usually setting in after about thirteen miles; but the thought of a bed and a shower drove me to try it. It was a solid tarmac trudge up and over the Black Mountain pass, pushing and pushing onwards, up into the clouds and down again, winding around the bends of the mountain road and into the wet farmlands on the other side. I kept checking my maps: seven miles to go and it was 3pm, two hours until sunset.

My feet started to really hurt, strong pain in the heels. I sat down and took my boots off for a while, the wet concrete soaking my legs. Adrenalin kicked in and I strode on, still a few miles to go as darkness fell, but I strapped my torch into my belt and continued, willing myself towards the bed waiting for me.

I walked in pitch black for the last hour, sweating up the last steep hill, pushing myself forward. I found myself focusing on a light ahead in the darkness and chanting to myself in a whisper over and over again, *That. Is where. I'm going. That. Is where. I'm going.* I was on auto-pilot, keeping myself in movement until I could reach the hostel and relax. Seven hours of near constant walking, fighting foot-pain, just keeping myself going and going.

I reached the hostel. It was closed.

The doors locked, the building dark, just a single light on above the central door. Oh... No way. I rattled the doors, I knocked, I chucked gravel up at the lit window, I shouted out. Nothing.

I was going to have to sleep in the wet tent. I loved my borrowed tent, except for one problem. In the mornings, there was condensation inside and out, so when I took the tent down it all soaked together. All day strapped to my rucksack with no chance for it to dry meant I had to put up a damp tent to sleep in. I'd been camping like this for three days running and was fed up.

I laid down in the wet tent, feeling my legs sticking out below me like stiff boards, the muscles tensed and held tight. I pounded my thighs with my fists in an attempt at tough massage, running my palms up and down until I felt them release a little. It took a good hour for my feet to stop throbbing, in all the many ways which they do: the bones, the ankles, the tendons underneath. I rubbed them and stretched and rubbed them and stretched until finally they relaxed. I'd walked too far that day and, in the end, for nothing.

I got up the next morning feeling rubbish – grumpy about the hostel and with stabs of pain running from my feet into my ankles. Too much distance yesterday meant I needed to take it easy today. It was a precarious balance; if I pushed myself too hard I'd have to stop, I could feel that my feet wouldn't take it. I walked until Myddfai where I found a visitor centre with lots of polite and interested people who donated loads of money. That made me feel better. They also mentioned a bunkhouse in Llandovery; I felt like I was owed a bed. I made it to The Level Crossing Bunkhouse and stopped. It was kind of a half day, even though I walked eight miles, but I needed it.

The hostel dormitory was empty apart from me; a quiet bar downstairs, just a single old man propping up the counter, grey and bearded. I talked to the landlady about what I was doing, and it turned out she'd had ovarian cancer. Fifteen years clear. It was good to meet someone who'd survived that long, given the low five-year survival rates. We had hugs and a selfie; it was a useful post to put online, remind people why I was doing this, prompt them to share the symptoms or donate. I had a steady stream of small donations into my tin day-to-day and a trickle of larger donations online, prompted by my regular social media updates. Every time a donation bigger than £30 came in it was a cause for celebration, thrilling that I'd inspired someone to give so much. I'd raised a few thousand pounds by now and was starting to believe the target of £10,000 was feasible.

I spent three beautiful days coming over the hills from Llandovery to Rhayader, the weather cold and bright, bringing the best of the colour out of the oranges and browns of dead bracken and fallen leaves, highlighting the whites and greens of sleeping foliage. This was the middle of the country, barren and bare of towns, with only scattered houses and thin ribbons of road laying a thin web of human presence over a land too huge to feel overcome by it.

In and out of safety I skirled, temperatures dropping down to near-freezing every night, mornings of frost-crusted grasses: hopping between nights out in the chilled wet leaves and shivering winds, and the hosted comfort of friendly hugs and hot meals.

The coldest night I spent outside was near the upper reaches of the Elan River. I said goodbye to my lovely friends Sam and Noel, walking a short way from Elan Village with them before Sam's pregnant belly held them to a short stroll, and we had long hugs goodbye.

It was a beautiful day in the wilderness, walking around the many reservoirs of the Elan Valley complex, eventually climbing away from the thin slivers of water and walking along a long straight valley with very few farms along it. The wiry, coarse grass still showed the soil to be that of the boggy, unfertile uplands. There was just a thin strip of tarmac road and the occasional car, this road linking Rhayader and Cwmystwth, climbing and winding across the Cambrian high ground.

I found a tucked-away flat place to make camp, held in the curve of a rise of ground. There's no relaxing when you camp in the winter, no sitting and staring before sleep. I couldn't even sit down in the tent without the insulation of my sleeping-bag around me, needing it zipped up to my chin, hood over my hat and head, any exposed skin on chest or hands would soon become numbed with cold. Winter camping meant constantly monitoring my body temperature, because once that was gone I wouldn't get it back without moving again. I was still in my three-season sleeping-bag, it was close to the margin of safety. I could feel the dullness of the surrounding cold, a blank-faced solidity that hits the senses like an open-handed slap. I was almost too cold to sleep, I hunched into a ball to shield my innards from molecular slowdown, pressing my little handwarmer heat bundle onto my lower back, which I'd found was the best place to spread heat around my body.

In the morning I reached up a tentative finger to find my breath frozen to the inside of the tent, scuffled the thermometer within eyesight and found a reading of -4°C. Pride and intimidation all at once, that I'd survived this night outside. To get up properly I had to brace myself for movement, poised to rip aside the covers and dress with speed and efficiency, not allow the unnecessary emanation of my carefully-hoarded body-heat. I'd only taken off the outside layers – my fleece waistcoat, my waterproof jacket and trousers – but they all had to be immediately put back on again to insulate me. Hat, gloves, neckwarmer. It had to be quick movement, no dreaming: jerkily dress, breathing hard in short blows and gasps, then immediately pack down the tent, frost crumbling away and dribbling down the fabric like windblown sand.

I couldn't bring myself to walk straight away, and sat on the nearby metal road-barrier to come to, unwilling to be fully awake.

The sun had risen but the surrounding hills were too high to allow more than a diffuse pink dawn light into the valley. A single bird flapped dark and searching across the stillness, and I watched the land sit in its cold until I realised I was slowly freezing to the metal, my bottom heating and melting the ice. I pulled my trousers away from the metal, small scratching sounds as ice crystals shattered, and walked away along the valley floor. Within half a mile the path turned away from the road and climbed a hill, still yellowed white in its night-flung frost blanket. I crossed a small river, the wooden bridge furred with ice-crystals and the water a blue-black jewel-seam between white banks. There was a low boulder a short way up the hill, glowing above the sunline, and I sat there to eat my breakfast, mixing water into muesli, taking sips of the freshness of the ice-cold liquid. The sun glowed from a misty blue sky, creating diamond flashing grasses, feathered in a thousand sparks.

It was hard to walk in such low temperatures. I kept dropping down into cold valley bottoms or plunging through forest. The movement kept me warm from the inside, but when I arrived at my host's in Llangurig that night and ran a bath, the hot water tingled against my cold, cold skin; a sign my clothing wasn't robust enough for full-time winter-walking.

I scaled Plynlimon in a day – much easier without my bag. Jenni, my Llangurig host, got her mother to take it all the way around the bottom of the mountain for me, 43 miles through Aberystwyth and up to Machynlleth. I'd take the direct route – a fifteen mile walk. I followed the rubble road past the Sweet Lamb rally complex, then cut away before it led into the Hafren forest for a steep pull up the grassy mountain to the frozen parts, where ice-crystals nestled in grassy hollows, clustered against the clawing wind. At the final fence white frost outlined every wire and surrounding grass blade; crystals electrified, standing outstretched to the grey air.

The rocky summit was a monotone blend, grey stone holding quiet within a coat of white. Each rock emanated cold, an infinity of freezing condensed inside it like the sad-eyed Groke. I'd climbed this journey's first winter mountain and it felt fine. Coated in woolly and waterproof layers, covered against cold and wet, I could sit happy at the top and eat handfuls of peanuts, savouring them in the window of time before inactivity lowered my body-temperature. My cheeks felt iced by the wind but I was so happy to be here witnessing this beauty, swallowing chill water from my blue metal bottle, my heart pumping good hot blood around my body.

It felt great, this slow mountain pull and an easy descent on the other side, down to the familiar friendliness of James and Vicky. I didn't stop to rest as often and could feel the power inside me. Released from the weighted cage of my rucksack, my body felt like an endless machine, reliably pushing me upwards from the ground, carrying me forward for miles.

I was back in Machynlleth the next day, picking up my bag, and then walking a short way out of town where friends in their little cottage lay on my path. I could stay there overnight before heading north towards Cader Idris. First I'd head up and over a pine-planted line of hills and down into Abergynolwyn, an easy day before heading out to cross the shoulder of Cader Idris at the head of the Dysynni valley. It felt like it should be a simple day, but I discovered I'd gone off the edge of one map and didn't have the next one. There was a small corner of my journey missing, the route untraceable, so I sat with my friends Ruth and Scott and pieced it together from their paper maps, taking photos of the route, listening to their directions of crossroads, lefts and rights and following tracks. It seemed simple, and I walked upwards with Ruth the next morning along the stone access-road into the forest, hearing her stories of growing up in this place, a dream holiday-cottage that she'd finally been able to come to live in. We crossed the stream that was her water supply, pushing through a rusted gate and into the forest itself, saying goodbye at the final tin-roofed cottage before waves of trees became all there were for miles ahead. The cottage doorway was a dark hole leading to a green-rimed dankness of ferns, moss and tumbled stone, remnants of farm life overtaken by compulsory purchases, dreams lying dormant awaiting potential purchasers to bring human settlement back again.

I followed the track upwards, winding in sinuous curves along the contour lines, sometimes tall waving trees alongside, sometimes the blasted aftermath of felled forest.

From Ruth's directions I knew I'd come to a fence eventually, but this seemed too soon. The land fell steeply away in front of me, but there were more pines ahead at the base of the hill, a square of green field in the middle of them. I didn't have a map to check my position, didn't know where I was in relation to these serried ranks of silent trees. I knew I needed to cross a hill and decided to head downwards, thinking I'd probably come out on the other side of the Tarrens. I climbed over the fence and descended the steep field, carefully placing my feet so as not to slip. Every step down was a commitment to continue, considering the difficulty of scrambling back up the slope again. Stubbornness prevented me turning back, retracing my steps, covering ground I'd already walked. It was hard enough to walk this land once, I couldn't face the hideous spectre of wasted effort.

At the base of the field there was no pathway and I plunged into the forest itself. It quickly became horribly difficult. The trees were clogged, growing feet apart, branches linking and mingling; there was no space between them, not even winding animal tracks, just thin twigs reaching and pine-needles falling like skin-flakes in a constant whispering rain against my clothing. All I could do was push and push against them, holding my arms against my face and using them to hold away the scratching claws that formed such a solid barrier.

I felt pinioned in all directions, a limp puppet in the grasp of blind branches. I could try and fall in any direction but I'd remain upright. I knew that if I hurt myself, if I placed my feet in a way that made me fall and break a leg, I could die there and no-one would find me until the trees were harvested, thirty years in the future. It had happened near here before. It was impossible to see me; no-one knew I was there, I'd taken a wrong turning, wasn't even on an expected path. No other human would come here until the trees were cleared, one by one – a great machine grabbing and chopping at them until my skeleton was released, bones dangling and swaying like Christmas ornaments, ragged clothing hanging in streamers.

I came to a place where the trees cleared, but found that it was because there was a series of steep boulder-drops; no earth to root trees, but gorse grew there, spiky, unfriendly gorse. I was forced to keep descending, picking through prickles, awkwardly lowering myself off the rocks to unknown footholds beneath, trying to keep a solid footing on writhing roots. I fell awkwardly, wrenching one leg to the side as I tried to keep my balance. It was an irritating, arduous slog and there was nothing I could do but keep descending. I'd committed myself to this stupid route the moment I'd crossed the fence and started down the steep, steep field.

Eventually, hours later, I emerged on the track and stopped to take a photo of myself: a sulky-faced woman in a needle-pinned bobble hat, green streaks of smeared lichen dirtying her yellow jacket. There were pine-needles everywhere; I pulled handfuls out from the back of my neck, my hood, hat and pockets, even found them in my bra that night. I'd been thoroughly investigated by the forest – pinioned, probed and discarded. There was no way I'd make that mistake again.

I looked around: a stone track going left and right and rolling hills of lined pine in every direction. I genuinely had no idea where I was and no map to work it out. I chose a direction – right – hoping it would eventually lead me out to somewhere I could identify. I was only five miles from my home town, surely I had to recognise the shape of the land eventually. I came down around the hills through a fox-hunt, dogs lolling and lolloping around the road as men in well-worn clothing, beanie hats and fleeces made the barest glimpse of eye contact, busy in their own world and used to being judged by those that don't know them. I eventually got a lift with one outrider who welcomed me into his jeep, long radio antenna waving gently above it. Seven foxes that day, he told me, all in the Pennal area. Pennal, that was where we were coming out. I knew it so well, could point out the houses where my old ladies had lived; I'd come here regularly as a care worker. I stood by the side of the road and a friend pulled over within minutes, giving me a lift back to the cottage I'd waved goodbye to that morning, Ruth and Scott bemused but happy to host me again.

I took a rest day, tired and irritated. I was waiting for my fantastic new sleeping-bag to arrive anyway, and would have to return to Machynlleth to collect it so I gave up again, in a small way, and waited there for it to arrive. The next day I tried again, waving Ruth off for the second time in the forest, resolving to be more careful. I came to the end of the track and continued upwards into the trees, but where I came to the dead end I looked around and saw a thin gap in the trees I should have turned towards, only a short fumble through branches before it widened out into a path: narrow dark peat lining a small stream, moss muffling the ground between the trees. The path was trodden away to dark peat where I walked, following a thin stream out towards another fence with endless misty ground beyond and there I was, on the right track to cross upwards and over, down into Abergynolwyn.

There'd been a confusion over phone numbers. Having no mobile signal, I squeezed into a phone box and spoke to a mystery voice, waiting in the dark and drizzle for the next strange person and their bed, not feeling in the mood for interaction. An awkward meeting in the dark, speaking to a silhouette, took me to a small house with an open coal fire where I could huddle close on the hearthstone, stuff my sodden boots with paper and sit quietly steaming while daughter Matilda jumped over my legs and mother Sarah made tea. It was comforting and homely. These were deeply ordinary people, with a hidden thread of quirk running through them, and the atmosphere was relaxing and happy.

Sometimes I felt I was in an endless chain of favours: tea in cafés, people buying me meals, getting ferried to a house following a Facebook message, clothes washed, bath run, food cooked. I couldn't even wash up in return, shrill rebuttals meeting any offer of help. Accepting it felt like a crushing responsibility. Guilt, I suppose. I felt overwhelmed by all the giving, unworthy. Each gift of help meant so much to me, it was a hand reached out to pull me along through a hard and unforgiving journey. Each time I received help it was a piece of tenderness that enabled me to relax from constant alert, always aware of my money dripping away or my personal safety.

I wanted to hug, to cry, to give heartfelt thank-yous but realised this made people uncomfortable. For me it was an important experience, for them mundane. I learned to accept their gifts quietly and gracefully, eventually gauging that this was ordinary generosity. I was just a houseguest for a single night, one of many in the course of years.

I realised that for many women, the drivers of my invitations and hospitality, I was just another person to be looked after.

"Do you want a packed lunch?" they'd ask, as I sat humbly eating their breakfast.

"Yes, if it's not too much trouble."

I didn't want to make a fuss, be a burden. But whizz, slap, slap and it was done: sandwiches in a bag with crisps and cake, and suddenly I was aware of their years of child-rearing, whether their children were tumbling and squawking around the house or long past university. I understood that I was just a small part of their years of care and tenderness, and that it was OK to accept this from them. I was mothered in small and large ways by hundreds of women in Wales, in awe of what I was doing, inspired to help in any way they could. I was doing something that intimidated them, sleeping outside, spending days alone. I was responding to my ovarian cancer, suffering for it, in a way that impressed other people. Some saw me as a woman alone in the world, challenged and in danger. Whatever their reasons, whether it was cancer or adventure or feminist-inspired, they helped me and it took me a while to realise that this was normal.

Gale-force winds and hail, said the forecast. I wasn't sure if I should climb Cader Idris. The route would take me away from Abergynolwyn and over the shoulder of it, climbing up to the head of the Dysinni valley – which ended in a curved bowl of land – and dropping down towards Fairbourne to take the railway crossing to Barmouth. I tacked my way up the side of the steepness, pausing at rock-scattered sheep-pens, the first places for farmers to contain their sheep as they corralled them down off the high lands for childbirth or medication.

Of course I climbed Cader! It's my favourite mountain and I was only a mile and a half from the peak. The winds were strong but the summit was clear; once I'd climbed out of the valley basin I could see it! I dumped my bag by the fence, stuffed my pockets with Sarah's sandwiches to eat at the top and set off, bracing myself with my walking-poles, wary of the hundreds of metres of rocky cliff that fell down to Llyn y Gadair on my left. The gusts were only occasional but they were strong, buffeting and bashing me, forcing me to stop and brace to make sure they didn't bowl me over. I went steadily to the summit, keeping at least a tumble and roll away from the sheer drop at all times, rocks gradually whitening with accumulated frost and hail, small patches of snow. I looked at the snow and worried: what would Snowdon be like further north – would I manage to climb that, too?

It started to hail, sharp needles stinging my face. I turned against the wind until it died down, standing like a statue and allowing the sharp points of pain to spatter against my water-proofed, padded back. The clouds moved quickly overhead, patches of sun-shaft brightness alternating with dark storm-grey, raking over the route I'd climbed.

Up to the trig point, a photo, a video, a sandwich in the bothy and down again to where I left my rucksack. Two and a half hours. I reached the bottom of the mountain at 3pm. I could have camped anywhere around there – it was all open, inviting land – but I had an invitation to stay in Barmouth, just five miles further on. I could do it, I thought, a bed would be nice. So I descended to the road, as daylight became twilight and then darkened to pitch-black, down the steep steep hill, pained feet pressing against the front of my boots, and finally across the 700m long railway bridge that spanned the estuary. The bridge seemed endless in the darkness. I concentrated on the small circle of my torchlight highlighting the planks under my feet, the wind whistling through the wires that separated me from the trainline. My feet were stones by this point, just thudding, blunt and heavy, down to the ground, over and over. A train rumbled past me, the whole bridge shaking. I shone the torch down to the water and felt dizzy as soon as I saw the sea rushing inland, white foam stirred by the tide and wind. I was a small thing in the face of the mass of metal, the elements of wind and water.

I arrived, wind-shocked, at the warm and steamy Mermaid chippy. After an eleven-hour walk through high winds and hail, battering myself up a mountain and down again, I was done in. Dianna had phoned ahead; I could have whatever I wanted while I waited for her to finish her spinning class. The lady behind the counter couldn't hear me – my voice becomes very small when I'm tired – but I managed to repeat myself a few times and make my request understood.

"Large chips, peas, gravy, mayonnaise, cup of tea and a can of coke." A meal for comfort, not nutrition. I ate it all, slowly and carefully, and sat back, sighed. Restored.

Dianna's home was comfortable and relaxed. She brought out the decorations; it was time to do the Christmas tree. I didn't believe so many decorations could even fit on one tree, let alone look good but she kept encouraging me,

"Put more on, put more on," and she was right. The completed tree looked wonderful.

She dropped me in Barmouth the following morning. It was a great day for walking but I loitered in the town, snuffling coffee and toast in the converted church café, African drums and woven bags hanging where the organ used to be, high ceiling painted with stars. My urge to be out there in the gale force winds, trussed up in my waterproofs and rucksack, fighting to see out of my tear-spattered glasses, wiping drips from my nose, shoulders hurting from my rucksack, pain striking into my heels every time my feet hit the ground... Well, it was strangely absent.

My childhood favourite rock-shop was now closed for winter, but I went to the other famous Barmouth bargain shop, where everything comes in round orange bins with shovels for you to help yourself to your choice of dusty muesli, dried figs, powdered soup or peanuts. I shovelled up a selection of chocolates and sweets, feeling a childish excitement over strawberry creams, honeycomb crunch, toffees, chocolate limes, pastel smooth dolly-mixture, hard jelly beans, soft jelly babies, chocolate smarties. Now I had a bag to dip into, give myself small treats every few hours, the pleasure of surprising myself with a varied sugar hit would help my spirits withstand December weather. I headed out of town, climbing up a steep, winding back road which started with small town houses that grew larger and more expensive-looking the higher I climbed, gazing back at the increasingly-costly view over the bay.

More high winds were on their way and I decided to take the lowland route, up the west side of the Rhinogs and cut through Bwlch Drws-Ardudwy. Most of the high route would have been fine to climb, but the descent from Y Llethr was a sheer slope that I really didn't want to tackle in bad weather. It had been difficult to climb back in the autumn, a sheer gravel-lined gash in the turf that felt almost vertical. Descending it would be worse: a horrible slow step with knees aching, balancing with walking-poles, feet ready to slip out from underneath me, especially when strong winds were battering and blowing. Instead, I took a path through the middle ground between busy coast and rocky hills, in a gentle landscape of grasses and sheep, ancient stone bridges crossing small streams. That night I slept in Cwm Nantcol, a small sweet valley at the base of the Rhinogs. It had the feeling of a valley end, only a thin pass snaking on between the two mountains, the farms occupying the fertile land in the valley floor. Stone-walled field edges crept up higher until they could enclose no more, leaving the sprouting wild land above, sheep released to roam and tame it as best they could. I came past the farms, out past the last stone wall, and trod down an oval in the bracken and heather to make a springy bed, pushing the tent pegs almost horizontally into the thin layer of soil between roots and rock.

It was -2°C in the tent in the morning but I'd been cosy all night; this new sleeping bag was such a good investment.

I walked the day through the mountain pass and into the forest beyond, coming out on the plains of Trawsfynydd, with just a few more miles to the edge of the reservoir where I could cross a long wire bridge and end up in the village itself. Trawsfynydd feels isolated in such open plains, the nuclear power-station looming from the other side of the lake.

There was a youth hostel here and I went in, pleased to find a cheap place to sleep. Once the reception closed I was alone in the building, a strange and lonely feeling. I ate a disgusting meal of tuna and noodles, the only food I'd found suitable in the corner shop; my brain was tired and dull, blankly staring at shelves of colourful packaging. I couldn't bring myself to finish this lump of claggy carbs, sitting alone in the empty faceless kitchen. Still, I woke at 4am to hear the wind and rain blowing outside my tiny bedroom window and was very glad I wasn't camping.

Next day brought me a walk through farmland around the Trawsfynydd reservoir; the rain continued to come, sheeting down on me and soaking me through. I had to walk with one eye closed

Base of Tryfan

Sunset on Western Anglesey

2000 mile celebration

Cloud inversion from the top of Snowdon

Descending from Snowdon

January oak apples
on Pen Llyn

Feet up waiting for a lift on Pen Llyn

Marshlands near Harlech

Sun dappled hill in the Dyfi Valley

Taking a break
on the way up
Aran Fawddwy

Peat pools near summit of Aran Fawddwy

Sunset at Newport, Cardigan

Wales Coastal Path markers were very useful

Seeing how my feet felt in the sea at Newgale

Swimming in the Teifi

Drying kit after a rainy night on the Pembrokeshire Coastal Path

Rain in Llanelli saying goodbye to Helen

Route planning for the Rivers Taff and Usk

Boots off for breakfast by Usk reservoir

Coming under the bridge for the last time

Evening firey sunset on the River Wye

Gifted coffee and cake in Builth Wells

At the finish line

against the amount of water that was driving against my face. I stopped in the visitor-centre café and poured water out of my sleeves. I was truly saturated, peeling off my waterproofs to let them dry as much as possible in the brief hour I could spend inside. I nursed a pot of tea and watched the rain beat against the huge windows. I felt scared of winter and needed comfort. Were the next three months going to be like this? Always wet and fighting cold? And what about Snowdon? The route lay directly over Snowdon; I'd feel really disappointed if I went around it. If there was rain down here there would be snow up there. Could I climb a wintry mountain with my huge rucksack and incomplete kit?

It continued to rain that afternoon as I walked to Maentwrog, the village that lay at the head of the Dwyryd Estuary, the first place where cars could cross the river. There was a large hotel there, the kind that was a coaching inn for several centuries, with large wide rooms and tucked-away nooks and crannies. I went for a huge Sunday lunch, a buffet where you can load huge spoonfuls of mashed potato and roast parsnips on top of your slices of beef and cover the whole thing in as much gravy as you like. I sat for a few hours eating and digesting the food, drinking a lovely pint, my waterproofs laid out on the surrounding chairs to dry out. The post-meal sloth grew and grew until I couldn't bear the idea of strapping on my bag again, heading out of the hotel to go and find a soggy place to camp for a damp, uncomfortable, shivery night. I booked a room. I really couldn't afford it, even though it was the smallest there was. It cost me £50 – more than I tried to spend in a week. I berated myself as I lay in the single bed; a plastic packet of biscuits and nice wallpaper wasn't worth the drain on my resources. I had to get stronger, had to manage properly what I was trying to do here, not freak out at the last minute and spend money I couldn't afford just to make my life temporarily easier. I stuffed in a cooked breakfast the next morning, ate endless rounds of toast, sneaking yoghurts into my rucksack from the buffet. Now I'd climb again, over the high land behind the Moelwyns.

There was a spooky valley of abandoned houses that led up from behind the railway line at Tanygrisiau, collapsed rafters poking into the air like a heap of bones, the whole valley empty, leading up to the disused slate mines of Cwmorthin at the top, stacked slate houses slowly degrading, tottering and leaning, roofs and windows gone. Cold air blew out of the mine entry, a hole in the hill that led into a dark and deep unknown. My torchlight showed nothing, the water-filled shaft-floor prevented me exploring any further, not that I was even tempted. I was heading another way I hadn't travelled before, around the spine of Cnicht and into the empty high territory, bypassing Beddgelert below me and leading towards a Snowdon approach from the East.

I slept a night up on the high lands behind Cnicht. The path led through thin grasses poking through a blanket of moss, and I found a spot where the land dipped and I could bed down out of the wind. There was even a small round pool not far away, stony-bottomed and clear enough for me to safely take water. It was a cosy night, no real frost and the wind ruffling the tent where it whipped over the rise of land from the west. The gentle lavender dusk picked the whitened wiry grass stalks out in rose.

It was a slow start again the next day, the usual routine of poking my nose out from my sleeping-bag before bracing to reveal the rest of me, packing up as quickly as possible before a final sit-down beside my full rucksack for as long as my dropping body temperature would allow it. I was high up in the hills but the land was gentle, swoops and rises and the lovely springiness of compacted peat to support my footsteps. I passed small pools of collected water and rusting pieces of ancient fencework. When I looked behind, past the knobbly peak of Cnicht, I saw the Glaslyn estuary where it joined Tremadoc Bay – low tide and silvered paths of water scribbled across the empty sands.

As I came to the top of the final rise, where the land dropped away down to the thin valley bottom and the road, Snowdon was there – unbelievably, hugely, right there. The whole mountain range was in view – I'd never seen it so clearly. Normally Snowdon appeared as a point, just a head crowning distantly behind other crowding rises, or a bulk seen crouched imposingly above. But across a wide rift of a valley I saw the whole thing, floating squat, weighty and...snow-topped. It was the moment I'd been dreading. I was supposed to climb it the following day. I'd known it was snowy, known I was heading for difficulty, but the visual assault of the huge mountain in its entirety brought a blank certainty. I couldn't get up that. I thought of the Watkins path ahead, sometimes a sheer tiptoe of rock footfalls in gravel and loose earth, the rattle of small stones ready to run away under each footweight, and sometimes a clamber between rocks, lifting each heavy boot knee-high to reach onto another bouldered step and lever up a heavy, burdened body.

I thought of my bamboo poles stabbing weakly at icy stone, badly held in closed fists, ready to slip and send me tottering and tumbling, weight-laden and clumsy. I thought of my boots, worn down and leaky, the rubber soles worn to slippery smoothness. I felt unprepared, unkitted-out for a snowy rock traverse and quailed in the face of it. Snowdon had loomed large in my mind during my frosty trek up the centre of the country, the most challenging part of my route; I hadn't wanted to acknowledge that I was unprepared.

I spent the night in the Pen-y-Pass hostel, feeling slightly separated from these happy young people who'd just spent the day ascending the highest mountain in Wales. I maundered in my bed, spreading kit out to dry and ignoring the fussy people who shared the dormitory. Shân, my north Wales stalwart, lived close to the next valley and I arranged to stay with her the following night. I could even leave my gear in the hostel, she'd pick it up during her commute and then pick me up later from the hotel just down the road from her house. All I had to do was walk over the shoulder of the Glyders, down past Tryfan and hitch a few miles to the hotel.

It wasn't a straightforward day. I wound upwards over swollen rushing streams, the water dusky blue and toppling downhill, swollen with ice-melt, and came up to the rocky shoulder of the mountain-top. Here was where I could detour up to the top of the Glyders, go and see the bouldered castle of the winds. But the clouds had descended and I was in mist already. A large patch of snow marked the place where the routes split, and I decided to see it as a sign of conditions higher up and descend instead. It was a relatively simple route down through the heather clumps and rocks, along the side of a swooping bowl that contained another mountain in the curl of it: Tryfan, a thin triangle of rock that was a sheer-sided scramble and the toughest Snowdonia mountain of them all. I'd pop out on the road that ran through the Ogwen valley and hitch a few miles along to the pub at Capel Curig. Which was fine until I became lost. The cloud thickened and I realised that I should have come to a sequence of lakes. Instead the heather and rocks hadn't stopped and I couldn't see further than about twenty metres to orientate myself with the map. I sat for a while, stumped, my waterproofs insulating me from the worst of the wetness, stopping to wipe the cloud droplets from my glasses and wonder, humorously, where I might be. I wasn't too worried, I knew that I'd come over the mountain and was heading in the right direction. As long as I continued to descend I'd reach the Ogwen valley floor, I just wasn't sure exactly where I'd pop out. A few hours of careful clambering later, I made the short hitchhike to the Tyn-y-coed pub with a man delivering tyres from Anglesey.

Rain had drained inwards, sweat had soaked outwards and I was saturated. I sat close to the coal fire and ordered a cherry brandy hot chocolate, promising to pay when my purse arrived. There were a few other walkers in the room, silver-haired and relaxed in their expensive kit. One started talking and eventually brought me some of his clothes to change into. He was right, I was never going to warm up if I kept the same damp clothes on. I reluctantly accepted his offer, feeling gauche and unprepared for the day's conditions, ready to change back into the damp uncomfortable clothes when I got picked up.

Shân collected me in a whirl of chatter and friendliness, home to hot water and a cosy sofa. We checked the weather forecast for the next day and it gave gale-force winds. I'd have to miss the high ground again, third day in a row. I'd take a valley cut through to the side of the Carneddau, winding through Llyn Cowlyd to reach the Conwy valley at Dolgarrog. Even the low route made for a hard enough day; down in the cleft shelter between the high peaks the wind blasted through the narrow valley and slapped the lake into white ruffles. It knocked me over several times, catching my blocky rucksack and twisting me off balance and down. I learned to watch the surface of the water and brace myself as another gust came rippling down the length of the lake towards me, finally ducking down behind the wall that separated the lake-valley from the boggy fields beyond, and breaking out my emergency mint-cake for fortitude.

I crossed into a wide, flat field and couldn't find the stile the guidebook promised; the grass kept breaking down into puddles and mucky wetness, making it difficult to find my way. There was a barn ahead with a van parked outside: Dulas Ltd, a Machynlleth company. Turning up at the barn door with windblown tales and foggy glasses, I poked my head around to see Dyfi valley friends. Waving my arms in the air, pouring a run of water drips from the elbow of each bent arm, I rambled about the stile and about my journey. Follow the pipe, they said, and you'll find the road down to the valley below. A thick black pipe ran from the dam at the end of the lake, I didn't ask why.

I sat in a haze of damp clothes in the Post Office at Dolgarrog, eking out a very welcome pot of warm tea and picking my way through a £1 bag of broken biscuits. The Post Office had a closed café in the corner, and I was allowed to squeeze into a table and wait for a woman to pick me up. She was a disappointment, glossy and closed, telling me I was crazy. I wondered why she'd opened her home to me if she couldn't handle the reality of a damp adventurer who simply made her feel nervous and unwelcome. Dinner was a precooked chicken leg brought home from a local food factory, eaten with oven chips and instant gravy. I watched *Frozen* with her son and gloomily ate chocolate. I wasn't in the mood for my host's reservation and didn't handle it well.

Sometimes I'd arrive at someone's house and, even though they'd chosen to invite me home, they wouldn't be relaxed. I'd just have to go with it, accept whatever they had to offer me, in a personable sense, whether they wanted to talk or ignore me, whether they were used to having people in their house or not. I couldn't choose how each person acted in their own home, whether they wanted to hear my whole cancer story or just chat about insignificant things – whether they wanted to offer me booze and have a celebratory night or whether it was an everyday tea. I had to react, to an extent, to whatever they had on offer. It was my job to make the situation comfortable: easing the effort of hosting a stranger was my payment for the reward of a shower and bed.

The end of the mountains had come in a swerving avoidance,

the late December weather forcing detours and anxiety. I didn't feel I'd failed, I'd done all I could given my abilities and the conditions, but the fact remained that, on this path, I'd gone around the base of Snowdon and not over it.

IRISH SEA

Holyhead

ISLE OF
ANGLESEY

Llandudno

Llangefni *Conwy*

Bangor

Caernarfon *Betws-y-Coed*

△
SNOWDON

Porthmadog

Pwllheli

Bala *Llangollen*

△
CADAIR
BERWYN

RHINOG
FAWR △
Dolgellau ARAN
FAWDDWY

Barmouth △
CADAIR
IDRIS

Machynlleth
△
PLYNLIMON

CARDIGAN
BAY

Aberystwyth

YSTWYTH

Tregaron

Cardigan

TEIFI

Fishguard

St David's

Haverford West *Carmarthen*

TYWI

Tenby

Llanelli *Neath*
Swansea

Rhyl

CLWYDIANS

Flint *Chester*

Wrexham

DEE

SNOWDONIA

DYFI

MOUNTAINS

Welshpool *Shrewsbury*

SEVERN

Newtown

Llanidloes

WALES ENGLAND

Worcester

*Builth
Wells*

Hay-on-Wye *Hereford*

BLACK
MOUNTAINS *Tewkesbury*

Llandovery

Llandeilo *Brecon*

BLACK
MOUNTAIN △
PEN Y
FAN *Abergavenny*

USK

*Merthyr
Tydfil*

Pontypridd *Newport* *Chepstow*

CARDIFF
Barry *BRISTOL*

BRISTOL CHANNEL

CAMBRIAN MOUNTAINS

WYE

SEVERN

WYE

TAFF

N

W E

S

0 Kilometers 30

0 Miles 20

266

ANGLESEY AND THE LLEYN PENINSULA

Route description: Part of the Wales Coastal Path which provides a continuous walking route around the whole coast of Wales. Although the route is obliged to turn inland on occasion, the sea is rarely out of sight. Most of the Anglesey coast is an Area of Natural Beauty and the two sections contain small fishing villages, estuaries and miles of sandy beaches.

Length:	221.2 miles
Total ascent:	6,330m
Maximum height:	411m
Dates:	31 December 2014 – 30 January 2015
Time taken:	31 days
Nights camping/nights hosted:	4/27
Days off:	5
Average miles per day:	8.5

I reached Conwy with a buzzy, Christmas-morning feeling. The end of the mountains! I'd done it, I'd bloody well walked from Conwy to Cardiff and all the way back up again, climbing most of the highest peaks of Wales on the way. I'd passed half-way, I'd passed the arduous and difficult mountain section: now all I had to do was turn left and walk around the coastal path from Conwy to Bristol, detouring inland to walk the length of six rivers. Roughly another 1300 miles; it didn't feel like much.

The next day came another celebration: 2000 miles walked! I set myself the challenge of finding party supplies in one of the three small villages along the coast between Dwygyfylchi and Bangor, eventually feeling phenomenally happy to find a fancy-dress shop in Llanfairfechan. I armed myself with a glittery top-hat and party supplies and walked further along the path to take ten minutes to sit down on the coastline, the field edge breaking away to shingle. I sat on a sunken piece of ground where the trailing fence-edge poked out into air behind me and wreathed myself in streamers, drawing a sign with multiple exclamation marks and taking a silly selfie to mark the moment. The top hat squashed into the top of my rucksack and left stray specks of glitter hiding away for weeks.

This was it: I was doing it, no matter how hard it was, I was still doing this. I'd propelled my way, in infinitesimally small pieces, to a journey of 2000 miles and I was still going. I wasn't going to stop, nothing could force me to quit this. A bubble of excitement rose within me, I was going to achieve the end of this journey, no matter how long it took me.

I'd reached this milestone just in time for Christmas. I took a break, going to stay with my brother in Derby, taking some time with family, putting my feet up. I didn't do much, just took a week to drink booze, play cards and cook meat-based meals. I felt a warm glow of happiness looking back over the past year: all I'd achieved and all the ways I'd been helped to do this. The scattered stars of my Google map showed me all the places where people had offered beds, all the places people had stepped forward to help me, a complete stranger, who'd chosen to walk thousands of miles and share it on the internet. Just because I'd had cancer. Just because I was raising money for charity.

I'd had help wherever I went, from hundreds of generous people, whether it was chucking a coin in the donation tin, giving me a cup of tea at the right moment or beeping their horns as they passed me on the road. I'd discovered community where I hadn't expected to.

People had used social media, the greatly lamented disconnector, to follow my journey, sending messages of support, aiding the spread of my symptoms-awareness work, giving donations. I felt a huge network of people around me, even as we all sat behind our smartphones bemoaning the state of modern Britain.

The beginning of Anglesey felt hopeful. My accompaniment changed from the blowing of grass in the wind to the crash of waves. Coming back from Christmas fattened and well-rested, I set out across the bridge to a largely flat island. The high peaks of Snowdonia were rumpled land, crinkled up behind me against the Strait. It was a relief from mountain walking, steep hill climbs and shrieking calf muscles. Snow had fallen thickly throughout the Christmas break, and the mountains across the water were white, shining fierce in the sharp blue sky. Even the foothills were covered now, lapping mounds all the way towards the higher peaks, inaccessible to the casual walker. I would have a break from the worst of the January weather here: walking by the sea would keep the temperatures higher than further inland, frost wouldn't coat the ground at night, and I could camp more easily, not having to stay alert and in survival mode.

I arrived at the eastern headland of Penmon as the day ended, the narrow lane widening to a flat, open headland with a lighthouse on an island close offshore. The wind blew hard against this exposed ground and I hunted around for a sheltered place to camp, avoiding the gaze of the blank-windowed campervans which were scattered around the parking area. Around the back of a closed café, shuttered against the winter, I found a small garden with an enclosed space, walled in on three sides. There was just enough room for my small tent and I sat happily in the dark, toasting myself with swigs of brandy and Coke, savouring two whole packets of crisps. It was New Year's Eve and I felt totally happy to be in this unusual place, celebrating alone. I felt tucked away, safe from the storm, even though gusts of wind were still bending the tent walls to press down against my face. It was annoying and intrusive to my sleep, but was nothing compared to the power of the air battering the headland.

I woke up dreamily at midnight to hear the faint bangs and booms of fireworks in Beaumaris, the sound travelling clearly across the water from further along the Strait, but otherwise I had a thick, black, deep sleep of a night. Happy New Year!

The following day was grey and bleary and I packed up as the rain started, turning quickly from drizzle to steady droplets. I knew that it would last all day and that storms were coming later. High winds and heavy rain were forecast to last all night. After a couple of hours' walking I became lost, losing the coastal path somewhere behind a farm and resorting to the road down to a stony beach, seaweed-lined neatly, marking the highest wash of water.

The rain was clear and steady, sheeting across the sea and hiding the other side of the bay. My route took me along a lane, the rain splashing directly into my face. It had been a few hours of walking and I was ready for a break. But where? There was nowhere that wasn't wet.

I saw a barn, climbed clumsily over the field gate, soaking wet and laden, but then couldn't work out a way to get into the building. The gates seemed impassable, tied together with numerous small intricate knots that I had no hope of retying. I paused in the shelter of the corrugated-tin wall, unwilling to go back out into the storm, so I turned again to the puzzle blocking my entry. There it was, I was too rain-shocked to see it at first; two gates alongside each other could be shifted apart for me to squeeze in between them and enter the space – no undoing knots, no fussing. I stood absorbing the quiet space, just me and a pile of old pallets, straw and shit trodden thick on the floor. I put my waterproofs straight on for warmth, then sat for a while watching the rain sheet down outside, flickers of wind shimmering the water like silver fish scales.

It was peaceful there. I looked around at the barn floor. It was a pretty ancient, leaky place, no real dry patches on the floor, and the pallets I perched on were green and dank with the beginnings of moss and overgrowth. I was tired and wet and didn't want to leave, but there was no point in trying to sleep here. Plus it was only 1pm, I had to walk on.

I found my way to the shore again and set to walk around the edge of the bay. There was no sand, just a flat stretch of slippery rocks, decorated with hanks of green moss that grew in the splash of the highest tides, reaching against the walls of the fishermen's cottages whose windows and doors faced away from the sea. I slipped and picked my way around the great curve of water, heading for the pub I knew was around the corner. I thought of sheltering there for a few hours, of tucking in and finding a camping spot somewhere nearby, waiting for twilight in the heated pub before escaping to the tent at the last possible point before bedtime.

Finally I was there, walking in to be met with a wall of noise and bodies. It was New Year's Day – I'd forgotten in the overwhelming struggle against the weather – and everyone was here to socialise, families and children and dogs happily crowded together.

I became intimidated by the people cramming every seat and table. There was no space for a huge soaking rucksack to squeeze through. Instead I found a tiny round table near the bar and made myself as small as possible, hidden behind the rows of people queuing at the bar, their bums backing onto me at head height. I spread some of my wet things onto the gentle radiator heat and set about making myself dry, first removing fresh clothes from my bag and then going up to change in the toilets, feeling very bedraggled and out of place in the glossiness and good cheer.

Soaked to the skin I stripped down in the toilets, and smoothed a fresh outfit onto my damp body. It took ages and people banged on the door while I was still about it.

I sat, stringing out a cup of tea, watching the wind blow outside, scudding plastic bags past the window and blowing people in through the doorway, laughing and jolly. I watched them all: happy families crammed round dark varnished tables, drinking and chattering, easy and relaxed, dogs in their under-table world, sniffing out scattered crisp crumbs, noses resting quietly on paws, searching for stealthy strokes, nudging against trouser legs. It was warm and cosy in the pub, I could relax in the invisible space where no-one else was. They looked past the solitary figure, didn't notice me. Normally it would have been heaven, but I was worried about where I was going to sleep. The pub garden was too exposed, a small triangle of sloped grass with sheer rocky walls; the wind would hit me hard if I slept there, rip the tent down. I went for a stroll to scope out where I could camp, the strong gusts making it hard to walk out there. Finally I found a doorway tucked around behind the yacht club, a curl of blown leaves in the corner of the concrete porch. Out of the wind was the only option: I couldn't put the tent up tonight, it would get blown apart. I walked back to the pub and started packing up, relieved to have found somewhere, even if it was a cold doorway.

Just as I was about to leave the manager, Sharman, came over, slipped a fiver into my tin and asked about the sign on my rucksack. She asked if I wanted to stay with her, once she'd finished work. I could stay at the table, small and strange and humble, eating crisps and reading a book as the pub whirled around me. She didn't tell everyone what I was doing, just quietly beckoned to me at the end of her shift an hour later, her quiet husband having bought me a second pint and packet of lovely salty crisps. I could go and explode my rucksack into her spare bedroom, covering cream linen frills and wooden hearts on the wall with hanging clothing, tarpaulin, tent. I went down to smoke cigarettes, drink tea and eat chocolate in the kitchen with Sharman. She was exhausted after her shift and we were all grateful for an early bed before heading back to the pub the following morning.

Steph called me at 7.30am.

"Can I come and walk with you today?"

"Sure, Ship Inn at tenish?"

"Great, do you need anything?"

Steph lives in Shrewsbury and when I passed through there on the River Severn, all the way back in March, she came out and walked with me for a few hours, carrying her 9-month-old daughter on her back. This time she brought the rest of her family, too, 5-year-old Ben and husband Pete. They'd come to Caernarfon for a New Year break and to walk with me again. We all walked for a lovely few hours tramping up and down the headlands of Moelfre, trailing in single file over rises and falls, with thick hedges protecting us from the worst of the cliff-edge drops, catching up on all that had passed for us both. It felt like minutes had passed when we arrived at their car. They took my rucksack ahead for the day's remaining miles, and promised to come out and meet me again in the spring.

People just kept coming forward and offering me things; the bus driver taking me from a host in Pentraeth back to my starting place at the Pilot Boat paid for my ticket and gave me £20, with the strict stipulation that £10 was for me and £10 for charity.

"People matter," he said. "You're doing a great thing and you need to take care of yourself."

I stood with him and talked about cancer, the devastating destruction of those we love, swaying in the aisle as the bus rattled around winding corners.

Steph had told me about her cousin Nikki who lived at the northernmost point of Wales, Llanlliana. There was a gigantic house which was run as a luxury holiday home and an island just off-shore: Middle Mouse, the truly northernmost point of Wales. I wanted to kayak over to the island to spend the night there, but in the end found myself in a caravan for the night with a headache and a sore throat. I only wanted to escape from friendly Nikki, feeling awkward and headachy in her kitchen with people coming in and out, curious children. She gave me a selection box of chocolate biscuits, Christmas leftovers, as well as a box of Lemsip. I retreated to the caravan and felt sorry for myself, feverish and bunged up. No kayaking for me. She looked shocked when I suggested it; apparently the tides were too strong to make an attempt like that and I felt too ill to push it.

My illness continued through the next day. I slept late in the caravan, dozing under the covers, pulling them over my head, willing the day away. It was blowy again, rain coming in a steady drizzle. I had to walk again but wished I could stay in bed. I took the afternoon to go around the western point of Anglesey, wind blowing on the exposed fields. The path took me on cliff edges, the land sloping down to the crashing white waves on rocks below. There was no hiding, the wind just came straight and block-solid over the grey water. I kept my head down, squinting ahead of me in short glimpses, eyes watering, face wet and reddened. This was a strange land, the wind blew my peace away, and I couldn't look around calmly, everything felt jarred and jumbled. Under attack, the wind pushed at me, every step forward against pressure. There was no time to appreciate the landscape, the beauty of the gentle fields, fuzzy planted grasses. There were strange chimneys in the distance and the path took me towards them: single pillars of stone, standing straight, spaced away from each other, an enigma of architecture, grassed field bases, edge of the land. What were they? Long defunct industry? The druids' last stand? A hare burst from under my feet and ran wildly away over the long, cropped field, no shelter in sight. I hadn't seen it until I was almost stepping on it, crouched against my looming predation. I felt blind, hunched, the rain shutting down my senses.

The wind was high and there was no shelter, the path winding in small humps and wriggles, a thin strip of trodden earth with exposed rocks to stumble over, gorse bushes to one side and the cliff edge on the other, falling away in sunken earthen wedges. I came at last to a forest, trees abutting the cliff path, allowing me to turn away from the wind, dropping down into the sanctuary of quiet pines. There was a pheasant enclosure not far in: a square of enclosed space, needle-carpeted, small openings at ground level for the birds to squeeze in and out with a track coming to it that wound away through the trees. I wondered if I would be disturbed by anyone coming to check the birds, but the flat area just outside the fence was too tempting. It was just the right width to pitch a tent and rest, listening to the weather. I was safe here, down behind the cliff edge, like a shell in the ocean as the waves rolled above it, the tent rocking gently, as the wind rushed in the pine branches overhead, washing them like tidal waters washed the beach below. Pine-needles pattered softly on my tent, depositing like grains of sand on the sea bottom, small leavings of the greater forces above me.

The next day I reached Llanfachraeth where I met a cameraman for an interview. ITV Wales were going to put me on their evening news, my first piece of television coverage. It was a good sign that I was being recognised as making a newsworthy journey; more coverage meant more people thinking about ovarian cancer. Seeing myself on TV was a horrible shock, though. All I saw when I looked at that night's news, of the images of me walking thousands of miles for charity, was the way my stomach folded over the tightly-clipped belt of my rucksack. I was snapped back to the unpleasant knowledge of how my body appeared on the outside: fat, foolish, ugly.

I didn't feel that way when I was walking, I felt strong and wonderful, my body capable and able, and my spirit felt beautiful, bright and shining. Surely my skin would show all the happiness and love I felt. But in the mirror it never did; I only ever saw my pudgy, saggy body, squinty eyes and crooked goofy smile. I loved my body when I wasn't looking at it, when I wasn't forced by the jarring image in front of me to accept that I wasn't all that attractive.

This dichotomy, this inner lack of self-worth, was something I wanted to make a public part of the journey but I never found the right way to write it down, slip it amongst the blog posts of mountain – climbing and camping, photos of sunset and sheep. It was far too big an idea for me to articulate, that my unpleasant relationship with my body was a huge and hidden part of this journey and maybe this negative attitude had contributed to my cancer.

Know your body and love yourself.

I was doing my best to raise ovarian cancer symptoms awareness in women and I wanted to say this too, as a way to encapsulate my thoughts on how to recognise cancer sooner.

I wanted to write a blog post that would talk about the way in which my experiences had shown me that I didn't respect my body enough to take care of it, and that might explain something about the way that my tumour had grown without me realising. I'd ignored my body's signals, the faint calling of cancer, telling me something was wrong as it swelled in my body, as it pushed my internal organs aside, as it swallowed my energy, siphoning the sugar from my bloodstream to fund its greedy growth. Part of the way this had come to pass was that for years I only paid attention to how my body looked, how it was of value to others – not how it felt inside. I'd always thought of my body in terms of fat and thin, its value as a purveyor of my sexuality to onlookers, as a scorecard held up to signpost my fuckability, beautiful or ugly, good or bad, pass or fail. I'd seen my body in such reduced terms, judging it myself before it passed the scornful gaze of others, pulling at my rolls of fat, wishing I was different, always finding my excess wanting. Had my cancer grown as I viewed the swelling of my body relative only to the amount I'd eaten?

But to make this idea public I'd have to tell a very personal part of my story – which was admitting to the fact that I really didn't pay attention to myself. In some sense I didn't think I was worth looking after. There was never the time and space to work out a way to frame it as I was walking. I'd write lists of things to do on my days off and sometimes the *Know Your Body* blog post would appear on one but it never got written, a subject too big for me to crystalise in a scant few hours of writing, too big for me to face.

Know your body and love yourself. Maybe the answer to improved health wasn't through fear, or inflicting punishing fitness or food regimes upon yourself, but true and better health had to start with nurturing, and nurturing had to start with valuing. Simply paying attention, connecting energy levels to nutrition to triggers to emotional states to workload – not masking tiredness with caffeine, or lurching between sugar-induced highs and lows. The subject whirled around in my mind during the hours of walking, mixed together with all my other preoccupations.

The afternoon of the ITV interview, after finishing filming, I walked over The Cobb causeway to Holy Island at the north-western corner of Anglesey, where I'd arranged to meet Peter who whisked me away south to Rhosneigr. He offered me the use of a holiday home there, I could even take a rest weekend in the gap between paying guests.

I drifted around in the huge house, careful not to make too much mess, always aware of cleaning my footsteps away behind me. The previous guests had left and, as there was a window before the next set arrived, Peter's wife Helen would delay cleaning it for a few days to allow me to be there in the wash of the previous family. There was a leftover half-box of chocolates which I ate, half a bottle of vodka in the freezer which I left alone. I acted exactly as I wanted but always aware that the house was a gift to me, and the eventual clean-up would be left to a woman who didn't need to clean up my mess too.

At first I used the house as a base to get buses from, trying to walk a little bit, down around Holy Island and along the coast to here, just south of Rhosneigr, but the timetable was too sparse and logistics too complicated to make it an easy way to walk. Covering a few miles helped me feel better about sheltering in the luxury of the big house, even though it was a meagre fourteen miles in two days.

My chosen bedroom was the large room at the top of the house. The floor-to-ceiling glass windows gave a view of the stretch of beach that lay immediately behind the house. There was a huge bed for me to sprawl in, luxurious white bedlinen, multiple pillows, a mattress topper for extra softness. The sand-coloured carpet was soft under my feet, and the room looked out to the curve of the west Anglesey coast. The Llŷn peninsula lay across the water, a toe of land poking out and turning south: it was out there somewhere, probably within view but the sky lay overcast and murky for my whole stay, sheets of grey misting the view, mixing sky and sea. I lay in bed at night and felt the wind slamming into the house. It rocked and swayed under the non-stop assault. There were constant small creaks and rubbing noises, the timber frame shaking under invisible blows, a humming of wind vibrating the loose pieces of the windows and guttering.

I pressed my nose against the rain-spattered glass, watching the white waves crash against the shingle below the house, gobbets of foam blowing through the air. The water washed against the small garden wall that enclosed a grassy area behind the house, raised slightly above the beach but otherwise liable for rinsing by the tide. I didn't want to go out there: didn't want to walk in the eternal, face-slicing, spirit-dampening rain, bracing my body against the buffeting gusts. So I called Peter and asked for one more rest-day.

My bones were hurting. In addition to the usual tendon pain underneath my feet I had sharp, stabbing pains in my ankles, shins and heels. It was hard to hobble round the house at night, so much easier just to lie on the sofa and watch TV, put my feet in the air and rub them, trying to ease the pain, relax the muscles and help my circulation carry away the poisons of inflammation.

My shoulders and neck also started to hurt while I was staying in this wonderful solitude. It was as if I was set to a certain tension while walking – pushing my body onwards, camping on hard ground, carrying a heavy bag, daily walking – but if I stopped for too long my body started to relax and hurt, the lessening of tension allowing my stressed muscles to let go and begin screaming.

My brain needed rest too; it was a blank, I had nothing to say on blogs and social media. I spent most days crafting beautiful words and insights as I walked with the wind and the hillsides but somehow, when I came to rest, I just wanted to sit and switch off, do nothing at all, my carefully nurtured words melting back to ether.

A couple of days became five and they had passed in a long blink. I'd glued my boots where they'd split along the sides, not feeling quite ready to buy a new pair yet. I'd also sewn up various holes that had appeared in clothing and rucksack, detangled hair whipped about by 40mph winds. I'd lazed on the sofa for long enough, turning the heating up and snoozing in a lambswool blanket, enjoying channel-hopping on the huge TV, allowing the days to pass in a finger-licking food-haze, regularly getting back up to refill my cereal bowl or make cheese on toast.

I could have stayed for even longer, but the following day brought a gap between storms. There was more bad weather coming but I couldn't wait forever. The holiday home would eventually have guests coming in and I couldn't avoid the inevitable; I was on a walk and that meant walking.

A man wanted to meet me. He'd been put in touch by Gail in Dwygyfylchi and responded instantly, sharing my links on Facebook, sending messages of support. I found out that his wife had died from ovarian cancer. He was a county councillor, a man of politics and action, supporting a campaign in Parliament.

I was conscious of his grief, felt that I had no right to intrude on it. It was too big a thing for me to treat in my usual light and casual way. I'd had this illness in name only, I couldn't lay claim to the same experiences as him, as his wife. It made me feel like a fraud in my glowing health, stepping out under the banner of cancer. We met in a wide, open car-park where a large building towered noticeably above the low surrounding dunes. As we shared a drink in the bar of the restaurant he offered to buy me a new pair of boots. I really needed them. The grips on my pair had worn down to smooth rubber and they were cracked along the edge where the leather met the sole, letting in water to dampen my socks and soften my feet, soaking a bad smell into the internal fabric. I didn't want to accept: a new pair of boots would be over £100 and it felt strange to accept such an expensive gift. I shied away from accepting money for myself, normally telling people to give to my chosen charities; but I had to think of the effect this man wanted to have and honour that, honour the sentiments behind his gift.

I pushed up the hill, leaning forward to take the weight of my rucksack against my shoulders, placing my feet carefully to dig against the slope and I thought of others who'd done the same. All of them had trodden in small steps, fighting the wind or basking in the sun. All had made the effort, step after step for hour after hour in pursuit of their own personal challenge, born from the joy of walking or the unexpected obstacles that living brings. My effort was just the latest of the many.

I came to the Barclodiad y Gawres burial mound about thirty minutes later. The mark of those who'd been here before me, this time thousands of years ago. I read the sign, detailing the known rites and customs of those long-dead people, details scratched together from patient collectors and chemical analysis, marks scored into stones, bubbling brews poured onto embers. Frog, toad, eel, limpet, grass. Muttering incantations, putting the dead to rest in this circle of stones, inside a heap of earth on a headland above the sea, thousands of years ago when the limits of the known world were far nearer.

There was a short corridor into the mound leading to the covered circle of stones within. Further in, near the barred entrance, I started to breathe heavily, sensing deep power emanating from the inside of the dark space. It was as if I'd been caught in a whirlwind of energy but was only attuned enough to sense little more than ripples, like a child playing on the carpet as the adults in a room discuss politics or divorce. At the metal barrier I stood and breathed, trying to feel what was coming from the ancient inner space. Like a bird hopping at the corner of my vision and disappearing if I looked directly at it, I could only try and sense, holding my instinct like fingers in the current, trying to feel something trailing through them. Tears fell down my face as I shakily breathed in and out, thinking of the people here, pouring their ritual into the earth, creating their sacred space.

I may know about the mechanics of cell division, or why we get rainbows, or where the sun goes when it disappears. I may be able to live without hours of daily foraging for food or talk to my sister in Mexico without seeing her face. But is my quality of life better than theirs? Am I more fulfilled? What did they know that I don't? What beliefs did they have that my culture has long forgotten? I truly couldn't imagine.

I came out, unsteadily, back into the crashing, unrelenting wind and continued under the bright sky, wondering whether life really is better these days: animals in cages, food made of emulsifiers and additives, and humans scraping and squeezing the last of the earth's resources into their greedy mouths. Did the mound builders live in harmony and die in peace? Do we?

I came to Aberffraw and went to a café where Rebecca Morris had told me to stop. She'd walked in and made friends with the owner, had tea, cakes, dinner and been invited to stay the night. I told the owner who I was, and we sat for a while, talking about her experience of Rebecca, the quiet, unobtrusive woman, tanned brown as a nut, who steadily walked the entire Welsh coastline.

"She sat over there," said Linda, the café's owner. "That's her seat." And so we sat there again in honour of Rebecca, and had our photo taken. One walker sitting in place of another, remembering her journey months earlier.

I said goodbye and walked away. It wasn't until I was almost at the gate that a man called after me. It was Richard, the craftsman from the workshop opposite and a friend of the woman I was due to stay with that night. He invited me into his space and I found myself having a conversation with another cancer-sufferer, a coper, using work and deliberate cheerfulness as his distraction from the fear that cancer can bring. We had a brilliant conversation about all kinds of things. It was as I was preparing to leave that he mentioned he'd met an inspiration of mine, Christian around Britain, the man who walked the entire British coastline while I was preparing for my own challenge, finishing his walk just a few weeks after I started out. Not only did he walk 7000+ miles, he slept rough the entire time, trying to get people to talk about the problems of homelessness in ex-servicemen. He slept in sheds, in barns, in toilets, and not once did this man crawl into a bed to ease the aches in his bones. Richard showed me a picture of Christian standing outside his shop, and then we took the same shot with me in frame.

They all came flooding in at me that day, those who walked before me.

I continued on my path around the island. Fighting to keep my balance on the stepping stones of the River Braint as the gale threatened to knock me over, unable to go onto the beach at Malltraeth Bay with the wind blowing a skin-scraping faceful of sand into the pine forest. The red squirrels were hiding, the snow remained on the mountaintops as I turned the corner at Dwyran and brought the Strait into view once again.

I took the weekend off in Alexandra's house at Menai Bridge, a fellow pilgrim who'd taught a course that my mother attended. I hadn't met her, she'd just offered her house when she heard about me; we exchanged messages and she told me where to find the key. I took a day to lie in bed and sleep, eating cabbage and rice and chocolate mousse, then a day to travel inland to Betws-y-Coed and buy new boots from the cluster of outdoor shops that nestle there, a small centre of outdoor specialisation.

Sitting in the bustle I considered my options, asking the sales guy about which boots could take crampons. When I returned to the mainland I'd be coming close to Snowdon once more; maybe I could detour inland and take the Llanberis approach, the gentlest and easiest route. Perhaps I could take this last opportunity to get up the mountain; I really felt sad about missing it out. I had a vision of taking a day to climb it, being as slow as I needed, taking great care, then, too late to descend in the dangerous darkness, tucking into the snow at the peak for a night of survival in my sub-zero tent, out of the wind in the shuttered café doorway perhaps. The shop assistant told me that the boots I wanted weren't suitable for crampons, they were too flexible and the metal attachments would fall straight off. He told me I could hire boots and I added this into the Snowdon dream. I'd hitch to the hiring-place and then to the base of the mountain with my borrowed gear. I really wanted to climb this mountain.

At the till I was recognised by the salesgirl. She called another woman over and they chatted to me about what I was doing, ovarian cancer survival, walking through the mountains in December and the storms of January, spending so many months on my journey in the pursuit of thousands of miles.

"I'd like to come and walk with you," said the curly-haired supervisor. "I've got a couple of days off later this week."

I looked up at this woman, into a pair of clear and smiling eyes. "Would you? That would be great."

I instantly trusted her, the kind of woman who is clear and unfaltering, sharp and capable.

"Would you like to climb Snowdon?"

The words tripped onto my tongue, spilling from my mouth in a moment of spontaneity.

"Yes," she said. "I'm a qualified mountain-leader."

The smiles grew in our eyes and became an adventure. We swapped contact details; she promised to find me a set of boots that fitted, to provide me with crampons and an ice-axe. I would walk away south for the rest of the week, enter the Llŷn Peninsula and then double back to climb Snowdon. I left Betws in a bubble of excitement; what had just happened? Was I really going to do this? I'd been so hampered by my inexperience, intimidated by the snowy peak and totally unsure of the best way to approach it. Out of nowhere, I'd made a split-second comment and found a woman who'd take me up the mountain.

We started early, driving to the car park at the base of the Pyg Track, suiting and booting up, wriggling fingers into gloves, legs into waterproof trousers and saying goodbye to the wagging tails and eager noses of Diane's spaniels, shutting them into the van for the few hours it would take us to climb and return. The mountain was heavy and grey, snow clinging everywhere except the vertical rock-faces which showed black against the whiteness. Long reeds spiked above the snow blanket but all else was hidden. The light was grey, heavy cloud close above us.

It was always a well-trodden path, even with the snow, although that brought its own problems where the footsteps of others had compacted the softness to slippery ice. We trod carefully, using our poles to balance against slipping. I'd foregone my usual bamboo flagpoles in favour of proper walking-poles; the handgrips were much better, much easier to hold without strain on my wrists, but I missed my flags. It made me ordinary, to walk without fluttering flags announcing my presence. We walked upwards and into the cloud, light filtering through the mist.

We stopped a couple of times: checking warmth, shedding a layer of jacket but keeping the insulation of fleecy waistcoats. The idea was to walk without letting a nasty layer of sweat build up on your body, there to chill your temperature as soon as you stopped.

The cloud was thinning, giving way, a clear blue colour coming through the mist. The snow was shining up above us.

We climbed above the cloud layer and out into a glorious, glinting landscape. It was a complete inversion: the clouds had dropped low down, filling the bowl between the peaks with a bubbling mist. The mountain tops stood tall and brilliant, bright white and gleaming. We still had hundreds of metres to climb but we'd be doing it under blue skies. We were at eye-level with the cloud, a smooth blanket of white, with only the wall of rock that's called Cribau sticking out opposite. Eventually we turned a corner and there was the pyramidal summit of Snowdon ahead. It was a clear and easy path, we just trod slowly and carefully upwards, stopping when it got steeper to strap on crampons. The shell of metal fitted around the sole of my boot, providing spikes to stick into the ice and keep a good grip. Diane showed me how to jam my foot against the ice, how to make sure the spikes held my weight, even when little of either foot was on a flat and level surface.

My breath condensed in white moisture droplets on the fuzz of my woollen bobble-hat. We needed gloves, double layers of trousers, fleece waistcoats and buff neckwarmers, even as we climbed in full sunlight. I never felt nervous – it was just a case of being careful of the cold. Diane was a perfect guide: monitoring without being suffocating, advising without being patronising. The walk itself wasn't problematic: it was her knowledge of what to do if anything went awry that I valued, as well as her ease of access to all the right kit.

We came around the curl of the final peak of the mountain, built by humans into a spiral to absorb the high numbers of people present in the summer months. I did a short video, to share the glorious view online: clouds far down below and the mountain ridges dropping away into the mist that stretched out to the horizon. I tried to talk, to mark the moment, but found myself crying, overwhelmed with the fact that I'd done this, that I was really here again. I'd come through snow and ice to reach the top of this mountain for a second time, the winter peak that I thought I had no chance at. I felt all the power of my journey that day. Diane had helped me to get here but it was my body's strength, my determination, my ability to stay safe that had brought me to this point, the culmination of over 2100 miles of struggle.

Coming down from the summit we sat for a while at the base of the rock, eating our lunch, making sure we were refuelled for the slippery descent. There were other climbers around but not many – I'd say about fifty people climbed the mountain that day, far fewer than the many hundreds who summit each day throughout the summer. Everyone was quiet and peaceful, admiring the view; nobody seemed compelled to make noise or draw attention to themselves. It seemed that the only people there that day were experienced mountaineers. I felt really moved, tried to express it to Diane but couldn't do it without sounding odd. To her it was unnecessary, she'd just brought me up the mountain. I couldn't express without crying how important it was that I'd made it up here, that I'd done what I set out to do and not shirked it – that I couldn't have done it without her help.

After a couple of hours of careful descent, I suggested she walk ahead. I could feel my feet cramping in the unfamiliar boots, their inflexibility was designed so that feet didn't bend and slip against the smoosh of the snow and ice. It meant that my tender feet met the tough boots and yielded. I felt them curling underneath, the familiar pain coming sharply. It made me irritable; I could feel myself wanting to snap and snarl, curse out loud. Diane wanted to get back to the van to see to the dogs and I was holding her back. Letting her walk on meant I could relax for the final two miles, allow my feet to step, step, step, at their own pace, a measured tread that was slower than most walkers but that would keep a speed that got me there, kept getting me there. It was a flat path by this point, coming around the two lakes, first Glaslyn then Llyn Llydaw, the rippled lower peaks mirrored completely in the still water, blue skies and sun shining bright on the snow and rock.

Penny, jolly and generous schoolfriend of my mother's friend, plus husband David and Jack Russell dog, hosted me all the way around the Llŷn Peninsula, generously picking me up and dropping me off every morning and evening. They lived in the centre of the tip of the stretch of land, a web of single-tracked, high-hedged roads stretching out in all directions, the canals by which to navigate this backwater: Wales' Land's End.

Penny's diligent ferrying back and forth meant I could walk further than usual, despite having trouble with oedema along my calves. Diane, also a sports masseuse, had looked very concerned as she treated me, telling me to sleep with my feet raised wherever I could. I pushed a pillow down to the foot of my bed, massaging my legs from toe to ankle to knee over and over again, trying to reduce the sharp tenderness that ran along the inside of my tibia, worrying it might be a walk-ending injury if it got any worse.

The weather stayed bright and brilliant all week, with a wind to freeze the drip from the end of your nose. I was glad of my bobble-hat and neckwarmer, pulled right up to cover my cheeks and ears. I walked into the wind until I turned the corner of Pen Llŷn into the cover of land, away from the side of the peninsula that was slapped by the wind coming straight from the Irish Sea and curling under into the cover of Cardigan Bay. Here was gentler-washing water, rocky coves giving way to wide flat beaches. I took some time at the sloping peak of Mynydd Mawr to stare longingly at Bardsey Island – it was another important island I'd missed out on; the boat transport didn't run at this time of year and I'd struggle to afford it anyway. A £30 return ticket for a four-hour trip was the same as my weekly food allowance.

From Aberdaron, past Abersoch and Pwllheli towards Criccieth, I walked on so many beaches, always accompanied by the wind, made visible by the grains of sand taken along by it. Hard gusts progressed in diamond ruffles, zigzagging white above the deep yellow hard-packed surface, hitting my legs, stinging and abrading.

The Llŷn peninsula passed quickly, thanks to Penny and David, enabling me to walk without a bag. I managed eighteen-mile days without problems, so different to my usual pained hobbling.

OWEN'S ACCIDENT

As I walked around the tip of the poking finger of the Llŷn Peninsula, I felt as if I'd turned a big psychological corner too: it was all downhill from here, just the coast and another six rivers to go. I woke up in Porthmadog on the 1st of February after a wonderful rest weekend, stumbling naked through another unused holiday home, blinds drawn, thinking of the day to come, more food to eat, more terrible television, another bath, more sleep, more writing. Bliss. I was almost there, just another few months of walking...

I settled on the sofa and found a missed call on my phone, an unknown number, a voicemail from a policeman with a broad Derbyshire accent, asking me to call him. The words were so simple that they didn't register at first.

"Your brother's car has been involved in an accident. There's a man in hospital in a serious condition: he was found in the car and we need someone to come and identify him. He's unresponsive and can't identify himself."

No further details, just "a serious condition". The policeman couldn't tell me anything unless the man was indeed identified as my brother. I called my mum, arranged that she would go directly to the hospital and then looked at train times. It was Sunday and there was only one train that day; I had to wait eight hours to catch it. Could I go on walking? *Serious condition*. What did it mean? What was happening over there? Would I want my family to come to me if I was in hospital in a serious condition? Of course I would. I didn't want to stop walking but there was nothing else for it, I had to go to Derbyshire.

After a day of tension and waiting, I finally left Porthmadog at

4pm. The train wound its way around the coast and estuary into farmland, then towns, then Birmingham, the Midlands, where there were buildings as far as the eye could see, no distance to the horizon. Finally, late that night, I had a lift into the heart of Nottingham where, waiting for me, lay my prone brother, the wise nurse at the end of the bed guiding him through his coma, machines beeping a jagged lullaby.

Owen had been put into an induced coma, to allow his body to cope with a head injury, brain swelling, broken bones. We gathered at his bedside.

"Can we talk to him?"

"Yes," they said. "It's his hearing that will come back first."

This talking was for us, not him. I was hesitant at first, stumbling over words that suddenly felt alien when spoken to a sleeping man. We had to continue to talk knowing that he wouldn't respond, knowing that our imprecations were unlikely to make an impression on his stern unconsciousness.

A car accident, they said. Slipped off the road in the dead of night. A mystery. No speeding, no alcohol, no other cars, no marks on the road. Only saved by a woman who drove past after midnight, saw a car in a ditch and had a strange feeling, called her daughter who told her to call the police who went to the spot and found a bleeding man behind the wheel, his brain battered and bones broken. His life hung there, death suspended by the safety belt, time ticking through the minutes between successful treatment and brain-death.

I whisper, croaked and awkward, that I love him and believe he will be fine. I don't know where the words are going, how they'll interact with his darkened mind. I imagined his eardrum vibrating, flashing the Morse code of binary nerve responses towards the silenced machine that is his brain and the message falling, jagged and jumbled, at the foot of a closed door. I didn't know if Owen was inside his body or if he'd gone away forever. He might have melted away into shadow at the foot of a tree on a rural back-road, leaving blue lights flashing on crumpled metal, turning blood to black.

We called his friends together, rallied the troops. He had a group of friends from school, from years of computer games and football, of spliffs in the attic and nights out drinking. Mountain bike weekends, grunts and piss-takings, long-held easy friendships. Now these men came to be with him as he mended, along with many others. There was nothing to do but wait, spending time at the small plastic-topped table outside the ward, different friends turning up every day, taking it in turns to go in and see him. It turned out that many people loved and cared about Owen – he'd made friends wherever he went. In the first few nights, when he was in intensive care, twenty people arrived to see him, gathering in different groups along the corridor, making jokes and hiding their feelings.

They took away the drugs keeping him sedated but Owen didn't move, didn't respond. Nothing held him there, no chemical cosh; he was just a man lying silently in a bed and not waking up when you pressed him.

"If he continues in this state for another two or three days, there's a very strong possibility that he'll die…"

We held each other, sometimes in tears and sometimes silent, my other brother walking into this meeting straight off the plane from Barcelona, his eyes wide in shock.

I saw men everywhere that looked like my brother – the shape of the shoulders, a flash of bristly beard, a thin upright back, a blazer, spectacles on a round, shaved head. I wanted to run after them each time, catch an arm and have them turn and be him, alive and warm and moving but the illusion always revealed the truth. *He's not walking around in the fresh air, he's upstairs inside, prone in bed and not responding. He's lying as if sleeping but you can't wake him no matter how hard you try. Don't shake his broken body, you'll only grind the pieces of his shattered bones. Only place your hands gently on his skin and pour your love out towards him, hoping that it will catch his spirit.*

Then Owen's eyes opened overnight, flickered into life. At first they were just moon-eyes, indiscriminate, wandering blankly over any surface. Then they contained recognition. He would see people, try to speak.

I learned, through regular consultants' meetings, to understand the reliance of every single thing that makes us human on an arrangement of neurons, nothing more. Everything that made Owen into the person he is was down to the interactions of his neural network, the strength of the connections between areas of his brain. His brain was only a series of nerves, their constant firings creating his entire reality, creating him, his bodily functions, his personality, his movement and sensory processing. Everything was up for grabs, nothing could be taken for granted. He might have woken up but could he see us? Could he walk? Could he swallow or shit? Could he remember who we were? Remember our shared history? Keep events in his head for longer than the time they took to fall out of short-term memory? Would he be angrier now? Sadder? Disinhibited? Would he speak in a foreign accent? Believe he was a spy?

We only knew that life had irrevocably changed for him, my lovely brother, but it wasn't clear just yet how seriously. While his world had changed again, so had mine. This time it wasn't a calamitous event changing my health and outlook, it was his. Now he was the one with a date that marked a before and after.

There have been times when life paused, when I lay at a field edge watching a wren hop gently between the twigs of an intricate

293

hedgerow, safe from swooping predators, just a short head turn from a face-to-face encounter. I'd keep my body still as I focused on the bird, subduing my movements so as to pay attention to it, to drink it in, everything else blanked out. There in Nottingham, the walk disappeared. I could do nothing except be with my brother as he struggled to bring his brain back to normality, back to a world that had suddenly become confusing and impossible to understand.

First he saw us, then he mouthed words, started to speak, rambling burbles, slurred murmurs, then he made sentences, became able to move more, was helped into a chair, helped to his feet, helped to walk. We watched as his feet crossed over and did not obey, a physiotherapist under each arm, keeping him from tangling on the floor. There was always a change the next day; improvements kept coming, steps grew straighter; he put clothes on, he played cards, chess, remembered names, laughed at jokes, his eyes bulging to absorb all the newness. We paced with him and tried to help him rest, tried to keep his concentration on a single object, tried to encourage him to eat and drink through his broken mouth, tried to keep him informed about his condition when facts were falling out of his head as fast as we put them in there.

All the other things I thought I wanted to do – walk another thousand miles, write a book, take a boat to the Black Sea, meet a man, have a baby – all seemed very far away. They didn't seem like anything it was possible for me to do at all. I could only wake up, have breakfast, go to the hospital, try and talk to my brother, answer his questions, hope he could eat something that day, hope he could hold on to the facts I gave him, hope that if we started a card game he'd remember the rules, hope that eventually he'd be able to leave hospital, to live by himself, hope that things would get better.

He had a shaking injury, small spots of bleeding which were scattered throughout the brain. No specific part was damaged, we just had to wait and see what would be affected, how his brain would cope with rerouting around the damage. It would depend on the strength of his neural network, on his ability to think around the problem. He'd always been a person who was pretty out there, who would come up with a joke, an invention, out of left field. I tried to imagine the type of brain he had, the neurons veering off into unexpected places.

This is what would save him, his ability to find new pathways where others had been destroyed. A brain isn't just a single track of impetus to action, it's a complex network of connections, each one conveying an individual piece of information: the seeds of strawberries, their taste, their texture, the fact they grow into plants, their appearance, their pattern on the fruit. Each piece of information could link to millions of others, memories of strawberries on cakes, in jelly, on days out, in gardens, picked with a grandparent, picked while listening to Wimbledon, a handful of miniature ones, warming sun on strawberry skin, the explosion of juice in the first bite, redness of ripening, lusciousness of swelling fruit, deep smell of strawberries in the sun.

Each of these points of information could have disappeared in a minute explosion of blood, never to be retrieved, and we had no idea which facts would come back and which would stay missing.

Owen was reborn, a Buddha brother. The layers of learned behaviour, of human culture were stripped away; he had no artifice, every thought came to his face and then his mouth. He was an innocent, trying to put out chairs and shake hands with the doctors when they only wanted to stay standing, chant their information and leave, trying to invite friends for a sleepover when they'd come for a few hours' visit. He was funny and ridiculous and we laughed at him, as we had always done; he was a man who made people laugh, was charming and funny, and somehow he still was, even as he paced up and down the ward corridor in bright green compression stockings, drooling uncontrollably, eyes bright and hair crazy, saying hello to everyone who passed him, my arm linked in his to help him balance, legs high-stepping in jerked movements, like an awkward robot, imitating walking from a set of written instructions.

He changed daily and we tried to keep up, went to hospital and sat with him, or sat outside while others took their turn. Days became a rota of visitations, a packing of lunches. We seized upon the gift of an adult colouring-book, my sister and I, colouring flowers as a way to hold still in the whirlwind, to live in the uncertainty without going mad. In the hours between leaving the hospital and going back the next day there were meals, showers and the passing of time until we could return again. I took up smoking again, as a way to escape the waiting area outside the ward, a way to add regular breaks into my day, a way to take back control. Some kind of subversion of enforced events, even if it was self-defeating.

After the first couple of weeks of daily car-journeys, once the emergency part was over and it started to be about recovery, I began to take some time out to walk to hospital. It was an escape from the life I found myself in, the stifling effect of being with my family all the time, the intense pressure of familial relationships. It was six miles, the quickest way. First a gentle canal-side pace, then cutting away to ploughed field-edges, approaching the roar of the M1, a muddy tunnel underneath it and then a mile of fume-crusted suburbia until, finally, a surprise stately home and deer park, nestled in the city's encroachment, frilled with tarmac, and on the other side of it, the huge hospital complex.

I tried walking further, taking the canalside detour, twelve miles all the way around to the River Trent and up into central Nottingham, admiring the narrowboats and their private community, the beauty of riverside life, their tidiness, their choice of rooftop adornments. The twelve-mile walk was more beautiful, but it brought the pain back. My feet hurt, the plantar tendons felt cramped and curled, sharp shooting-pains spread into my heels and I feared for the future of my body, feared that I'd permanently damaged myself. I realised that my body had nothing left; I was bone-hurtingly, crumplingly tired.

As days became weeks it began to dawn on me that it was going to be OK; Owen was getting better; this was positive. He moved into a room of his own on the Major Trauma Unit and it felt good. He was walking, talking, he appeared to have full control of his body. His mind was still all over the place, unable to settle, unable to concentrate, unable to make rational self-care decisions, but he was progressing. I felt my mind churn as I turned away from the idea of constant worry and negativity. I'd been stuck there for four incredibly intense weeks.

Before this, before the 1st of February, my life had been fixed and focused on one thing: completing the 3300 mile walking target I'd set myself. I'd walked through pain and bad weather, up and over hundreds of hills, down into tree-lined valleys, scattered hundreds of sheep. My heart flew free above me and, despite all the pain and privation that walking in this way involved, I was happier than I could ever have been in a job, in a house, entangled in the snares of a so-called civilised life.

Now I was torn. My focus had been ripped away from the walk and onto my brother's life: first his survival and then his small achievements before finally turning to his long-term future. Owen was getting better, the flickering open of his eyes in that first week had turned, seven weeks later to a recovery of sorts. He wasn't better, he wasn't the same. But he was alive; he could return home to live alone, manage his own life and start to think about returning to work, he had that much of a future. If Owen was better, that meant I was free again, free to return to my old life. But what was that? It was walking.

Walking is healing for me. I walked myself fit after surgery. I walked to Bristol to see if I was still myself after cancer. As I walked these three thousand miles I was creating calmness within myself, building an appreciation of my qualities, the strength that gets me through, the joy and positivity with which I approach each day no matter how exhausted I am.

I knew that I'd need to walk to feel better about my brother's difference, about the new, damaged state he found himself in as he lay blearily in hospital, vulnerable, in pain. Once I was certain that he was safe I'd walk to move away from fear, away from the pressure, the trauma, the uncertainty buzzing in my head. Walking would bring fresh air to my brain and body, a certainty that I can cope with change, that there are more things in this world than one woman and the near-loss of her brother.

My sister lent me money so that I could finish my challenge: a final thousand pounds to hoard and savour and only let slip away incrementally on cups of tea and tins of mackerel, treats of toast and chocolate bars and the occasional pint. I was so skint, gone beyond poor to near-destitution, living on fumes, my savings almost gone. The walk had taken months longer than expected and it was so hard to always live under budget. I was still trying to live on less than £50 a week, £35 if possible, a £5 daily budget plus a window to overspend into. I'd always overspend but the mental limit helped me restrict myself. This level of budget was incredibly hard to keep to, even though my main expense was food; the cost of not eating at home, not able to buy in bulk and store the extra, meant it was more expensive than usual. The few weeks of work in November had helped but I was tired of skimping and worrying about money, tired of having nothing coming in and always going out. I was always berating myself for adding cake to my pot of tea, or crisps to my second pint. It was exhausting, especially when I was berating myself for something so minimal. I really needed those treats, for calories as well as morale.

It all felt a bit futile now: this walk, this sunshine, these cancer charities. I'd spent almost two months on a knife-edge, waiting to see if my brother would return to health, balancing there with my family, keeping us from tumbling over into argument, keeping the right people informed of his condition in the right way, keeping close to Owen as he came back to himself. The buzzing, intense pressure of phenomenal worry had become normal. I'd totally zoned in on him and the structure of hospital routines, and as that intensity of concentration receded I felt hollow and sad.

I knew that this would change, that I'd come to feel different in time. I just had to keep acting as if this were normal and the jumble inside me would slowly unravel, leaving me free to enjoy the final thousand miles. There were months of walking the Welsh coastline still to come, another six rivers to follow and a target of £10,000 to raise for charity. I went back to Wales because it was the only thing to do; completing the walk was the only thing that existed for me.

I felt like Rip van Winkle in reverse; in this tale, it was Wales that slept in stasis, not me. I would return from a strange dream to the same life – same mountains, same sea, same gossips in village shops, same ovarian cancer, same boots, same rucksack, all seen with new eyes. It was me that had changed. I'd been to death and back again and now I was different.

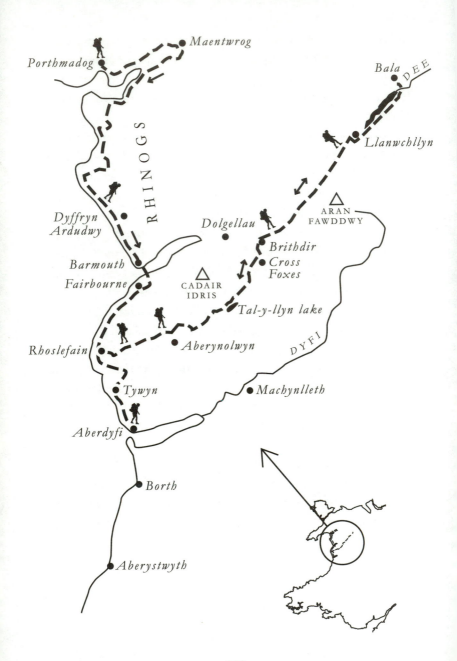

300

THE MARY JONES WALK

Route description: A trail created as a memorial to mark the route that Mary Jones walked to buy a Bible in 1800. Mary was a woman who, in her sixteenth year, walked twenty-eight barefoot miles from her mother's squat cottage in Llanfihangel y Pennant to Bala, carrying the money she'd saved for six years to buy a Welsh-language Bible from Thomas Charles, an influential preacher. He gave her three, so impressed was he by her dedication.

Length:	26.5 miles
Total ascent:	1,259m
Maximum height:	300m
Dates:	8 – 13 April 2015
Time taken:	6 days
Nights camping/nights hosted:	3/3
Days off:	0
Average miles per day:	14

I was walking while wanting to hide. I was hiding while wanting to walk. It was a strange week, this time of return, of spring, of newness, beginning again. I felt immediately happier on my return to Wales, the warmth of the colours, the sharp increase in the distance of my horizons. How could I feel sad when I walked alone over hillsides, the grey flat sea far below me, sheep and their lambs mixing and calling, sleeping curled against each other, nestling at field edges?

No more being hemmed in by grey buildings, exhaust smoke hanging in a flat landscape, so flat that canals provided most of the nature-walking. Here I found blue sea, sun sparkling on lakes, vivid purple heather lining small paths that wound through low hills. Anglesey was in the distance, patches of snow gleaming on high mountains as the sun coloured my face down by the flat marsh edges. Instead of a walk to hospital, always thinking of schedules and the beginnings and ends of visits, I now had entire days and open landscapes, grass springing back under my feet as sheep raised their heads to watch me pass, their noses flaring after a trace of my scent.

This made me happy, listening to the rain fall thickly-wet as I lay dry on a dusting of dead leaves and bat shit in a quiet, long-forgotten building, arcs of spider web hanging in the corners. The daffodils, the dawn chorus; deep swellings of joy came with the rediscovery of positive sensations. Stress had obscured the knowledge that a beautiful world still existed away from hospitals, large-scale machines created to manage the squirming, filthy nature of human illness and death: contain it, sanitise, streamline. In hospitals there's no life, no real, raw, messy, contaminated, interwoven living.

My feet felt better; the pain of long overuse had been dimmed by two months of inactivity, and instead I could pay attention to the gentler sensations of the stretching and strength of my leg-muscles as I began to walk again. It was a nice time, to walk gentle distances in the spring freshness, hair waving in the sunlight.

I enjoyed a great deal of that first week away from Derbyshire; the sensory part of walking Wales lifted me. But I also felt deeply sad at times; there was a lot of delayed shock that needed to trickle out. Owen had almost died and we'd been with him every moment as he fought back to health. I wanted to fix him, I wanted him to be better and there was nothing I could do to make it happen. He was ill and I was far away from him. I felt desolate and broken. Normally I'd hide, hibernate. I was 35 years old and I knew my ways by then, the ways I dealt with stress: solitude and unhealthy food. You may think that an extended daily walk would provide the solitude I needed, but it didn't somehow. I needed to hibernate, not sit alone on a rock in an open landscape. I needed to be left undisturbed, not on alert to the possibility of a farmer on a quad bike buzzing over the horizon, or a fellow walker at the next stile, ready for a hello and a cheery conversation.

I had a taster of private space with Dianna in Dyffryn Ardudwy. She knew what had happened and thoughtfully made me a bed in the caravan in her garden. I'd explained to my online followers some of the immensity of what had happened, to account for my sudden disappearance from daily updates. I made polite conversation but retreated as soon as I was able, escaping to the caravan balancing a tray containing teabags, a jug of milk, a cake-tin, and a glass bottle of blackcurrant whisky.

Cooking being one of her ways of caring, Dianna showed me her tenderness by baking me a cake. Foil-wrapped eggs were spaced, like turrets, at regular intervals around the edge of a chocolate Easter cake. I delicately consumed the entire thing, slice by slice, and sloshed whisky into a wineglass, savouring the dark and sharp-sweet flavour. I drank as much as I could without seeming to have drunk it at all, afraid of my urge to empty the bottle. I wanted to destroy myself for a short evening, but knew this wasn't the answer to my stress, only a way to add more to it. I'd been a heavy drinker in the past and knew this was a destructive instinct that I shouldn't listen to.

The sun and signs of spring did me a power of good. I felt my heavy heart lifting as my feet trod gently across the miles down from Porthmadog and around two estuaries. I was walking in Wales and walking back to myself. My time was my own again, to be filled with my own simple desires: to walk, to sit, to eat and to sleep. My limits were defined only by a far-away target: the promise of home, a return to Machynlleth and an end to walking. But it lay a thousand miles away, deep in the future.

I turned away from the coastal path at Rhoslefain and headed inland to Abergynolwyn to begin the Mary Jones Walk.

I wanted to walk barefoot to mark her journey, but my tender feet squirmed at the idea. They'd grown soft and weak in their protective casing; there was no way I could walk a mile barefoot, let alone fifty-six.

First, though, the Mary Jones Walk started with a break, an empty house that was too good to resist.

"I'll leave the key under a rock for you," said Sarah in Abergynolwyn.

I intended to stay there for one night and then walk away towards Bala. I meant to keep walking, I needed to; after all these breaks and interruptions, there was no time to lose and I didn't have the money to stretch things out needlessly. But it was an empty house and I so badly needed to do nothing. So I did, staying there for three nights, walking a few miles on Sunday afternoon but mostly sleeping until late morning and trying to write, trying to get my feelings out, begin processing as the calmness of walking Wales seeped back into my alarmed brain, long set on alert by danger to my tribe.

The part of me that wasn't berating myself told me that it was OK. *Calm down, you can take as long about this as you need, you can always borrow more money. It's been an intense two months and you obviously need some time alone to do nothing. Take it. Sit all day and write. Have baths. Sleep as much as you like. Let the fear out, feel the effect that the stress of your brother's accident has had on you: the weeks of worry and focus and hope. Allow yourself to stop. Allow yourself to heal.*

Eventually, after a few days away – first down in Bristol to go to my own hospital appointment, and then to visit my brother in the neurological rehabilitation ward – I was properly ready to start on this section of the walk. Owen was well enough not to need a constant family presence but I couldn't just leave him altogether; he was vulnerable and we had to be a major part of his life for a while. I'd go back and forth until the end of the walk: first a week of walking and then a break to visit him, then two weeks walking before visiting him again, then a month. The gaps would become longer and longer as we became more certain of the shape his recovery would take. My own hospital visit was a quick tick on a to-do list. I was in no immediate danger and had other things to worry about than the 4% chance of my cancer returning; my brother had a life-changing brain injury and I was in the middle of a 3300 mile walk. I was more worried about my feet than my ovary!

I set off from Abergynolwyn at 11am, spinning out a last few moments at Sarah's breakfast table before I put my boots on and went out to walk. Again. I crossed the valley and climbed up to a back road that led into the forestry and the farms that border Tal-y-Llyn. I'd not seen this side of the lake before; the road curls alongside on the opposite side. I walked along, enjoying the sunshine and fresh green countryside. Just half an hour's walk and I was already far away from roads and buildings, from everything except nature. Perfect.

The path wriggled up and down above the lake, descending into small gorges to cross streams and ancient abandoned farmyards, trees growing out of crumbled ruins. My grandparents had honeymooned here, in the early 1950s. I looked at different outbuildings, trying to imagine where they might have stayed, thinking about the life of a newly married couple sixty-five years ago, driving to Wales in their Austin 7, their hopes and happiness. What would a 50s Welsh cottage be like? Indoor toilet? Heating?

Furniture? Linen? They would have had the absolute basics without the rural tourist industry of today – no such thing as a five-star holiday cottage.

The lambs were coming again, the knock-kneed joy of jumping babies. I walked through fields full of brand-new lambs napping in the sun, struggling to co-ordinate legs and brain. One particularly brave lamb didn't run away with its mother, but stood, stared, came over and smelled my legs then curled up beside my foot. I couldn't resist crouching down and taking a few photos. A lamb close up!

At the end of the lake, I dropped down to the road and passed the foot of Cader Idris. There was a short period of road walking – pretty dangerous on this fast and busy stretch – but when I reached the head of the mountain pass the road opened up into the wide valley, and I could turn left to walk over the reedy moorlands before arriving at the Cross Foxes, a large hotel at the T-junction marking the ancient stopping-place. There was time for a quick pint at the hotel and to put my feet up on the sofa, before I was ready to walk around the small hill towards Brithdir, looking for somewhere to sleep. I got distracted by an old barn, walking into the field it stood in, entranced by the view of Cader Idris to the left and layers of hills, blueing beautifully in the fading light. It was a wonderful view but I couldn't find anywhere that felt right. Ground too lumpy, stones scattered near to the barn walls.

Eventually I came to a cycle-track that led over open farmland. The flattest spot was on the path itself, another place I wouldn't normally sleep but decided to chance it. I laid out my bed and ate my evening meal – the usual flavoured couscous soaked in cold water, mackerel, grated carrot, mayonnaise – an unappetising idea that tastes loads better than it sounds! It was cold that night, I had to put a scarf over my head and face and my nose was freezing, but the hardship was worth it for the sight of the moon rising over the hillside.

I sat up to watch the pre-dawn light flood the view below me, eyes taking a while to focus, gluey from the cold night air. Around me, dew beaded every grass-blade; it was a fresh morning, just a little bit too cold for me to jump out of bed. I should have done though, about half an hour later came the buzz of a farmer's buggy. Oops! He had to make a detour around my sleeping spot; it was obvious I'd camped there but he just nodded to me.

"Morning."

"Morning."

It was ten miles to Llanuwchllyn and another beautiful warm day. Summer warm, too soon for me; I still had my white winter skin and thick clothing. I went a few miles to the edge of a forest, stopping for breakfast on some tussocky tree-roots, sitting and admiring the thick mosses and fallen leaves. But I must continue, I must always continue. The path took me along quiet tracks, high up on the valley side.

Below was the modern road in the valley bottom. It would have been a toll-road 200 years ago and Mary Jones couldn't have afforded that. So instead I experienced the old tracks she might have walked – tree-lined, winding, the ways to travel before tarmac and car engines came into being. Up and down went the day, from farm to farm towards Llanuwchllyn.

I trudged on, feeling surprisingly tired and rubbish. A row of four excited pensioners perked me up, sitting outside their caravans enjoying the sunshine. They gave me a fillip of validation, a water top-up and £30 for my donation-tin. I imagined that I'd probably see them in exactly the same place as I retraced my steps, walking the path in reverse on my way back to the coast. I went on a bit further but was struggling. I stopped for lunch, which was a carrot and a stray chocolate bar from the bottom of my rucksack. Boots off, feet propped up in the air, scouring my rucksack for remaining scraps of food. As I carried on walking my head ached more and more; I think it was the hazy light and its effect on my flapping flags, the white edges fluttering in and out of my vision. I sat in the Eagle Inn, Llanuwchllyn with my head in my hands and phoned Fiona, my host east of Bala, to see if she'd mind picking me up, pressing a little upon her good nature given the eleven-mile distance. She came, though, took me home and made me comfortable in the caravan. I tucked up with a meat pie and peas, bed by nine thirty, woolly blankets and the radio.

The next day, washed, rested, I felt better. From Llanuwchllyn to Bala was an easy, flat five miles around the lake and I could sit for a couple of hours in a café, getting given free tea and chips by a lovely Irish waiter. It was a beautiful, beautiful day; the greens and blues of the woods and lake glowing bright and relaxed in the sunshine, and I felt so glad to be doing this. I'd followed the likely path that Mary Jones came to buy a Welsh Bible, 200 years ago. What kind of money would I raise if I saved for six years? How many books could I buy? She bought one. How different my life was to hers, my needs fulfilled with ease, millions of books available to me, delivered to an address of my choosing, bought with my disposable income.

The route follows ancient trackways and drovers' roads, mostly high above the valley bottoms where the marshes or toll-roads would have been, many years ago. Thinking about Mary's life back then, her experiences, the most I could do was stare at the view and wonder what wasn't there.

I did well with my own body too: not at Mary's level, twenty-eight barefoot miles overnight. No, it took me three days. But that was good enough; I'd managed sixty miles in five days, averaging twelve miles a day which, for me, was flying. My body felt full of power, my legs were strong with muscle; just my feet held me back, my poor strained plantar tendons.

Arriving in Bryncrug, having reversed my route over another two days of walking and camping, I was almost back at the coastal path again, sodden from a surprise rain-storm. I was too lazy to put my waterproof trousers on, as usual, so got soaking wet as usual. I'm no kind of survivalist. I'd spent the previous night in a barn – no shelter out on the open moorland of Cwm Hafod Oer, and I didn't fancy crawling into a soggy, windblown tent so I found a wooden bench in the shelter of a quiet barn. Remove the sack of lime and the empty sheep-drench tin and, bingo, there was my bed. The farmer came in after dark, unexpectedly.

"I'm sorry," I said, frozen on the bench, an interloper in his empty property.

"No problem," he said, more concerned about the dead lamb in the pen in the corner.

They'd been so quiet I hadn't realised there were animals in there. He shooed the mother out, cursing. I saw her the next morning, hanging around in the gravelled enclosure, head drooping, limping.

I'd meant to camp on the night of my arrival in Bryncrug, in the wet again, but Sarah was only five miles away, over the hill.

"I'll pick you up," she said, like the big-hearted nurturer she is. I had no signal until Bryncrug but there she was, at short notice. "Yeah, no worries, love, I'll be there in half an hour."

I had a bath, rubbed my feet, bedded down on her sofa.

Sarah took my bag ahead so I could walk freely, past Tywyn and then along the long beach to Aberdyfi, treading the line between the silvered dunes and the tide, sun reddening my face, sand soft under my boots, a thread of footsteps laid out behind me. I treated myself to a cream tea when I reached the town, then it was a walk along the road to a holiday apartment, thanks to Paul at The Old Stables. It was lush, luxurious and all mine for the night. What generosity!

THE DYFI VALLEY WAY

Route description: A beautiful walk tracing either side of the Dyfi river, from Aberdyfi up to the peak of Aran Fawddwy, near Dinas Mawddwy, and returning on the south side of the river to finish on the opposite point of the estuary at Borth.

Length:	101.4 miles
Total ascent:	6422m
Maximum height:	876m
Dates:	14 April – 5 May 2015
Time taken:	22 days
Nights camping/nights hosted:	1/21
Days off:	10
Average miles per day:	11.1

From Bryncrug to Borth I didn't stay too long on the coastal path before I detoured inland again. I'd spotted the potential for a circular route during my route planning. The Dyfi Valley Way ran along one side of the river from the sea to the source where it dribbled off the peak of Aran Fawddwy, and traced back to the sea again on the southern side. One hundred and eight miles of familiar territory, this was the place I'd called home for the two years before I set out on this journey. I'd have friendly faces and warm beds for the whole length of it.

The Dyfi Valley Way began in Aberdyfi and finished in Borth. To make sure that I could say I'd walked the whole of the Wales Coastal Path I decided to walk it to Borth, then retrace my steps to Aberdyfi and set out on the Dyfi Valley Way, continuing south once

I reached Borth again. It meant I walked the panoramic way between Aberdyfi and Pennal three times, as the Dyfi Valley Way followed the same route!

Here's the farm where I cut through a field to the road, here's the house where the road runs out, here's the horseshoe mark cut deep into the boulder, here's the double-locked gate, here's where that dog barked at me, here's where the beautiful flowers are, here's where I cut through the woodland. On again now, for the third time, all the way to Pennal where the Dyfi Valley Way took a left, heading up the valley away from the coast and through the forest, down to Pantperthog.

I gave Polly a ring and stayed with her family for one final night. I'd had three nights in a bell tent in her garden as she ferried me between my trekking points, giving me the rest I needed and absorbing me into the typical chaos of a house containing young, adorable children.

It was a peaceful day heading up into the Dyfi Forest towards Dinas Mawddwy, padding along through closely-planted pine trees, along dry dusty packed-rock roads, finding paths that led between the isolated farms and houses which had survived the compulsory land-purchases. I passed derelict Capel Soar, slate slabs slowly being pushed from roofless walls by the trees which grew there in place of a congregation. Once this valley would have held farms, workers' huts, a school; now peaceful ranks of pine stood silent, bird calls echoing through the trees.

I got frustrated in the final few miles before reaching Dinas Mawddwy. The unwalked path ran out into a sea of brambles, impossible to push through. I had to retrace my steps and cut along the side of the pine forest, stopping every so often to watch the fighter jets flit alongside me, their shadows racing to catch them up along the steep hillsides.

I didn't last long in the company of hospitable Kim and his two friendly dogs. Despite the dogs insistently pushing their noses into the crook of my elbow, I fell asleep on the sofa by eight: sun-blasted, mile-weakened.

The next day I set out to walk to Llanuwchllyn and back again. I'd climb up and over Aran Fawddwy and then return around the base of it from the opposite side of the river, coming around Creiglyn Dyfi Lake where it curled into the crater side of the mountain. Thirty miles in two days, crossing a mountain: a tough journey. My feet didn't normally let me walk so far.

Oh, the bed was so comfortable, some kind of mattress covering I could just sink into and spend the day on but no, not yet. I hadn't earned a day off, not with all the breaks I was taking to go and see my brother. I got up, met Jackie as she came home, bleary-eyed from the night shift, saw her off to bed and set out, my rucksack carrying the bare minimum for an overnight camp.

First I met Clara, who came to accompany me for the first few miles towards the base of the hill climb. We walked in the sunshine, promising a hot day ahead up, the back roads passing small farms, sheep roaming, lambs bleating for their mothers. Clara turned back eventually, normal life calling, and I climbed on, coming to the steep beginning of the mountain, up a few hundred metres, stopping at a water-trickle to wash off my sweat and sun-cream, reapplying again. I climbed and climbed with frequent pauses, excusing myself that it was to admire the view, looking back at how far I'd come.

Eventually I was at the cairn marking the top of Aran Fawddwy. There was a white heat-haze covering the far distance, but I could make out the distinctive lumps of the Rhinog range, tracing in my mind my couple of days climbing up and down them with Stu. Nearer to me was the brute lump of Dduallt, the mountain I'd walked to in search of the source of the River Wye, the Arenigs further away to the north; I'd walked around them, dropped off near Llyn Conwy by Alun, the friendly farmer. Then coming, down to Bala, there was the blue puddle of Llyn Tegid that I'd walked around. Below was the valley I'd walked alongside last week, following Mary Jones' path. I retraced my footsteps across this view, saluting the months of effort and satisfaction.

Walking slowly down the ridges towards Llanuwchllyn, my knees ached on the downhills. I tried to estimate the time I would arrive: 7pm I hoped. Enough time to rest a bit and then try for another few miles before sunset; the next day would be an eighteen miler unless I knocked another couple off tonight. It was 7.10pm when I staggered towards the car-park by the bridge, too tired to walk the extra quarter-mile to the pub, no time to linger there anyway. I took enough time to take off my shoes, sit on a rock, eat my evening meal and wiggle my toes. Then that was it, I heaved up my bag once again and walked slowly on aching feet towards the valley at the base of the Aran ridge, looking for a place to sleep.

I found it after a couple of miles: a perfect piece of old, ungrazed land, crumbled stone wall near a stream, oak-tree canopy and a flat piece of ground in the centre. I kicked some chunkier twigs to the side and settled to rest, watching the stars come out between the tree branches.

Early start the next morning, pausing for breakfast once my stomach started rumbling. I looked up at the ridgeline of the Arans above. The outline was familiar and I realised that I was heading towards Nant-y-Barcut, the farm I'd been taken to when I was offered a bed in Llanuwchllyn by Heledd. She'd called the outline of Aran Benllyn above the farm 'the old man', saying he had his hat on when the clouds covered the peak. Should I say hello? My path would take me right past her front door. I thought it over as I walked up the lane towards the farm. Perhaps she wouldn't remember me; it had been almost a year. Perhaps she'd think I was crazy, some smelly hobo with an equally odorous rucksack turning up uninvited. Maybe she'd think I was ridiculous for still walking, plodding on like Don Quixote, endlessly in search of 3000 miles. I came closer and decided to put these foolish thoughts to one side. I had to knock, just to say hello at least. Of course Heledd recognised me, she was following me on Facebook! It all worked out, nice cup of tea and a chat and I was on my way – without rucksack!

Heledd had offered to take it to the other side of the hill: a steep climb for me, a detour around the mountain pass for her. She kept asking if I wanted a sandwich; I kept saying no, being proud, being independent, but at the last minute I relented, said yes, it would be nice. I only had sugary treats to last me until I reached Dinas and a solid meal that night.

It took three hours for me to reach the church porch where Heledd had agreed to drop my bag. At the head of Cwm Croes, where the farm-track ended, I passed Cwm-fynnon, a small, low farmworker's cottage, the shabby door held closed with orange twine. Three butterflies battered desperately at the cobwebbed window, wings worn thin in their torment. I tried to open the window and help them but it was no good. I unwound the door handle and went inside to the remnants of an older way of life. Broken red-rose china on a table, ancient ashes in an open grate, a wooden pew against the wall. The fluttering of the butterflies against the window was loud in the sleeping cottage. I closed my hands around each one in turn, raising them to the open window and freedom, then left the cottage, rewinding the twine around the doorknob, looking around furtively as I walked away, unsure of my right to enter.

I walked, crab-wise, up the steep valley-head and down the other side, joining the small Dyfi stream where it wound and tumbled down from the Creiglyn Dyfi Lake. Eventually, after a steep descent and a road-walk in burning sunshine, I reached the shade of the church porch, finding my rucksack and the packed lunch Heledd had made for me. Deep delight as I lowered myself onto the cool stone seat to enjoy this unexpected feast. Sandwiches, crisps, cake and fruit. Such a small thing for her, an intense joy for me.

I walked on: just six miles more. I could see the valley split where I'd walked with Clara the previous day, the head of Aran Fawddwy receding behind me, the conjoining of valleys ahead of me where Dinas Mawddwy nestled into the unseen dip, the settlement at the crossing of routes.

Made it. 7pm, just in time to see Jackie before she disappeared for the night shift, inhale a big plate of spaghetti and salad, stroke the dogs for a while, chat to Kim, shower, bed.

I broke the walk again the next day, going back to the Midlands for a few days to welcome Owen home from hospital. I didn't like entering the urban area, with its car fumes and UKIP posters, houses pressed close together. To stop and start was also frustrating; it felt like I wasn't properly concentrating on either thing, but it was the way it had to be. Owen was coming home after three months in hospital and I wanted to ease him into his first week back in a house. He lived by himself and would suddenly be expected to do all the daily tasks of a normal life: washing up, cleaning, bill-paying, cooking, monitoring his hunger, his fatigue. It was all new to him, yet completely familiar.

He listened to his music collection, hearing the freshness of the music for the first time but simultaneously experiencing the memories that special tunes fired for him. He was OK and not OK, all at the same time: free to leave hospital and enter back into his own life, but he'd completely changed, whereas everything else

316

remained the same. The strangeness of his brain injury didn't show on the outside. It wasn't an easily labelled disability, but apparent in an unusual way of expressing himself, a strange blankness with certain words, a difficulty in organising himself, needing long periods of rest. There was no guarantee that he was capable of returning to work. Yet his situation contained so much joy, he was alive when he very much might not have been; our family's love for one another was unexpectedly at the forefront of life and constantly reinforced. We were all really happy to be around him, laughing at his foibles, making humour out of his mistakes, cheering when his broken jaw healed well enough to allow him to put a whole crème egg into his mouth, the way he'd always liked to eat them.

I registered to vote during this period, as a person of no fixed abode. The solemnity of what I'd done, the official labelling of myself, settled on me for the first time. I'd actually made myself homeless, so fixed was I on the idea of telling women about the symptoms of ovarian cancer. The journey had overtaken everything else in my life, there was nothing else. No home, no work, nothing else to fill my time. Walking was all I wanted to do, walk and raise awareness, collect donations. Was this obsession OK? Was my mental health intact? Other fears preyed on my mind too. I currently had less money and security than I'd ever had in my life. I had no idea if this was safe or reasonable, just that I had a way of living that worked for what I wanted to do right now. I had a system that allowed me to walk long distance, I knew how to cope with it, I had the right kit and just about enough money to finish what I'd started, to walk roughly another 1000 miles. That was enough for now. The future could wait, whatever shape I was making for it.

Back in Dinas Mawddwy I shouldered my pack again, heading back to the sea where I'd walk around the coastal path and down to South Wales, through sun and rain and wild nights and strangers' beds, through experiences unknown. I passed through the houses and hands of many friends in the Dyfi Valley: Tom and Laura, Vicky and James, Ruth and Naps, Annie, Megan, Kate...

The next time I saw Machynlleth would be at the end of the walk. I'd walk around the coast of South Wales, detouring inland to walk four more rivers and that would be it, just up the River Wye and home, back to Machynlleth for the final time. I swapped my boots again; this pair had walked 1000 miles and were bulging and cracked, slip-soled tired travellers, bent and worn by their journey. I stocked up on small things from my supply-dump, chomped final chocolate bars and posted supplies ahead to friendly addresses in Bristol and Pembroke. That was it, I was heading south. See you at the end, Machynlleth and friends!

CEREDIGION AND PEMBROKESHIRE COASTAL PATH

Route description: The most beautiful area of the Wales Coastal Path, the Pembrokeshire coastal path in particular is a long established National Trail, opened in 1970 – a spectacular cliff coastline walk in many places, providing views of the rugged northern coast and then rounding the corner at St David's to the softer rocks of the south coast and its many sandy beaches.

Length:	240 miles
Total ascent:	12,826m
Maximum height:	167m
Dates:	6 – 31 May 2015
Time taken:	26 days
Nights camping/nights hosted:	8/18
Days off:	4
Average miles per day:	11

The days were longer now, and the temperature had risen. I luxuriated in daylight, took breaks without fear of losing body-heat or walking time. I slept outside without a tent once again, plonked myself anywhere in green-grassed solitude, no longer having to stop at 5pm twilight or immediately snuggle into my feather-lined cocoon.

Summer days meant carelessness, stretching out on my back, wriggling into last year's dry bracken for a post-lunch catnap. Summer brought scent: hot coconutty gorse, fresh pine fronds, thick carpets of bluebells, grass, greenery, growth. The land was returning to full, fecund life and my first few weeks of the coastal path were spent enjoying full bluebell-power.

Without having to fight the weather, walking got easier. The series of enforced breaks seemed to be doing my feet a lot of good too – first the six weeks of no walking as I orbited around my brother in hospital and then the regular breaks to go and visit him. My daily distances started creeping up – fifteen, seventeen, nineteen miles.

There seemed to be no stories to tell; this incredible life was normal now, I just kept walking. My sister came for five days, and we walked together. She'd come from Mexico for a summer of family visits, coincidentally timing her flight with my brother's accident, arriving just a few days after he woke from the coma. We'd spent a couple of months together in the maelstrom of his recovery, tight together in the same house, loving and supporting each other through this incredibly hard time. My sister was my calm place, my source of wisdom. Now it was time to relax together, for her to visit my life and share the wonder of what I was doing. Together we traversed the short seventy miles of the Ceredigion Coastal Path, where the land came from the flat plains of Ynyslas and Aberaeron then gradually climbed and climbed, the ripples of land becoming higher as we grew closer to Pembrokeshire, the cliffs higher and the drops to small beach coves steeper.

Walking with Rose made me realise how fit I was and, conversely, how unhealthy I was. She'd always been thinner than me, with a different, more athletic, body type. She was willowy, I was sturdy and rounded. It was OK, I wasn't jealous, just appreciative of how beautiful she was, proud of her for looking so good. She went to the gym regularly at home, had taken self-defence, core strength training. I felt slightly defensive about walking with her.

Sometimes I felt as if this wasn't a challenge at all, that this was just a beautiful walk with loads of people helping and supporting me, making life easier. Then Rose came to walk with me and I jokingly pushed her up steep slopes as she slowed down, helped tend to her blisters and realised that this was in fact a huge challenge; I'd just toughened up over the course of it, incredibly so. I helped her as she struggled with a too-heavy bag, feeling the pain of wrongly-fitting, borrowed boots and realised that in comparison I was worn in, finally, after months of exhaustion!

Rose also showed me something about my diet. She ate a mostly vegetarian diet with very little processed food in her everyday life, and I realised our hunger was different. She needed to eat regularly and often, not quieting her system with handfuls of sugar. Her metabolism was different to mine, her hunger came strong and deep and wouldn't be satisfied with a handful of peanuts, needing regular, large meals whereas I was satisfied with what she called snacks.

While walking with her I started to move away from sugar as fuel, to foods that would provide energy differently, more slowly and for longer. It still had to be picnic food, however – raw food, able to be transported in a rucksack. Hummus became a staple: carrots, tomatoes, oatcakes and hummus. I felt my body react differently. I had fewer exhausted drops as the quick hit of high sugar energy ran out. I began to see that maybe this was why I was fatter than her, that I put my body in a constant churning and saving, that my body was fixed on energy storage because its supply came either as feast or famine. My metabolism was fixed in winter scarcity, holding onto what came in because it never knew when the next good food would come; she lived in a summer of plenty, always eating what she needed, not forcing her body to hoard energy. It was a glimmer of another life, not something that I could easily fix, but bringing the spark of an idea that if I wanted to change my body, to be healthier, it wouldn't be by imposing a diet, but changing my entire attitude to food.

We started along the Pembrokeshire coastal path. The first section of the path, from St Dogmaels to Newport, was reported as one of the toughest. No water sources or settlements for fifteen miles. After fourteen glorious cliff-top miles, we arrived at 6pm, stumbling and sun-shocked. The BBC told me it would start raining early the following morning so we bumbled around in Newport, trying to decide what to do. Try and squeeze two of us into my one-man tent or seek some form of shelter? An old lime-kiln? A barn? A bus stop? The porch of an empty holiday home? We were hungry, really, and in no state to make decisions, so we fumbled and demurred, played cards in a pub, went to eat expensive pizza and finally, as the last of the light ebbed from the sky, erected the tent on a field edge, a mile from Newport.

Sunset lay on the surface of the rocking water out in the bay, metallic layers of light gold leafing the tide, highlighting the plume and spray of waves further out. We sat watching it, in peace, eventually noticing four fox-cubs playing and gambolling in the next field. They jumped and stalked one another, rolling and leaping. The nearest one saw us, sitting quietly in our lurid, unnatural colours, and their body language changed completely. Low to the ground and slinking, they stalked towards us, creeping and investigating, coming as close as they dared, beady eyes shining, before marking us as harmless and returning to their mown field home.

All was dreamy and perfect until my sis came back from her final wee.

"Sis. There are cows in the field."

There were and they were coming to investigate. Up sticks, roll beds together and hop over a gate into the next field, unfortunately a lot more sloping. Not much sleep, painful hips, aching back and bleary faces in the morning. Sometimes wild camping is like that.

5am, the wind started blowing, 6am, right on time, the drizzle started and we got up. Pack away, waterproof up, a couple of slices of cold pizza, and we set off to an incredibly wild and windy Dinas Head and then a long trudge to Fishguard, windblown, tired out. These early starts would be the way to walk really long distances, twelve miles by lunchtime, if we could handle the exhaustion. My fit sister hurt all over, was hobbling, feet throbbing.

"Welcome to my world," I said with grim satisfaction, and probably a hint of sibling smugness. "You'll enjoy it eventually..."

The Pembrokeshire Coastal Path was where the coastal landscape really changed. Rosie left to make other family visits, and as I walked further south the sea became a glorious turquoise blue, shimmering seductively. I saw my first grey seal, thousands of bluebells, stuck my feet in streams, climbed endless steep cliffs, slept in fields, was sniffed at by wild ponies extending tentative, quivering nostrils. Around every corner was a brand new bay, jewel-bright sea lapping at the rocks. Wildflowers grew profusely, thick clumps of them everywhere, the air was thick with fragrance. Speedboats looped circles in the bays below me as I walked high on cliff edges, my feet following the foot-flattened dirt path.

The sun beat down on me, unrelenting. I was wearing factor 30 and my skin was still burning; spending so many hours outside made it unavoidable. I saw cormorants, gannets, gulls, a myriad of small brown birds perched by my sleeping-spot, fluttering above me with beaks full of caterpillars. The caterpillars! Tiny black ones, tiger-striped ones, porcupine-quilled orange monsters. I put my boot down next to the path-stranded ones, they climbed up and I hobbled to the edge of the path and flicked them into the long grass. I assessed the path for sleeping places out of habit, finding snug dips with soft grass linings, hollows where the rock was giving way to gravity in the slow motion of centuries.

These things were just small highlights in days of steady steps, hours outside, hauling myself up slopes or along cliff edges. My hair blowing in the wind, I just kept walking.

I walked, I rested, I waved my flags, I ate, I met friendly people, I gave out symptoms-cards, collected donations; pound by pound they trickled into my tin. I kept going.

There didn't seem to be peaks of excitement anymore. I was surrounded by beautiful things and kind people every day, and instead of the jumpy, flushed peaks of joy there was simply a deep satisfaction that life was as it should be. I walked, I managed my pain and discomfort, I covered the miles. There was nothing more; it was simply a matter of mileage. I had come 2600 miles, I had struggled through pain, winter, mountains, turning my legs to steely trunks. There was nothing left for me to do but finish this; another 700 miles, more or less, give or take. I just needed to put one foot in front of the other until it was done.

I sensed, faintly, that I had become obsessed, that in order to succeed at this walking challenge I had gone beyond a passion for symptoms awareness and talking to women about ovarian cancer. I was shoehorning my experience into every encounter, giving out cards, putting them on tables in cafés, up on noticeboards, leaving them in hosts' houses to pass to friends.

Tell as many women as possible. Walk 3300 miles. I was doing it. I would keep doing it.

There is always a path when you're following the coast, but especially in Pembrokeshire where the places closest to the sea are rocky and uncivilised. I'd look down at the next bay and see a path winding down to it, a cut in the gorse and thorny hedge which my eye could follow to the stony beach. The path trickled along the stones, heaped at the highest point of the wash in a gradual slope from the sea, and then down a sharper drop to where the bushes began.

I enjoyed the feeling of rounded, sea-washed shingle shifting under each step, although it was difficult when it went on for too long, sapping my energy through the movement of the stone.

The path clearly rose up with the shape of the next headland, a strip of brown worn into the earth by the repeated pass of feet tracing the edge of the land, an endless ribbon laid down to follow around every corner. I passed my eyes over the land, finding the trace of others' feet, a marker for me to follow, unquestioning, trusting. It wasn't grass that I walked on here, but dozens of tiny plants, tougher than grass, that could withstand the daily blow of offshore winds, nibbling sheep and the tread of feet. The ground was a mosaic of plant life, budding and growing together, wind-seeded. But mostly there was a thin stone path, as wide as two feet standing side by side, and my ankles brushed the tips of the grasses as I strode. In places the path gave way to rocks cleaned of earth by the repeated pass of feet. Bushes rose to either side, remnants of stone walls grown through with vegetation. Spigot bursts of gorse, studded with bright yellow buds.

The path rose and dipped between harbour and headland. It was a ragged, rugged coastline, fragmenting away into the sea, a line of waves rippling and breaking at the shore. The rocks sat in waves too, ridges lapping away from me, a line formed under immense pressure into wobbles and curves.

I'd turn a corner and see, stretching away, another headland to manoeuvre, or the haven of a dip inland: a place to stop, maybe a toilet or a café to sit at. The harbours were mostly set to catch tourists now, the flat boat-stands emptied to hold car parks instead, cafés and pubs waiting ready with glossy menus to empty wallets and ring tills. I could stop anywhere, laze out on the grass wherever

I wanted, but somehow these harbours made marker points, targets to achieve before I could rest.

A week into Pembrokeshire, walking barefoot on the sands of Newgale, my feet felt like shelled prawns. Cramped and clawed they slowly relaxed into the sand and then struggled to revert to their usual positions. It was the final two miles of the day and I'd decided to walk them in a straight line along the long, flat sands. I never take my boots off and dabble my feet in water, it's too much effort and would disturb the carefully stuck-on strapping that helps to save my feet from so much pain. But that day I put my bag on a rock and eased off my tightly laced leather ankle-boots, pulled off four sweaty socks – two thick woollen ones and two thin cotton liners – and wriggled my sensitive feet into the sand. Unused to the sensation of anything abrasive they squirmed; it was exquisitely ticklish.

I took my poor feet to the sea and let them bathe in the ripples of the shallow tidal wash. I felt sorry for them, they'd suffered so much. I walked the entire two miles of Newgale Sands barefoot and it was painful, especially for my Achilles tendons, but I continued hobbling because I wanted my feet to stretch out in a safe place. The sensation of barefoot sand walking made my steps very small and tentative, and I trod carefully and slowly along the sand, thinking about stretching each part of my feet as they pressed against the buoyant, yielding grains. I took steps on tiptoe and steps on my heels. It felt lovely, raising and lowering my heels to stretch my calves into different positions. At the end of the two miles I went up into the rocky, gravelly edge where fields started to meet sand and made camp among the fading bluebells.

From Newgale to Tenby I had help all the way. I was passed from house to house for 100 miles of walking, my rucksack a suitcase to rustle through at the end of a day, never strapped on for a day's tread, never a stone upon my shoulders. Three families helped me, first

John and Jo in Spittal, then Helen and Simon for a night in Pembroke Dock, and Lynn in Angle. They all had their own reasons for coming forward. Jo was a belly dance student of Mel's, inspired by my bravery; further east towards Carmarthen, Simon had fought his own cancer battle; and Lynn was a keen walker who'd heard about me through Facebook sharing. I started to ramp up my distances, managing regular eighteen-mile days. My body felt good, I was a machine, flying along the rugged coastal path, full of physical power.

During that week I met Sarah, another woman who was making her way through to the other side of ovarian cancer, relying on Target Ovarian Cancer and online support to navigate her way through a suddenly uncertain, fear-filled existence.

I felt nervous as I approached our meeting point: the road bridge crossing into Pembroke Dock, high above the River Cleddau. We walked towards each other, small figures coming far from either end of the mile-long bridge, growing closer until we embraced, wind blowing hair into our faces.

There was small talk until we reached the pub and could embark on the real thing: the exchange of cancer stories. Gary, her partner, bought drinks and smiled quietly, familiar with this relaying of history. We shared our diagnoses: holding up fists to describe the size of tumours, describing the unfolding, the progression of a cancer diagnosis, the details of the gradual discovery that all was not well – that in fact, something was truly terrible. She had an ovary that had burst as the surgeon went to touch it. I had a mystery fluid that filled my lungs, disappearing as the doctor stood poised with exploratory needle. We were traumatised still, years later, sharing memories of our naked, hurt bodies, exposed and quivering. Each nugget of detail assumes mighty importance in the traumatised teller; we knew how it was when your mortality was in question and all you could do was wait, hoarding small scraps of information to give definition, to give hope.

We shared the before and after of cancer, of finding your way in a new and uncertain world; post-upheaval everything's changed and you must navigate your way in this new landscape, try and return to yourself again. We shared our shock at diagnosis, our ignorance of the symptoms and common desire to take action: action as healing, action as strength, action to make other women more aware, to give them the power we didn't have back then, before everything collapsed – knowledge of their own bodies and awareness of the symptoms, what to look out for and what might change.

It was a short meeting; they had to get back home after their holiday and I walked on, towards the house where I could stay that night. Hugs outside the pub, a quick photo and they were gone. I felt a bit stunned when I left Sarah, reeling from the quick dip into another's cancer story, and later in the evening I realised how far I'd come from that world, from the chaos and fear of major medical treatment.

Three months after my abdominal surgery, back in early May 2012, I went for a walk one day. The sun was starting to warm the fields and I wanted to discover the beautiful surroundings of my new home, my new beginning post-illness. I went to find my way through the oak woods that covered the side of a huge rise of land as it forked away from the road my house lay on, and separated into a side valley. Coming out into a field of long grass I lay down under the blue sky. The sun was bright and I felt the warmth of fire on my skin, the moist grass underneath me, full of the wetness of growth, plump and lush buttercups and fat, wide blades of grass. There were vivid greens and blues, the white of the clouds. I felt this sensory world for a short time, trying to absorb the beauty of the land around me into my sad post-cancer mind-set.

I felt positive and hopeful, pulling up my clothing in a gesture of healing, allowing the sunshine to hit my pale and violated skin, thin pink scar running the length of my centre. It was a few moments before I realised my thoughts had turned inwards, hands on belly, mind inside it. I'd disappeared into worry, thinking over my cancer – the chances of reappearance, the hurts of the previous months, the stress and worry and tension.

Cancer had been hovering in front of my face for months, causing a blindness to all else, even obscuring the fact that it had enveloped me. It was only when the sun brought me out of it for a short time, showing me another, lighter way of being, that I noticed when I returned to the fear and darkness.

When I met Sarah in Pembroke Dock that day, it was three years since my tumour removal, major surgery and cancer diagnosis, and I finally trusted my body again, to carry me for miles every day and not collapse. I'd walked back to normality over thousands of miles, nights of camping, days of sunlight, of soft grass, of beautiful views and contemplative solitude. I'd walked my way to health; my body was strong, solid with muscle, resilient, tough. Capable, trustworthy.

The challenge I'd set myself was so big it had eclipsed cancer. It had taken such total focus to walk 3300 miles, such a concerted effort, that I'd burnt the fear of illness out of myself. I'd walked 2700 miles of the planned total; I was strong and healthy, cancer felt behind me. I might be talking about ovarian cancer, handing out symptoms cards, raising money for two charities, but it was all for others. My own cancer story was almost finished, I'd come through to the other side. Two more years of check-ups before I could get the official all-clear, but already I felt free.

It was the 28th of May 2015 and I sat at the tip of West Angle Bay, looking out at St Ann's Head across the mouth of Milford Haven.

It was one and a half miles away across the water, refinery ships gliding serenely through the gap, the daily to-and-fro of oil deliveries. It had taken me two and a half days to cross between the two points, over forty miles of walking around the urban stretches and industrial edges of the bay, passing two oil refineries, a power station and four small towns. This journey had taken me almost fifteen months so far, and I'd covered exactly 2700 miles. I calculated the totals that night as I sat at the kitchen table in Lynn's fisherman's cottage. She would have me to stay for the next three nights as I walked around the peninsula and back east, through the sheltered and luxurious green beaches of southern Pembrokeshire, very different to the rugged north coast. I checked through again, I'd walked 2700 miles, which should mean there were only 600 to go. But the numbers didn't make sense. There were at least 270 miles of coastal path left, plus the second go-around of the Pembrokeshire coastal path once I reached the head of the Teifi River at Cardigan, plus four south Wales rivers, plus the Wye Valley Walk back to Machynlleth.

I looked again at my planning book, where I'd listed the paths and totalled the distances, first in the planning and then noting the actual distances as I finished each path. They were different. The planning list was missing many miles. I'd failed to take into account all the linking distances I'd walk between the paths: the twenty-five miles into Bristol from the end of the Severn Way and out again to the start of the Offa's Dyke Path; the extra fifty miles to walk the Mary Jones Walk in reverse back to the coast; the 100 miles from the end of the Cambrian Way to the start of the Coast-to-Coast Path.

I sat back, a fool. In my panicked pre-walk jabbering I'd come up with a total that didn't exist. I'd been focusing so hard on walking 3300 miles and now I was going to get to that amount while I was still awash in the journey, shore nowhere within sight. I didn't know how many more miles there were to go, it would depend on the river routes I took. I calculated each path as I walked it, adding or subtracting small miles depending on the actual routes I took, not simply accepting the prescribed totals. Never mind, I'd just walk the path I'd set myself and work out how long it was at the end, laughing to myself for my stupidity. The number didn't matter; the days, steps and endurance were the important bit, the people and the beauty felt never ending.

In the couple of days walking between Angle and Bosherston, I made sure to pause at the Green Bridge of Wales, a huge sea-arch next to the Castlemartin firing range. The sea was white and rough there, thumping and roaring, a lacework of white water, a thrown jumble of spray, angry heavy slaps against the rockface. The water contorts and sways, rushing inwards and back on itself to meet in a central swirl of confusion until another incoming swell overcomes and hurls all back again to hit the rock.

I wanted to play on the Green Bridge of Wales, to climb over its ridge and dive from its huge awkward shoe, resting humped on the flat rock. But to swim through the huge circle of stone and sea would be to die; looking down from such a height had turned it toylike.

I had a farewell meal with Lynn at Amroth – pie and chips outside on the patio while a minibus dispensed dressed-up women, a touring birthday party which giggled and tottered around us as we ate. Then it was a day spent walking behind the firing-range on the peninsula at Pendine, miles of clear yellow sands along the edge, following the Dylan Thomas Birthday Walk – info boards and chiselled quotations through the woods – and the Laugharne Corporation's cocklers' path into the town, where Gez and his friendly family awaited. They opened their beautiful home to me, small children moving out of the playroom so I could enjoy the double bed, scratched drawings laid to welcome me, and a delicious meal of sausages and dark Puy lentils.

The next day I continued on beaches and through the woods that lined the estuaries, the sky running patchy clouds to shadow water-pooled tidal sands, all the way to Llansteffan where I sat on the wall separating car-park from beach and looked over to the small houses of Ferryside, across the Tywi estuary. That was where, once the train came in the mid-19th century, Welsh people would welcome poor tourists, fitting the holidaying miners into their attic spaces and spare beds. Accommodation was arranged by letter, people coming for their regulation two weeks by the sea before flitting away home to resume the smoky harness of underground labour. How lucky I was to be able to take a year and a half away from work. What seemed like hardship to most, living on counted pennies, sleeping in field corners, was freedom to me.

Ferryside was only a mile and a half away across the river mouth, but I'd walk at least 300 more miles before I set foot there. I was going to turn away from the coast, buy maps in Carmarthen and follow the River Tywi up to its source before walking across to the Teifi and down again to the Cardigan coast.

THE RIVERS TWYI AND TEIFI

Route description: The two longest rivers that flow completely within Wales, both noted for their sea trout and salmon fishing, have a combined length of 148 miles. Their sources begin within 10 miles of one another and end 26 miles apart at Cardigan (Teifi) and Carmarthen (Twyi).

Length:	130 miles
Total ascent:	unknown
Maximum height:	460 m
Dates:	9 – 17 June 2015
Time taken:	9 days
Nights camping/nights hosted:	6/3
Days off:	0
Average miles per day:	14.4

Following a river is a wonderful experience: witnessing its beginning, manifesting from a sloping hollow of hillsides, the ground fecund with water, saturated. It trickles down through peat and mosses, gurgling, until it coalesces and a pool is born, overflows, water running down the side of the hill, around stones, pushing away flecks of earth, carrying them with it until it finds a grounding of stones to run over, always downhill, meeting other trickles until a stream emerges. This is the source of many a Welsh river: no surprise spout from the ground, no fountain of clear underground water, but a draining of the water-heavy hills, a gravity-born collection of rainwater drainage.

This is how rivers begin their runs to the sea, and I love to follow their journeys, through all their many faces: small, trickling, mist-laden moorland streams to shaded pools, trees drooping their branches down into the water; branch-choked, weed-filled country rivers, fish chasing in and out of shadows; deep cool water, cows coming, lowing, to drink; wide curves and loops culling the earth to shape sickle-moon ribbons through flood-flattened valleys, falling into gorges, rushing, pushing around boulders. Grain by grain the water carves holes in stone, shaping the land with its transient, unyielding force. Finally the river widens, becomes a great, unknowable mass growing away from me, fresh with the scent of leaves and earth, folding flat against the tang of salt, becoming sea.

These are the rivers of Wales. We fish in them, trade on them, drink from them, grow towns around them. Around us they move, silently slipping from land to ocean.

First we followed the Tywi, my sister and I, after she returned to walk with me for a final two weeks. There was no preordained route this time; I had maps and a will to follow the river as closely as possible. Walking away from the sea at Carmarthen it seemed that many people throughout history had already had the same idea. Trackways had grown into tarmacked roads that stuck close to the valley bottom on either side of the water. We had a couple of long days of road walking: hot, sticky, boring, faintly dangerous, looking out for cars, making sure they saw us as they rushed – sometimes too fast – towards their important destinations. We walked, drank water, pausing at bridges or in the welcome shade of tree-lined gardens. Sometimes the river came into view, shrinking incrementally as we passed the small streams flowing into it and we'd pause to admire, say hello.

In time we reached Llandovery. The river changed from there, growing smaller, straighter, with no wide valley to twist around in.

It came down from the hills and we followed it up towards them. The farms got bigger, the soil thinner, mountain sheep having to range wider for nibbles of juicy grass. Humans had wrought change to this river, damming and trapping it, filling valleys, drowning habitat until the river rose to the hilltops and became Llyn Brianne: a jagged, stretched reservoir that provided drinking-water for part of South Wales. We walked six miles around the curving edge, cars appearing far away and passing us minutes later. Out to the bridge on the other side and we were in the mid-Wales highlands: pine forests and wet moorlands, the river smaller now, running white around boulders, blurring at boggy edges.

We stopped overnight in Dolgoch hostel – a strange dark building, still with a feeling of scratched survival in a harsh landscape. It had huge stone-flagged floors, gas pipes running along the walls for lighting, no mains electricity, solar showers, reminders to boil the water before drinking. We'd meant to make it to the bothy that lay a few miles further up the valley, but it was too far that day so we paid and collapsed gratefully into the soft sponge-beds, sleeping thick dark sleep in the silence of the valley. Rain came overnight and stayed the next morning, mist whitening the hilltops and hanging thick in the trees. We suited and booted up and pressed on – to the source!

The river thinned to a friendly brown stream and we forded it, only ankle-deep, cold water tingling my tender feet and leaving them freshened. The next ford was not so friendly – knee-deep and wide. Luckily, just as we reached it, four Land Rovers came along behind us. Sticking our thumbs out we grinned, and they took us through the next three river crossings. I felt bad about cheating 200m of the walk away. But only a tiny bit. The small guilt was worth the time and effort saved wading. We got out where the river, a stream by now, split in two.

The Tywi disappeared into pine forest where it would slowly melt away into bog; there was no track to follow any more, just a reedy, wet mess of land to cross. Saying goodbye to our lift we took the track curving around the side of the hill that birthed the river, looking at the ground where the water drained down and formed the trickle that became the torrent that became the path we'd just followed, all the way from the sea at Carmarthen.

Less than five miles away, over the rolling smooth hills, lay Llyn Teifi, source of another river. A beginning that would, again, trickle down, gathering strength, and carve a path to the sea.

The clouds thickened, tiny droplets of rain misting. The decision had to be made; do we go directly over the hills or follow a path down into the valley and back up again? No compass meant we chose safety, not wanting to get lost in disorientating cloud. So we walked, following bridleways through the dank and dripping forest, tree roots holding peat sludge, wetness everywhere, leather boots long since saturated. We walked into mist, following sheep tracks over hillsides to a farm, then a track, then a road, before branching up to another farmhouse – abandoned this time, rabbits scurrying away from the front garden. We peeked through the windows. Ripped wallpaper hung from the ceiling, the remnants of an elderly life still inside the house, left to be a rotting time-capsule: wooden chairs and a worn laminated tablecloth, no-frills washing-powder and rusting tins of custard. A small museum of Welsh life.

Dumping the bags by the shed where we could return to them later, we went lightly upwards, into Cwm Teifi and towards the lake, water rushing downwards past us and the mist clouding, confusing the path. Finally, we climbed the side of the dam, to the silent stretch of Llyn Teifi.

We each took a ceremonial mouthful of the Dolgoch-boiled

River Tywi water and spat it into Llyn Teifi to mark our journey. The two rivers mingled and ran away from us and we followed them down the hillside, back towards the sea.

Good times with my sister. It was easy to be with Rose; she'd lived the same life, knew exactly how our upbringing had shaped and distorted us. We could talk over ourselves in a way that others would take years to understand, with an immediate understanding and tolerance of one another developed over a lifetime. Each of us was an influence and wise woman to the other, using our individual strengths.

We climbed up to Twm Siôn Cati's cave and explored the slanted boulder walls, a small shafted opening above letting in a beautiful light, picking our way from the rushing white River Tywi below.

We slept in Rhandirmwyn Church porch, waiting up the road until a service had finished and the parishioners had trundled home; I told her the story of Sue discovering me and the unexpected breakfast, glad that it hadn't happened again. Turning up a second time meant I was a tramp, didn't it?

Another six days of descent brought us back to the coast; swimming in the gushing river, cooling sunburnt shoulders, giggling and messing about in rests under bridges, posing for silly yoga photos, eating ice cream. We stopped in Maesycrugiau, guests of Menna and Paul who'd heard me on Radio Wales. They were lovely – good Welsh people, descended from farmers, running their own small business. When I described walking around Llyn Clywedog, seeing a farmer who turned his quad-bike off in anticipation of a chat, Paul knew the man; he was the son of the farmer who'd bought his farm from Paul's father. It was a wonderful coincidence, the kind of interconnectedness that's so typical of Wales.

Rose was travel-hardened, used to this kind of itinerant lifestyle. She'd lived a transient life over the years, taking her bag to Spain and beyond, to the Americas. This was easy and relaxing once she'd done as I did at the beginning: found the right shoes and taken most of the stuff out of her bag. We knew how to live like this, scouting for sleeping spots, packing food into bags.

It was a fantastic week or two, dipping back into mid-Wales after the coastal journey south. I was having fun! My body felt good, feet weren't hurting too much, the sun was out, and around 700 miles still to go.

Once we reached St Dogmaels, I sat on a bench by the river mouth and contemplated. To get back to Carmarthen, the place I'd left the coastal path, and continue walking east, I had two options. I could walk inland from Cardigan to Carmarthen – which was roughly thirty miles and would take two days – or I could follow the coastal path all the way around Pembrokeshire again. When I'd designed the walk I thought I'd definitely walk around the coastal path again. But I didn't really take into account that it was 180 miles of the most rugged coast in the country. There was a lot that I didn't take into account before starting this ridiculous journey, though; and rightly so, because if I'd really absorbed just how difficult and painful it would be I probably wouldn't have started the whole thing in the first place.

So here I was, with a choice: the planned 180 miles or a thirty mile shortcut. Although I felt great every day, underneath the exhilaration and wonder I was totally exhausted. The walk was taking way longer than I had expected; budget and body needed me to finish by the end of the summer. Despite my tiredness, the whole precarious enterprise rested on the fact that I didn't quit, didn't give up and didn't make it easier. I laughed at myself, shrugging in resignation. Pembrokeshire was so beautiful, I was going to walk around it twice.

IRISH SEA

Holyhead
ISLE OF
ANGLESEY
Llangefni
Llandudno
Rhyl
Conwy
CLWYDIANS
Flint
Chester
Bangor
Caernarfon
Betws-y-Coed
Wrexham
SNOWDON
SNOWDONIA
Porthmadog
Bala
Llangollen
Pwllheli
DEE
CADAIR
BERWYN
RHINOG
FAWR
ARAN
FAWDDWY
Shrewsbury
Barmouth
Dolgellau
CADAIR
IDRIS
DYFI
Welshpool
CARDIGAN
BAY
Machynlleth
PLYNLIMON
SEVERN
Newtown
SEVERN
MOUNTAINS
Aberystwyth
Llanidloes
ENGLAND
YSTWYTH
WYE
Worcester
Tregaron
WALES
CAMBRIAN
Builth
Wells
TEIFI
Cardigan
WYE
Hereford
Hay-on-Wye
Fishguard
Llandovery
Tewkesbury
St David's
Llandeilo
Brecon
BLACK
MOUNTAINS
Haverford West
Carmarthen
BLACK
MOUNTAIN
PEN Y
FAN
Laugharne
TYWI
Abergavenny
Angle
Tenby
Llanelli
Merthyr
Tydfil
USK
Swansea
Neath
Porthcawl
Pontypridd
Newport
Chepstow
CARDIFF
TAFF
BRISTOL
BRISTOL CHANNEL
Barry

N
W   E
S

0 Kilometers   30

0 Miles   20

344

WALES COASTAL PATH
FROM CARDIGAN TO CARDIFF

Route description: Another section of the Wales Coastal Path, repeating the Pembrokeshire Coast and incorporating the Gower peninsula with its northern salt-marshes and southern sandy beaches before reaching the more urban areas of Swansea, Port Talbot, Barry and Cardiff.

Length:	372.75 miles
Total ascent:	unknown
Maximum height:	167 m
Dates:	18 June – 27 July 2015
Time taken:	40 days
Nights camping/nights hosted:	7/33
Days off:	12
Average miles per day:	13.3

This penultimate stretch of the walk started with a wonderful family visit, all four of us – my brothers, my sister and me together – in one glorious weekend, to celebrate our successes and to spend time together as a sibling unit. I'd prevailed upon the generosity of walk-follower Natasha to lend us a holiday cottage near Fishguard, one of her converted outbuildings. I couldn't imagine that four of us could successfully blend into a wild-camping field-corner, and Owen was still healing. We looked out for him, arranging the cooking and logistics. He was alright with us, fitted into the unit we'd known all our lives; it was only when talking to strangers that his brain injury became more awkwardly apparent.

We came around Dinas Head together, in sunshine this time, turning around to look at the two bays laid out behind us. Dinas was an almost island, frozen in the birthing, man-made concrete ditches preventing further tidal fragmenting of the umbilical strip.

After my siblings' visit came another break: off to Glastonbury Festival again. I didn't want to go but it was very necessary to earn an extra few hundred pounds. It was hard, though. I worked the night shifts there which meant completely reversing my body clock. Used to early exhausted nights and dawn-wakened mornings, that week I worked until 3am and tried to sleep during the day. It was the usual raucous good fun, but I felt quiet and withdrawn, preferring to try and rest, read a book. It was a struggle to boost myself to the extrovert behaviour needed to keep festival crowds entertained.

It was hard when I returned to the walk too. I might not have been walking for a week or so, but I'd been spending energy in a different way; my body ached from constant standing and late nights. I was offered the use of a friend's holiday cottage out at Strumble Head. At first I thought I'd stay there for one rest day, but my heavy and aching body said otherwise. When I wasn't walking, starting again felt like the worst thing in the world; in no way did I want to hump a painful and tired body outside for ten hours a day. On the way to the cottage, flush with festival wages, I bought enough food for three days and spent a couple of days on the sofa, eating scones and cream, crisps and toast and cereal. Finally, late on the third afternoon, I grudgingly caught the bus away from my cottage cocoon, back to where I'd left the walk ten days earlier.

It was going to be another wonderful 180 miles around the beautiful and friendly Pembrokeshire coast and, best of all, I wasn't going to camp for any of it. I had hosts lined up all along the way: a combination of eight different houses, three having me for more than one night. These angelic helpers, with their varied ways of finding my journey – through internet or newspapers or word of mouth – and their varied reasons for offering to help me (cancer or adventure or just kindness) would ferry my bag around and pick me up from the coast. It was going to be easy and lovely, revisiting lots of the lovely people who'd helped me the previous month.

First, though, I met someone new. Lyn picked me up from the sea at Abercastle and took me away to her house inland for a cosy night in and delicious food. She was bright and cheerful, wearing splashes of colour on scarves and jewellery. Lyn would have liked to come out and walk with me but couldn't go far; she had to watch her dog run along the beach instead of moving with him. Tumours throughout her abdomen were sapping her strength; chemo drugs and their aftermath were taking her energy. Lyn had stage 4 ovarian cancer; her tumours weren't removable and were not going to go away. All her treatment was about extending life, rather than saving it.

She had the BRCA2 gene, which gave her an 85% chance of getting breast cancer too. She mused aloud about whether to have a preventative mastectomy. This was a heavy burden to bear; cancer is a brutal illness that requires equally brutal treatment. This was what I was trying to prevent, with my own journey; I wanted women to catch this cancer sooner than stage 4, when there was a better chance of survival past five years. Lyn did too, also dedicating a lot of her energy to fundraising and awareness-raising.

It was hard to discuss certain subjects with Lyn. I felt her upset quivering deep beneath her determination, and knew there was a lot we wouldn't talk about. Who was I to capsize the carefully constructed sailboat made of silver and art and shells and lipstick that she was using to bring herself safely through her cancer storm? Why should I remind her that the ocean is deep, and eventually we all end up sinking to the bottom? Knowledge shatters illusion, and sometimes illusion is what we all need to survive, to paint ourselves a picture of a different life, using that to bring ourselves through the hard times. I'd been taught to dwell in my pain, but Lyn showed me a different attitude to hardship; the keep-on-keeping-on, the rise-above, the shake-it-off. Lyn was navigating her circumstances with strength, determination and positivity, and I was awed. It was an honour to meet her.

Back in Tregaron, as I descended the River Teifi I'd met Paul for a pint. He'd emailed me during his preparation for a walk around the coast and the Offa's Dyke Path, a 1000-mile circle around the edge of the country. I'd given him advice about blisters and rucksacks and blagging hotel rooms. Later on, in Pembrokeshire, I met Gareth – big smile and a baseball cap – coming towards me on the way to St David's, two weeks into his own circle around the Welsh outline. They were both cheerful and gregarious and I loved being part of their supportive club. Like long-distance travellers Hannah and Rebecca and Alex, these were people who understood how to battle against the aches and pain, how to draw strength from stubbornness of will and keep yourself going when motivation becomes low. They knew how incredible and wonderful and transcendent this was, how it would leave you sore and thankful, completely exhausted but in no way ready to quit. We cheered each other on via Facebook and Twitter, tracking each other's progress.

John and Jo took up the strain as I walked around St David's Peninsula and the northern part of St Bride's Bay, having me to stay for another few nights. It made it so easy; they cooked me huge delicious dinners and John walked with me whenever he could, pacing me really well with his long legs and 4mph stride. I loved playing with their bright and funny boy, Jacob. It was a relaxed and friendly house and I felt like I was at home, as I had done in so many places. The magic of a welcoming and happy family made me feel cared for and loved, despite spending so much time alone.

The weather oscillated between heavy rain and bright burning sun but it didn't matter, I was always en route to a house at the end of the day. Whether I was sweaty or rain-sodden I was always walking to a place where I could clean my clothes and my body, start again the next day with fresh hair, dry fabric against my skin. It was such a relief. My mileage went up and up: twenty-one miles, sixteen miles, twenty-three miles...

Walking twenty-plus miles in a day is, for me, a matter of keeping up a steady rhythm, watching my rest-breaks, timing myself on my hourly mileage, keeping it going, walking all day, rarely stopping. My legs powered forward, my thighs taking the force when each booted step struck the ground, my calves springing me forward for the next plunge to earth.

I push, I push, I push, in the groove that other walkers have made before me, grasses brushing my ankles, nipping the bud-growths from fresh green brambles that attempt to hang across my way. Most of the time there was a cliff falling away to my right side, a sheer drop down to jagged rocks submitting to the wash of the turquoise water. The sun beat down; I walked on, sweating, pushed forward, didn't stop.

I'd pick a spot on the map – Broadhaven, Dale, Freshwater East, Amroth – and set myself the task of reaching it before the day's end, before sundown, before my friendly host came to pick me up. It meant walking fast for hours, twisting my hips from side to side to bend around the slower walkers, those without urgency, no mission driving them on, slipping through curves in the path, bending forward to ascend slopes without slowing my pace, pushing up on strong muscles to climb the steps out of yet another idyllic small harbour.

Passing beaches I looked down at small coves with solitary trails of footsteps, inviting hours to be spent exploring, meandering over smooth sands, staring into rockpools, teasing fingers over the pull of tiny tentacles. I saw all that, the leisurely hours I could have spent, and I walked on – no time for detours.

I walked past small cafés, wind-shelters, sandcastles, dogs racing for tennis balls, crowded caravan-parks. Past headlands, islands, jetties, speedboats and tinkling boatyards, jovial boat owners, pensioners clipping flowers in quiet suburbs, lawn-strimming, bringing shopping in.

On beaches there were always children: crying children, sunburnt children, children running scampering into the sea. Once, an entire family wearing jeans and hoodies waded into the water while a rounded mother, arms crossed, waited at the water's edge. One wrinkled woman in a headscarf sat at the beach edge and watched her grandchildren finding special rocks to show her. Flecked rocks, marbled rocks, heart-shaped ones, drift wood, beach glass.

I passed in the background of every tableau: a fat woman, in black, walking quickly on my own quiet mission.

It became hard to keep updating my blog. There was never enough time to sit and write, especially when I was spending every evening with hosts. Days passed and I walked, rested, met new people and somehow, when I came to look back on it the minutiae had slipped away. Did it matter where I sat to rub my feet? Or the ten minutes I spent watching seagulls curve upwards on clifftop wind currents, swooping and jockeying for territory? Or the packet of sandwiches wrapped in paper and secured with a rubber band that I opened under the table in a café, only drinking tea because it was too wet to sit outside for free? All these small details of every day, wet grass shedding water into my boots, a line of sheep standing patiently with their backs to the wind, the heavy ache of my tired thighs as I pulled up onto another stile, a line of wooden-edged steps stretching up into the side of yet another hill; all felt wonderful, beautiful, extraordinary, indistinguishable, mundane, normal.

Had I been doing this too long? Was I no longer able to document it? I ate my breakfast in a field, finding a suitable flat rock to sit on, swilling out the bowl from my water bottle, drying it on my knee, repacking it in my rucksack, as I'd done hundreds of times over. The excitement of the new had subsided into comfortable repetition.

I suppose it was another stage, another state to experience. I was a walking-machine making its way towards the predetermined destination, satisfied with its simple, mechanical life.

I left Lorna and Gez in Laugharne, saying goodbye to their cute children, all eager eyes and scattered toys, and headed out towards Carmarthen. I was going to wild camp that night; for the first time in ages I had no host arranged. Lorna offered to take my bag ahead to a pub in Llangain and I eagerly agreed, welcoming any chance to walk without the usual 14kg on my back. Steady trudge all day in the hot sunshine, up and over Lord's Park, with a view across the tidal estuary back to Laugharne and ahead to Gower. I reached the pub at 5pm, not too tired after fifteen miles but ready to search for a place to sleep.

The barman hauled my bag out from behind the bar and said, "There was a man in at lunchtime, said you could stay at his campsite."

I looked and there in a side-pocket was a piece of paper sticking out of my donation-tin. It was an invitation and a map.

"You gonna go there or what," said the barman.

"Yeah, I'll go there," I said, "that'll do," not thinking how strange it might seem for me to be so relaxed about potential sleeping places.

I followed the map through the village back-roads and found Ian and Angela at the end of it, running a campsite and offering free nights to anyone walking for charity. Ian talked a lot, I'll be honest, but they showed me where to pitch up on the lovely flat, short grass, invited me in for dinner and even opened a couple of bottles of Prosecco in my honour. A lovely, lovely couple, just doing their thing and doing it very well in a quiet village in Carmarthenshire.

Next morning, up to say goodbye, I left them a card and walked off. I was definitely going to wild camp that night, somewhere near Ferryside. First, up to Carmarthen where I sat mindlessly in a café for a couple of hours (a necessary part of my journey) and received a message. It was from Helen, the person who'd offered me a place to stay in Llanelli. "I've got friends in Kidwelly who can have you to stay, they'll come and pick you up from Ferryside. Peter and Frances: here's their phone numbers."

Peter was very efficient, texting me the car details and an identifying photograph. I just had to get to Ferryside by six. It was a bit of a struggle and I made it by seven instead: getting lost in a derelict farm, no signposts to show me the way out. Eventually Ferryside came into view and there she was as described – Frances, come to pick me up.

"So how do you know Helen?" Frances asked. I had to admit that I didn't, not at all. She was just a name on a Facebook message and an offer of help. I was a stranger to her and therefore to Frances, just putting my trust in what was coming forward.

Frances and Peter were very nice but I was tired, so tired. I'd been walking for two weeks straight and needed a day off. I planned to have one on the Gower, just find a place to put my tent and lie quietly for a day, letting my feet rest. They were starting to throb painfully again, as they had for most of the last year, the plantar tendons strained beyond stretching. Their only resort to cope with the pressure I put on them was to rip away at the heel-bone, small sharp pains making me feel as if tiny tears took place each time they flashed through my heels. I needed to stop, rest, give them a chance to heal.

The next day I had to walk to Llanelli: nineteen miles. I plugged away, through fields and hillsides at first, over to Kidwelly but then came a tough stretch. The path took me for three miles alongside Pembrey airfield, heading towards a section of forestry, then a two-mile beach walk before I could turn inland and find a cycle path. The gritty forest road seemed to last for hours; every time I came to a corner I'd think, *this is it, now I'll see the beach ahead*, but no, there was another section of road, stretching away into the distance. Finally I came to the beach but that was even worse: a long straight piece of sand, kite buggies rattling along it but not another person to be seen.

I was looking for a café which marked the place to turn inland. Far away in the distance were some dark posts sticking out of the sand. I walked, finding places where my feet didn't sink in and sap valuable energy. The dark objects came closer; they were the skeleton of a huge fishing boat, left there to rot. Far, far away in the distance there was a line of rocks, built to break the force of the waves. I trudged towards it. When I reached the rocks, far, far away in the distance there was a van parked on the sands, small stick people milling around it, flying kites. I trudged on. When I reached the van, far, far away in the distance there were some flags, the RNLI stand. That was where the café was. I trudged towards it, raising a grudging hand when the kite buggies waved at me.

Reaching the café I collapsed on a bench. Boots off, lie back, cup of tea, check the internet. Oh, damn, rain on Sunday, the day I was hoping to camp on Gower. That would mean a truly unpleasant day off, trying to relax in a wet tent. Perhaps I could ask Helen if I could have a day off in her house, although I don't like to ask for more than people are willing to give. She was going away for a night, though, and it would be really nice. Argh, I'd have to at least ask.

But first, more walking. I found the beginning of the cycle-path and trudged on, resorting to music to help me move my feet. I wasn't going to make it to Llanelli – my feet were too painful for that – but I could at least get to Pwll, a respectable seventeen miles.

Helen and her friend Penny came out to pick me up. I was tired as usual, not able to make much by the way of conversation. Helen regaled me with travelling tales and I felt a funny, relaxed spirit within her.

"Could I stay here tomorrow night, while you go off to St David's?"

"Of course! Make the house your own! Here's a key, I'll be back on Sunday afternoon."

Helen's home came with a hammock, in which I spent most of the forty blissful hours I spent there. I didn't see anything of Llanelli but a nearby supermarket and the white, clouded sky through the windows as I lay prone, rocking gently back and forth, reading Helen's books. I stretched every piece of my body, washed my clothes, and had a good session with the tennis ball (my favourite bit of kit – you roll around on it to give something like deep tissue massage) and most of all I snoozed, naps between every bit of activity.

I was restored: not fully, but enough to keep injury at bay and allow me to walk a little further.

The next day came easily after my day off, posting the key back through Helen's letterbox with a note of deep-felt thanks, and setting out to walk around the Llwchwr estuary. There was water falling from the sky as I walked away, soft wet thick water that came steadily. That night I really would wild-camp again, out in the wilderness of North Gower salt marshes. I got soaked through in the heavy rain, but the storm passed over by the time I came the final few miles onto the peninsula, sun breaking through as I came past Penclawdd. I made camp on the side of the road where trees grew, guessing that this was where the tidal water didn't come. I'd picked samphire as it grew neon green in the muted mud and grass of the village edges and pressed it into my cheese sandwiches, enjoying the crunch and tang of the sea. Ponies grazed far out on the flat green, the setting sun haloing them in yellow outlines that flared bright against the black clouds massing over Llanelli, far on the other side of the estuary.

After a slug tried to slurp its way across my sleeping face at about 5.30am, I was wary of further investigations and slept no longer. I bent my way out of the wet tent and scared a bunch of wild ponies that had wandered to the edge of the marshland nearby, then sat quietly on a bench until one brave pony, with luxurious blonde punky hair, came close enough to smell my hand. His dreadlocked mate hovered in the background.

The edge of the sea had crept to the other side of the tarmac overnight. It trickled and seeped, lapping, gently rising, overflowing earth and running down to fill dips, pouring into small gorges, creating islands. A maze of blue pathways now lay where yesterday was undulating green.

Within an hour, as I followed the road leading along the edge of the marsh, the water had receded, leaving wet mud and gurgling grass once again. I wanted to walk eighteen miles that day, if I could. There was a pub at Worm's Head where I could charge my phone and get some food. I wasn't carrying many rations and would resupply when I reached the supermarkets of Swansea. So I walked – road at first. Breakfast on a roadside boulder at seven, a man with a lovely fluffy collie stopped and offered me a bag of freshly dug potatoes. "No thanks, kind stranger, I don't carry a stove." The path turned to fields and then sandy forest edge before dunes lead out to a wild windy point. This was the closest I'd be to the Carmarthenshire coast, before I turned and changed direction, heading around the point of Gower Point to walk east. I waved goodbye to Laugharne and Llanelli, the last time I'd see them on this journey.

Eventually I reached the nests of mobile homes, caravan parks and

Burry Holm, the island at one end of Rhossili beach. Ahead of me was an age of never-ending beach, three miles, and I must plod the ghastly length of it in order to reach the pub. Tiny dots in the distance marked where people ran their dogs, close to the ascent to Rhossili village. It felt like hours, the background cliffs never seeming to get closer, the sand too wet and clinging to stop for a proper rest. Eventually I made it, feet throbbing, but in plenty of time to put them up, read a book, eat some food, drink two pints of good ale and charge my phone. I headed out to sleep behind a wall with a view of the Worm's Head island, white waves splashing up the full forty-six metre height of it.

I started to push at this point, aching to get to Cardiff where I would turn inland again, walk my final pair of rivers and then to Bristol where I'd walk up the River Wye and finish. Finish the walk: only another 400 or 500 miles and I'd be done, this would be over. I could start pushing for eighteen or nineteen miles a day, focused on the end-point, only thinking about getting myself to the finish. My feet were hanging in there, just about.

My mum came to walk along the Mumbles with me. She lived there for eight years and it's where I was born.

My parents left Swansea too soon after my birth for me to have my own memories of it, but I feel a connection all the same. Swansea, my birthplace. Clydach, the home of my grandfather's family. This is my Welsh blood, this is my Welsh birth, but still I hesitate to call myself Welsh. I grew up in England; so did my Welsh grandfather and my half-Welsh mother and my English father. My culture is English and, although the differences between Wales and England are small when viewed on a world scale, they do exist. To be Welsh is to be local. To be intensely connected to one place, to know its history in great detail. I've walked the land of Wales because I love it and in loving it I've come to know it well but it's a different sense of nationality. Wales is my adopted country as well as the place of my birth; I'm from here but not of here.

I met people upon people over the following week, spent nights in B&Bs with my mum. She'd come and walk with me for the odd half-day and then go to visit friends, or spend some time reminiscing in Swansea while I walked the 100 miles to Cardiff.

Almost in Cardiff, I took an accidental shortcut from Cadoxton, walking straight ahead at a roundabout instead of turning right. It cut out a whole four miles of the coastal path, leaving me joining Penarth at the pier a whole hour early to meet effervescent Arry, the woman who holds the record for the first and fastest completion of the Welsh Coastal Path, in a run averaging twenty-six miles a day for forty-one days.

We walked across the barrage and into Cardiff city centre, as I absorbed her story. She didn't talk about how hard her run must have been, just stated a few casual facts about her journey, leaving me to realise the impact of her statements and her absolutely incredible achievement.

Later, I met up with an old friend for a few drinks and then went to another friend's house for a bed: nice catch-ups in a week of meeting person after person, none of whom I really knew. I'd pushed hard to get to the city, walking almost twenty miles a day for over a week. I loved meeting all these wonderful friendly people. I had to admit, though, a small part of me was yearning for the solitude of high open hills and nights in a tent. I wondered how I'd feel when I actually got there.

RIVERS TAFF AND USK AND
WALES COASTAL PATH TO BRISTOL

Route description: The rivers Taff and Usk both rise in the Brecon Beacons within 15 miles of one another and trace parallel paths to join the Bristol Channel at Cardiff and Newport respectively.

Length:	189.5 miles
Total ascent:	unknown
Maximum height:	500 m
Dates:	29 July – 9 August 2015
Time taken:	12 days
Nights camping/nights hosted:	6/6
Days off:	0
Average miles per day:	15.8

Leaving Cardiff was surprisingly difficult. I headed to the shops to buy more maps; I was going to walk up the River Taff and down the Usk to Newport, but there were no predesigned guidebooks or marked trails. I stopped in at a café on my way to the River Taff, and unfortunately chose a really good one. It served iced coffee in pint-sized glass jars and had a soft leather chair in a quiet corner of a room full of mismatched tiling, irregularly-placed mirrors, table-lamps and large windows. I did some writing, a couple of hours passed, and suddenly I found myself greatly desirous of a day off, the urge to walk completely absent, my body feeling heavy and tired. So I gave in: a night in a hostel, bag of crisps and a film, and set off again the following morning.

Well, kind of set off. I walked towards the river, and stopped in at Wales Online to meet a journalist. I was having my photograph taken for newspapers, shoulders back, stand straight, look confident and smile. I found I was able to smile and bear it, not shrink away in an embarrassed grimace. The photographs showed a confident, happy person, tanned, with thick, sun-lightened hair – incredibly different to how drained I felt inside. Finally I found myself in the castle tearooms ordering a Welsh breakfast (laverbread scone, nice touch), spinning out a final hour of procrastination.

Something had changed: my energy had gone. I just didn't want to walk. All my energy, all my focus had gone into one thing, pushing my body forward to walk for thousands of miles. But it was all an illusion. I could stop at any time, I just didn't give myself the option.

I'd made the finish-date public that week, told everyone I was aiming for the clock tower in Machynlleth on the 22nd August. It wasn't a random date: I'd arranged festival work the following week. If I made it I could meet my friend Sam's baby boy. If I hadn't made this arrangement I would probably have dawdled, slept late, finished early and arrived in Machynlleth a week or two later. Something happened when I named the date; I let my guard down and let the finish, the thought of no longer walking, come flooding into my mind.

Now, as the end was so close I could almost touch it, I thought ahead to the time when I'd be able to stop walking. The temptation to stop putting my body through all this effort was bleeding into the present moment, and I was simply running out of steam. My body felt heavy; I had no impulse to move, no energy. The Taff trail was no help either: hard tarmac under my feet made them hurt much sooner in the day, and there was a constant oppressive vibration of traffic noise following me as the path wound beside the A470. Time seemed to pass incredibly slowly. There was no joy in my walking, I felt close to tears. I wondered where I was going to sleep; the Merthyr valley seemed to be a long conjunction of town after town, each one bleeding into another with unwelcoming industrial areas at the edges.

It was a couple on bikes who saved me from urban camping that night. The guy slowed alongside me, asking me what I was doing.

"I'm going to talk for a bit," he shouted ahead to his partner.

After a few cursory questions he offered me a camping spot in his garden. I took a quick sideways glance, assessing this open-faced, Lycra-clad Valleys man and said, "Yes". So, out of nowhere, I found myself walking a few extra miles that day as I talked to the well-travelled Dai about his many experiences, on the way to his house just up and out of Pontypridd.

"It's just up this hill," he'd say. "It's just next to that pylon," while I tried not to tell him that my feet had gone way past how far they could walk that day.

I made it, feet burning, had a meal and a shower and camped in their garden, clean and with a belly full of pub carvery. Dai dropped me back into Pontypridd early the next morning, by car this time, thankfully.

I had a pretty rubbish day on my way to Merthyr, nestled at the head of the valley. All tarmac and worry about where I would sleep that night, again. I skirted the town, too wary of all the negative things I'd heard about the place. "Merthyr," people said, and gave a knowing smile as if we all knew without saying it what a terrible place it was.

"They're all a bunch of headers up there, love," a man in Abercanaid warned me, beer swinging in his carrier bag, the smell of more coming off him.

I stopped for half an hour of phone charging in the Merthyr Tydfil ex-servicemen's club. People spoke to me, asked me what I was doing, gave small donations. All as normal really, my pre-judgements clouding a properly immersive experience of the town.

I walked to the very edge of the town and beyond, not wanting to be caught camping out by the youths who came to the underpasses and bridges at night to smash glass and drop their empty cans. The sun was almost setting when I made it out to the first few farms beyond the town. On the edge of the forest I found a tall tree growing beside a stony track, and behind it a patch of smooth grass edged with mossy stones and foxgloves, where I could lie down and feel safe. The full moon rose behind me and I pulled my sleeping-bag around me against the cold night. I woke a few hours later to the sound of an animal near me, so close that I could see the shape of it moving and snuffling. Flicking on the light from my phone I saw a hedgehog, biting and sucking at my Welsh flag, undeterred by the flash of light. I moved the flags closer to me and it scuttled away, leaving me to the peace of the night.

There are animals out there we don't know about. We see them in black glimmers at the corner of vision, flicking in and out of sight. They are the rustles and calls in the night, the unexpected scat, the thin weaving paths that don't seem to lead anywhere, the squeezed-aside wire at the base of fences. They have learned to survive in the spaces we don't take up, and we'll never know – because if we did, we selfish humans would kill them in our desire for total planetary dominance.

The next morning found me rested, but no more motivated. I spread my kit out in the warm morning sun to dry off the overnight dew. I ate breakfast and read a book, no urge to move at all. It was hard, so hard to get going. There was very little impetus to lift my bag and take the steps that would lead to throbbing feet and exhaustion yet again. I knew that there was a hostel about twelve miles ahead and the temptation to give up early and hand over some money in exchange for a hot meal, shower and warm bed was overwhelming. My target was always there, hovering in the background, and in order to meet it I must always be fixed on forward. I walked to the hostel, slowly, pausing often, feeling weak and sad.

Something changed on the way there, though, as I walked out from the confining narrow valley into the more open hills of the Brecon Beacons. My mood lifted as the horizon widened. I found myself walking on sheep-mown turf instead of tarmac, the path ahead winding up and over a hill instead of twisting through housing estates or under roads. The roar of traffic faded, the road signs fell away and it was just me, a map and the wild, living land again. I felt at home, realising that, of course, this was the kind of walking I loved.

I slept at the hostel, filled my belly with as much food as I could and set off to find the source of the River Usk.

It helped a lot, walking through the open land. I felt better. All the problems were still there: a looming finish-date, a few hundred miles still to walk, rain, wet tents, painful feet, practically empty bank account. *I can do this*, I told myself; *it's not an impossible target. I just need, as ever, to keep walking.* Most of these problems had been constant throughout the journey; there was no reason why they should have overwhelmed me in the final month of the odyssey.

There were horses up on the shoulders of the Black Mountain, where dew formed on grass tips and rain hit the mountainside, trickling down from the heights of rock above, becoming the River Usk. I walked across the short tussocks of mountain grass, a band of roving ponies grazing close to me, the only human to be seen. I sat for a while and watched them, shaggy manes fluttering in the wind, grey clouds hanging low over the hilltops. A herd, small colts staying close to the safety of their mothers, they talked in the touching of noses. They were pale colours: grey dappled to white, light browns, all with a white stripe down the centre of their faces.

Underneath the sharp heights of the Black Mountain I searched for the Usk, walking over the wide open space, matching the shape of the land to my map contours, until I came over a shoulder of earth that popped down into the dip. Here it began, the nascent waterway, a liquid path for me to follow back to the sea.

It was a pretty mechanical few days, following the River Usk back to the coast, starting alongside a babbling baby and then accompanying its transformation into a respectable river. I was happy to take easy, flat stretches along the Montgomeryshire canal path where the river wound, curved, and meandered alongside.

I was up at 6am, walked as much as I could for the day and collapsed into sleep wherever I could camp. I still felt like crying lots, but I wasn't sure exactly why. I wasn't worried about what would come next, after the walk, I just knew that I'd rest and allow it to happen: how I would earn money, where I'd live, whether I'd try and write a book – the answers would come, in time. I had an idea that had been germinating for a while; I wanted to walk across Europe. Five years previously I'd kayaked the length of the Danube and just as I was settling down to a winter in an empty house in a small Bulgarian village, trying to process the fact that I'd paddled across most of a continent, I was diagnosed with cancer and had to start processing that instead, cancelling my plan to walk home to Britain.

For the last five years I'd been dealing with what was directly in front of me, not thinking about the future: first the unavoidable cancer, then the walk which arose as a way to deal with it. Now the future was open again, I could do anything. It made sense to go back to where I'd left off. I felt a definite sense of, *oh, right, where was I? What was I doing before all this kicked off?*

My mind had been chewing over this for months, always wanting to start worrying about the next thing, and I'd always pushed it to one side, telling myself to concentrate on this walk, to keep focused, not worry about a future that wasn't here yet. Now the end was so close it was hard to keep focusing on today. The whole thing – the enormity of 3700 miles, raising money for charity, the audience I'd created, thousands of people following and interacting with my social media posts, the huge and epic seventeen months I'd just experienced – kept flooding to the fore; it was overwhelming. I had to push it away, stay present, stop thinking about the 3700 miles and focus on that day's fifteen.

In Brecon I made some calculations. It was fifty miles to Newport, then I'd walk back to Cardiff, seventeen miles. Next I'd head over to Bristol, fifty-four miles, before turning around and walking up to Machynlleth along the Wye Valley Walk, 144 miles. There was also that thirty-mile section of the Offa's Dyke Path that I missed when I had a cracked tooth. So that was 295 miles to walk and eighteen days left to do it in. I couldn't take a single other day off, even have a slow day, if I was going to make it in time. Scary. The pressure was definitely on. After 3400 miles I was ready to stop walking, but I couldn't just yet. In fact, I had to up the pace.

Once I reached and left Bristol I'd be able to relax somehow: there'd be only one route left, the Wye Valley Walk. A finite number of miles and a finite number of days. Simple.

One precious night, near Llanfair Kilgeddin, I got to sleep in a barn. It was such a rarity and I loved it every time. I was comfortable, happily stretched out in the dry, massaging my legs and feeling snug. My tent was wet from the previous night's camping and more rain was coming. I was so sick of waking up in a wet tent, rain on the outside and condensation dripping on me from the inside. Yuk.

The next night was precious and valuable in a different way. I got invited to sleep in a pub on the outskirts of Newport. I'd walked in exhausted after a hard slog from Usk, the last five tarmac miles bringing pain. There was nowhere to camp on the edge of this big city that didn't feel exposed or unsafe. I'd be creeping around on field edges where they bordered houses and roads, too many cars passing, too many eyes to see me trying to hide. Grass fringed grey with road dust, hedges speckled with tossed plastic. I thought I'd stay in the bar until it got properly dark and then creep into the churchyard next door. It was too visible for a twilight pitching.

But camping didn't happen. The barmaid offered me tea, soup and a place to charge my phone. I sat parallel to the big TV and watched people's fascinated faces as *Bake Off* played; all sexes and ages turned to the screen and licked their lips or commented, their conversation stolen by the construction of a Black-Forest gateau. Eventually my host came over and we talked, she was living upstairs and suggested I sleep in the bar; she'd bring down a duvet and pillows to fit into the corner seating where I'd tucked myself. I didn't know why she chose to do this but I was so, so grateful. This journey was full of random acts of kindness from strangers and friends alike.

From Newport I set off along the coastal path to Cardiff. There was only a short seventeen-mile section of coastal path between Cardiff and Newport, but if I turned inland at Cardiff and popped out at Newport I'd miss it. What was an extra two days in a seventeen-month journey? Nothing. And yet without those two days I couldn't say I'd walked the whole Welsh Coastal Path. So they had to happen, as did all the other ways I'd been stubborn about my route, getting dropped off exactly where I'd left off the previous day, making sure I walked in between the various paths. This was why I wanted to walk the missing thirty-mile section of the ODP that I'd skipped when I broke my tooth. I'd felt the omission burning at me for months.

On my way back east I met Paul again. He'd set off from

Aberystwyth and walked north, all the way around the coast and down the Offa's Dyke Path. I met him in Newport, on my way back from Cardiff towards Bristol. We messaged and messaged, trying to gauge timings and a place to meet. He was faster than me – everyone was faster than me – but I didn't care. We hugged, thrilled to be meeting again in the middle of our respective adventures, sharing the highs and the excitement, comparing tales of blisters and unexpected beds. I'd dared him and Gareth to walk over the top of the Newport Transporter bridge, as I'd been dared to do so by Paddy Dillon, the kindly guidebook-writer who'd been sending me advance copies of his books as they came out: first Glyndŵr's Way and then the Coastal Path.

Paul met me in Fanny's Rest Stop Café on the west side of the bridge, saying it wasn't too bad. We chatted for an hour and then parted, him heading west with another six weeks of walking in front of him, me going east, with just another three. Then it was my turn to walk over the top of the bridge and it was truly terrifying, suspended 60m above the river with only wire mesh to walk on. I couldn't look down; seeing the gaps in the wire underneath my feet revealed a fear I didn't know I had. I'd had to climb up hundreds of tiny, twisting steps in the supporting tower – no way was I going to reverse and go back down again, take the suspended car-platform underneath. I had to look straight ahead, take baby steps and hold on tight to the guard rail in order to be able to complete the walk. But I saw it though, silly selfie included.

It was only two days from Newport to Bristol, walking around the flatlands of the estuary edge, seeing the two bridges so far away in the distance and then finally coming to walk underneath the concrete enormity of the new bridge, its swooping curves a mathematical beauty. I felt very slow and sleepy, taking breaks often. My body was heavy and ached but I couldn't stop, I'd come too far.

The flags at the end of my walking-poles were tattered by now; I'd long since given up trying to delicately unhook them from every grasping branch and bramble and would rip away in irritation at this check to my pace, leaving tiny threads in my wake, clinging to thorn talons.

They served me well, these bamboo poles, base slowly grinding away against rock and road, shortening the length grain by grain, my hands slipping upwards as the pole shrank away beneath me until my hands were pressing against the flags, material flapping against my face.

Finally, there I was, seeing the sign for Bristol city on a long, boring roadside cut into the centre. It was August 2015 and I was a bit behind schedule. In fact I was eleven months late; I'd planned to arrive here last September, to fit in with my hospital timetable. But I was here; I'd done it, I'd walked 3500 miles, and raised thousands for charity on the way, and that was what mattered most.

Tomorrow I'd start the last part of the journey, home to Machynlleth along the River Wye.

370

WYE VALLEY WALK

Route description: A walk that follows the meandering river Wye from its opening into the wide Bristol Channel at Chepstow, through the apple orchards of Herefordshire, rising to the moorland source on the side of Plynlimon.

Length:	137.9 miles
Total ascent:	5,579m
Maximum height:	481 m
Dates:	10 – 22 August 2015
Time taken:	13 days
Nights camping/nights hosted:	5/8
Days off:	0
Average miles per day:	15

I started the Wye Valley Walk with an ending: meeting the final marker stone for the Wales Coastal Path, the route I'd followed north to south in between inland detours, since May 2014.

I slept late in Bristol; the thought of rain put me off leaving the house, and I delayed and prevaricated before eventually accepting that what I really wanted to do was go back to bed for three hours. It meant that I arrived in Chepstow, a fifteen-mile walk across the Severn Bridge, after 8pm. I walked through the town, thinking about finding a good chip shop and walking out again to camp, but first I wanted to find the coast path monument. Eventually there it was, tucked all the way down by the River Wye, with a quiet park beside it and a little wine bar discreetly sending music into the peaceful evening. I hung around, persuaded someone in to take a couple of photos of me at the marker stone, and looked around. *Maybe I'll treat myself to a celebratory meal in the wine bar*, I thought. *Sod walking more, it's already close to 9pm, maybe I'll sleep in this bandstand that's just sitting right here in the centre of the park.*

It was deserted already, and I had a strong feeling it would be a peaceful place to spend the night. And that's what I did: a three-course meal in the bar, chatting a bit to the other customers and the friendly barmaid, but mostly sitting quietly and enjoying the good hot food before going outside in the dark and making up a bed in the bandstand. It was a warm night. I sat for a while in the silence, feeling the shape of the night. It wasn't the most relaxing place to sleep – public places never are, especially those where you might be stumbled upon by other people – but I settled eventually, after the clock struck 1am.

The only thing I made sure of was to wake up early, setting an alarm, not wanting to be caught by morning dog-walkers. It worked. I sat up, seeing a chicken pecking around, bustling for territory with the skulking gulls, put my stuff together and was lacing my boots as the first dog-walker appeared at 6am.

I walked further and further away from the coastal path. How strange that I was finished with the sea, it had been by my side for so long. All there was left was one river; I was going to follow it up to its source and I'd be home and finished. I didn't know how to feel about this impending date. Happy? Sad? The exhilaration and the exhaustion pulled at either end of the emotional spectrum, leaving me settled in a middling numbness. I was sure there was more, underneath, but it didn't matter. I didn't have to feel anything, just walk fifteen miles every day in order to make it to Machynlleth by the 22nd August. There it was, further days of pain, tiredness and treading the thin edge into injury; but only a finite amount of days. The end was near.

Leaving Chepstow and heading north it was just an ordinary day, as far as ordinary goes for me. The Wye valley was very beautiful; I walked through old forests, trees reaching high above me. I walked sweating under the weight of my rucksack, climbing hills and dropping down until I reached Tintern. Boots off, feet up and a couple of coffees; I gave my heels a chance to rest. Then I walked an hour more before stopping for lunch in a bus-shelter next to a busy road, then walked some more before being overcome with tiredness. It happens sometimes, in the early afternoons. There was nothing to do but sleep for a short time, half an hour or so. This time, three people walked past and laughed at me as I huddled in the forest by the side of the path. It is very hard to be exhausted in public and without a safe space to retreat to.

I woke up, chugged some water and walked some more, following the winding, gorge-like Wye valley, so lush and full of trees, until I reached The Boat Inn, Redbrook, a tiny and excellent pub on the banks of the river, which offered a multitude of barrelled ciders. I drank a pint here, rested and rubbed my feet, then walked a couple more miles before I looked for somewhere to sleep. Another day closer to the end.

I was finally too tired to even pretend not to be homeless any more. I'd slept on the lawn beside the boat club in Monmouth, the hedge providing the merest sliver of cover from passing dog-walkers. I didn't care any more about safety, about night-time marauders, about looking like a hobo. I just needed to sleep and it didn't matter where. The bridge carrying the roaring and gritty A40 in Ross-on-Wye was concrete and brutal. I took a Chinese takeaway with me. It was shit food, again, but I was on the edge of town by the time I realised there weren't any more chip-shops. The uncomfortably bumpy surface where the bridge faced onto the river was deliberately designed to stop people sleeping there;

the careless cruelty of society makes life even harder for its most desperate citizens.

As I sat under the bridge, my evening was made glorious by the most unexpected of sights. Fifteen swans swam slowly against the current beneath a blaze of a sunset: roaring pinks and golds, orange, red and peach-splashed, glowing across the whole sky above the black silhouettes of tree-lined water, all the colours reflected below so the swans trod water in a jewelled ribbon. I hunched awkwardly on the inhospitable concrete and munched prawn crackers, a small happy bystander in the corner of this heavenly picture, before retreating behind a column and making a bed on crushed glass and gravel, dry and comfortable for another night.

The Herefordshire burr was blurring into a Welsh lilt as I progressed up the river's course, and I realised that underneath the boundary, these borderlands were a place where separation dissolved. People and their long-held relationship with their surroundings, their years lived with the same weather patterning the same hills, knowing the same neighbours, watching blossom, fruit and leaves falling from the same tree. Divide it by nation if you will – distant governments setting invisible lines, drawing maps above our heads – but cultural identity starts with people and land.

In order to walk the missing miles of the Offa's Dyke Path that I'd skived out of when my tooth broke, I took a couple of days away from the Wye Valley and felt like a stubborn bastard as I did so. Rebecca and Phil, Knighton-based good eggs, had me to stay, shuttling me around so I could walk the miles and return to their home easily. I came face to face with Gareth again, as he came south on the ODP after walking all around the top of Wales. Rebecca and Phil hosted both of us for one fantastic night. We sat around their ceremonial barbeque table: three 1000-plus-mile walkers, sharing stories.

Detour completed, I went back to the Wye. I didn't know how it was happening; time was running away from me yet pulling me with it. The end was coming, it was unavoidable. I would finish the walk the next week. I couldn't wait to stop. I was incredibly sad. The finish. It was unimaginable, yet it was coming, it would happen. I was forcing myself forward to that point. It had to end.

The end of the walk would be a moment in time that I'd already decided upon. The following Saturday: eight days, fifteen miles a day until then. My body was exhausted: feet hurt, pain shooting through them and into the bones of my legs. Every day was an effort, a blur. I saw people, experienced beautiful things; I don't remember them. I was focused on walking, a slow grind until I could stop.

The Wye Valley was beautiful, lush and full of crops; the rain only served to make them flourish. I was walking through with no time to stop and wonder. I had to walk hard every day, my body so tired the necessary mileage took all day.

I didn't want the end to happen. I needed it to happen. I couldn't stop it from happening. I loved this, and yet I needed it to stop.

The walk had become a mania. I was completely overwhelmed with the thought of finishing – never mindful, never simply sitting and absorbing my surroundings. I was always taking photographs or writing a Facebook update or thinking, my mind churning with the pain, my potential reception, the future, the experience. I couldn't take it in, I wasn't present in it any more.

There's a brief period of time I do remember. Walking along the edge of a wheatfield, the path was a strip alongside the farmer's planting so narrow I could brush my fingers along the crusty grain tops as I walked. I heard a crackling, so faint that I couldn't focus on the source, it seemed to be all around me. I stopped and sat down, staring into the wheat, listening. It was the sound of the grain husks popping open in the sun, individual creaks and pops becoming a whisper of crackling, the swelling and growing of the grain becoming audible. I sat for a few minutes and took it in. Only in the silence did I realise how constantly my brain was chattering. How hungry am I? Where's the next water coming from? Where will I sleep tonight? How much do I hurt?

Sometimes I smelled food: walking through a village, quiet houses lining the river, set back by their long gardens sloping down towards the water, quiet trees trailing. Lunch came towards me on the air, spools of scent trailing out over the water. It was the smell of civilisation, noted for its rarity, noted for the days I spent with nothing but the scent of the fresh wild wind, the smell of earth and mosses, of sheep, their woollen musky tang.

When I came to human places I walked into much more intense smells, clouds of rose scent from pampered, preserved plants in cultivated gardens. I'd walk past people and sniff at the fog of detergent or perfume that trailed along after them. The smells of cooked food and roasted meats wound sinuously out of kitchen windows.

I realised that I was separated from all of this. I was part wild, had become a piece of the natural world. I squatted to piss as naturally as sitting, bent my hips low down to the ground, rested my weight down onto my heels, reaching underneath to wipe myself. I found my gaze sharply turning to birds where they fluttered in the trees, noting their movement, marking them. I looked for the traces of animals in my path, noting the scat, the scratches, the trails of foxes, badgers, hedgehogs, small mice and shrews. I saw squat shapes along the paths I walked, waited for shadows of movement, of animals scuttering away from my own clash and clamour.

I was become wild, my humanity dropped away over a year of outdoor living, careless of showers and scents and shopping, forgetful of where to sit, of dirt on my clothes, of dirt on my hands, of a day's timings and schedules. Uncaring of appropriate behaviour, of anything but walking.

I entered Wales again at Hay-on-Wye, after following the Wye's winding through the rich lands of Herefordshire, paced onwards towards Builth Wells, Rhayader and Llangurig, grinding out the final miles. I stayed in a hotel in Rhayader. It was supposed to be my final night of camping, but it was a wet and soggy day and I wimped out; everything felt too difficult, my weakness coming on in the final moments of the walking day.

Coming towards Llangurig, only a quirk of the rising of the land separated the Severn from the Wye. One rolled south, the other northwards, running away from each other and only meeting again hundreds of miles later as they entered the sea. This rise, preventing the two newborn rivers connecting, signalled the beginning and end of my journey. I began on one side of it and followed the water. More than a year later I was following it back again on the other side, thousands of miles covered in between.

I spent the next night with Jenny in Llangurig before walking up and over Plynlimon, the final climb. It was a hard and wet slog from the upper reaches of the Wye to the summit of the mountain, a final reminder of just how tough things could be. No path, just a plod along boggy stream-edges, water shedding from every waist-high burst of reeds and grasses, soaking me to the skin.

I reached the final boundary fence at the heights of the mountain and paused for a while before descending down to Talbontdrain. My old house would be host to the final night of my journey. Here I was at the top of the mountain again, and I'd walked 3700 miles. I didn't know how to feel. First cancer then walking had consumed the last four years of my life; this had been so big for so long and now the circle was almost complete, it was almost over.

I walked down Machynlleth's high street, with its familiar grey buildings and wide pavements, squeezing past shoppers and pedestrians, their blank faces unconcerned at the epic nature of the journey I was ending. There was the clock tower again, the end of the journey coming towards me. Once I was there I wouldn't have to walk any more; it really was the end. Friends and supporters were waiting, blowing horns and cheering. My steps dragged as I walked down the street. It was the final 200m of thousands of miles and I was scared.

A thought slammed into my mind, so huge and absolute that my steps faltered and I had to stand still for a second and face it. *You did this because you had cancer. All this. All these thousands of miles, struggling forward against the limits of your own body, always pushing on and on. This was all because of cancer.* Sobs welled up within me, huge, wet, nameless tears. All the pain of the previous four years had brought me here: this stupid thick pink growth that appeared where it shouldn't, all the illness and worry and then the inspiration and the walking, the people, the donations, the love and care I'd been shown. This thing that I'd tried to shake off, that I'd tried to treat as if it hadn't affected me – I saw that everything I'd done was because of it. I'd done all this because of cancer and now it was ending.

I came to the group and stopped, I didn't know what to do. I'd set out on a journey to walk an unthinkable, eyebrow-raising number of miles and I – silly, vague, plump, unprepared, determined, strong, stubborn me – had actually bloody done it.

EPILOGUE

A year after my cancer came, on the first anniversary of my operation date, I was in Mexico with my sister. We went to an agave bar with spray-painted walls and sat upstairs on a sofa with fairy lights and plants dangling down into the patio space. I poured a shot and said goodbye to my right ovary.

"You grew a tumour and tried to kill me and now you're gone. I let you go. I'm sorry this happened."

Then I poured another shot of the thin, sharp spirit and I said thank you to my left ovary.

"Cheers, Leftie, well done! Thank you for not taking up the cancer and growing it yourself, thank you for continuing to produce periods with such monthly regularity, thank you for continuing to maintain my hormonal balance in the face of such abdominal upheaval."

I'd never said thank you to a part of my body before; I'd never appreciated it for working as it should, all the quiet tickings and churnings which it carried out on my behalf every second of my waking and sleeping hours. My body was so strong and worked so well I didn't even notice how perfect it was. I'd only ever focused on the ways it failed me, the ways it wasn't good enough, the ways I wanted it to be different.

That anniversary, when I said thank you, was the beginning of true healing; I'd spent a year doing the immediate things, the sleeping and the sit-ups, the swimming and the therapy, the gentle walks and the good food.

I realised when I was weak that I needed to stop fighting it, that I had to stop denying my vulnerability and allow it to happen. For a short but vital period of time I had to allow myself to fully feel that pain in order to recover from it.

Part of healing is acknowledging hurt, part of healing is working at getting better, and part of healing is putting that painful time behind you, seeing that you no longer have to fear it. You're done with it; let it go, this trauma is no longer a necessary part of you.

The end of healing comes when you can acknowledge that the hurt is over now, that it has gone – and left you different.

> We shall not cease from exploration
> And the end of all our exploring
> Will be to arrive where we started
> And know the place for the first time.
> *T. S. Eliot*
> Little Gidding, Four Quartets

FINAL WORDS

Ovarian cancer most commonly occurs in women over 65, with women over 50 at increased risk.

Approximately 350 women are diagnosed annually in Wales, 7300 across the UK.

Approximately 200 women die annually in Wales, 4100 across the UK.

The five-year survival rate is 46%.

Symptoms are commonly mistaken for IBS.

Diagnosis is usually made when the cancer has spread beyond treatment.

Please take a moment to read and absorb the symptoms of ovarian cancer; one day it might help you or someone close to you live longer.

- Persistent bloating – not bloating that comes and goes
- Feeling full quickly and/or loss of appetite
- Pelvic or abdominal pain (that's your tummy and below)
- Urinary symptoms (needing to wee more urgently or more often than usual)

Occasionally there can be other symptoms:
- Changes in bowel habit (e.g. diarrhoea or constipation)
- Extreme fatigue (feeling very tired)
- Unexplained weight loss

- Any bleeding after the menopause should always be investigated by a GP.

Symptoms will be:
- Frequent – they usually happen more than twelve times a month
- Persistent – they don't go away
- New – they are not normal for you

Author's Note

There are discrepancies in some of the stated mileages in this book.

First is the total length of the walk. When I created the route and calculated the total number of miles I made a few mistakes, didn't take into account the linking distances from one route to another and spent most of the walk thinking I was walking 3300 miles. I had cards printed, put it all over the website. It wasn't until I'd walked 3300 miles and hadn't reached the end of my route that I realised I was bad at maths. The final total was 3718 miles, but I talked about 3300 miles throughout the planning and for fifteen of the seventeen months the journey took.

The mileage given in each chapter heading may not add up to the total miles walked (3718). There were days when I took detours or walked extra sections. Routes have changed since I walked some paths (the distance given on the official website for the Cistercian Way has increased by forty-eight miles). I've found discrepancies between guidebook mileages and website mileages for certain routes, and I also walked miles between each official path (for example, the 100 miles between the end of the Cambrian Way at Cardiff and the beginning of the Coast to Coast Path at Rhossili). I also walked different sections of certain paths at different times (for example, Offa's Dyke Path Chepstow to Welshpool in early April, Offa's Dyke Path Welshpool to Prestatyn in early May, after the Glyndŵr's Way and recorded in the Glyndŵr's Way chapter). I have my own record of the actual miles I walked, but it's difficult to represent them clearly in this book when I've divided each section by the name of an official path.

ABOUT HONNO

Honno Welsh Women's Press was set up in 1986 by a group of women who felt strongly that women in Wales needed wider opportunities to see their writing in print and to become involved in the publishing process. Our aim is to develop the writing talents of women in Wales, give them new and exciting opportunities to see their work published and often to give them their first 'break' as a writer. Honno is registered as a community co-operative. Any profit that Honno makes is invested in the publishing programme. Women from Wales and around the world have expressed their support for Honno. Each supporter has a vote at the Annual General Meeting. For more information and to buy our publications, please write to Honno at the address below, or visit our website: www.honno.co.uk

Honno, 14 Creative Units, Aberystwyth Arts Centre
Aberystwyth, Ceredigion SY23 3GL

Honno Friends
We are very grateful for the support of the Honno Friends: Jane Aaron, Annette Ecuyere, Audrey Jones, Gwyneth Tyson Roberts, Beryl Roberts, Jenny Sabine.

For more information on how you can become a Honno Friend, see: http://www.honno.co.uk/friends.php